G000256320

Bob Thorogood was born in Nort
fifteen to make his way in life; starti
through the building trade and eventually finding his true calling
as a Police Officer. He is married with two sons and a daughter
and still lives in Northamptonshire.

Bob Thorogood

Behind the
Call of Duty

Copyright © 2006 Bob Thorogood

The moral right of the author has been asserted.

Apart from any fair dealing for the purposes of research or private study,
or criticism or review, as permitted under the Copyright, Designs and Patents
Act 1988, this publication may only be reproduced, stored or transmitted, in
any form or by any means, with the prior permission in writing of the
publishers, or in the case of reprographic reproduction in accordance with
the terms of licences issued by the Copyright Licensing Agency. Enquiries concerning
reproduction outside those terms should be sent to the publishers.

Matador
9 De Montfort Mews
Leicester LE1 7FW, UK
Tel: (+44) 116 255 9311 / 9312
Email: books@troubador.co.uk
Web: www.troubador.co.uk/matador

ISBN 1 905237 90 1

Every effort has been made to respect the privacy of all those
people whose lives touched upon that of the author. Where possible and
relevant, names, places and dates have been changed to protect the
innocent. However, by its very nature an autobiography deals with
real incidents in the life of a real person. The author sincerely hopes
that no offence is taken by any individual mentioned in this book.

Typeset in 11pt Times by Troubador Publishing Ltd, Leicester, UK
Printed in the UK by The Cromwell Press Ltd, Trowbridge, Wilts, UK

Matador is an imprint of Troubador Publishing Ltd

Among the many reasons for writing this book, I wanted to create a lasting memory for our children Martin, Carolyn and Peter, and our grandchildren Vanessa, Joshua and Zane (and any more that come along), to remind them of their background and their origins. Therefore, I dedicate this book to them.

I would also like to thank my wife Jackie for all her help and patience throughout the time it took to write, and also to Richard Cowley and Irene Lewis for the tremendous assistance they freely gave in editing and correcting defective grammar.

Finally, I would like to say to all those who were involved in the incidents recorded, that though they might recall some of the facts differently or from a different perspective, these are my memories as I recall them and they are all true 'to the best of my knowledge and belief', as they say in some circles!

Chapter I

Flora (Flo) Thorogood lived with her husband Richard (Dick), their daughter Florence (Florrie), son John Richard (Dickie) and baby Alan in a large house in Stoke Newington in London's East End. It was quite a large house but it needed to be because they shared it with her family. Life was not easy because the Second World War was into its second year. Florrie and Dickie had already been evacuated to Northampton but Alan, at only seven months, was too young and had to stay with his Mother.

In typical Eastend style they got by. The popularised image of life in the war was of everybody heading for the shelters as soon as the sirens started and then spending the night singing songs and having a convivial time in a converted Underground station. It made a good story and a great image of the indomitable British spirit. Unfortunately it wasn't like that for everyone.

The shelters could be cramped and uncomfortable as was the one they used one night in 1940. The bombing had been going on for months and it was very heavy every night. People were tired of having their rest disturbed again and again but when the sirens started to wail, the whole family grabbed their clothes for yet another night below ground.

When they got to the shelter, it was already crowded but they found themselves a place. Flo and Dick snuggled down with young Alan. Flo's twin sister and their mother and father were next to them and they made themselves as comfortable as possible.

The noise was like an express steam train thundering through the night as the bombs started to fall. They were closer than usual and the whole family was feeling nervous. Dick tried to comfort Flo and the baby but nothing seemed to settle them. Eventually, Dick got up and went to speak to Flo's sister and parents.

Everyone said that if you could hear the whistle of the bomb it was not near enough to get you but this one sounded really close. Then the whistling stopped for one heartbeat and the whole world erupted in a nightmare of fire, debris and smoke. People were screaming in pain and fear. It had been a direct hit on the shelter and it left both of Flo's elderly parents, her twin sister, and Dick all dead along with many others.

Flo was (amazingly) uninjured and Alan had no more than a small cut on his lip. Flo's only thought was to get as far away as possible from this nightmare and, grabbing the baby, she ran from the shelter into the street. She started walking through the devastated streets of Stoke Newington. How long she walked she had no idea. To her, it seemed like three days and it probably was quite a long time because, by walking away from the scene, rescuers could not tell if they had been blown to pieces and, consequently, were not searching the streets for them.

The following paragraph is an unedited reproduction of a letter from my mother's parents to their son Bert (my Uncle) who was in the RAF in November 1940. Allowances have to be made for their grammar and spelling. It is quite amazing how casually they referred to the bombing and death that surrounded them and how tragic it was that, within a year, the incident I have described above resulted in the deaths of Mr and Mrs Smith and 'Frank' who had already lost his home.

Letter from Mrs C Smith
60 Shakespear Walk
Stokenewington N16

Dear Bert just a line hopeing this will find you in the best of Health as it levesus all at present exsept frank he has had his home burn up he had a Excenley (incendiary?) Bome through his house and he has got no home now it is a good job lil and baby is away we have had them all Round us all this week. Thay have been trying to find me by the way I have had a letter from your girl from Kensinton and she told me she has been going out with you and would I send her your address I have not done so yet shall I send it to her let me now as this is the first letter I have had sence you went back we are all tierd out for the want of sleep the huter has just gorn and we are running for our dugout so you must excues this righting you know the girl smith, well she has just died. I don't think there is a lot more to say we are being Bombed 6 and 7 times a day so you can see there is not much time so I will Draw to a close sending cake so goodbye I remain your loving Mum and Dad ??????? (unreadable)
XXXXXXXXXXXXX

Eventually, my mother was found and taken to a rescue centre. From there she was evacuated to Northampton to join the other two children but of course no one there would take on a whole family of what were known locally as the 'Vacuees'. The reputation that Londoners had with the locals was not good.

Stoke Newington was probably as bad a place to come from as anywhere if you were in Northampton and looking for charity and a warm welcome. The ways of Vacuees did not sit at all well with the close-knit shoemaking community. They were drinkers, they spoke 'wiv a fanny accent' and worst of all they sometimes used that 'F' word – well, all the time actually.

Now, I wouldn't want you to think that my Mother was some kind of lost little woman in a strange town. She just wasn't like that. She was six feet tall and well built. One legend that went with her was that a man once made improper advances to her twin sister. This resulted in him being lifted off his feet by the neck and held against a wall by my Mother until his face turned blue. She was not to be crossed lightly.

When she arrived in Northampton, the family remained split up with various families in the town. Where she herself stayed at the beginning, I have no idea. She was never very forthcoming on that subject and, as you will see, my own background was confusing to say the least.

I do know that, before too long, she managed to get a job at a local dairy (Bramptons). It didn't pay too well but there was a house that went with the job. A little house at 3 Oakley Street, which was one of many built back-to-back in terraces for the labourers who built the railways in the days of Queen Victoria.

Of course people were quite primitive in those days. No one had a bathroom or an inside toilet. There was, literally, a tin bath which could be placed in the kitchen and filled from a copper boiler, fuelled by an open fire, also supplying the warmth to get undressed by. Imagine the scene when Mum was taking her weekly (or fortnightly) bath in the kitchen and one of the kids wanted to go to the outside toilet. This meant getting the candle and the old newspaper, averting their eyes as they passed through the kitchen and going up the garden to the toilet.

I wasn't there for that of course but I know it was so because it hadn't changed much when I came on the scene. The Mangle. This was the other ubiquitous item in those houses. If bathing was not a certain activity every week, the Monday washing certainly was. It was done in the same, open fired copper boiler with a washboard and lots of hard work. The housewives would spend many hours putting each washed item through the rollers of the mangle and squeezing the water out of them before filling the line with the billowing garments. Well, not too many garments because not too many people wore underclothes and even shirts only got changed when they needed it.

I know the mangle was a dangerous beast as well. The women had to get the clothing into the rollers and then turn the large handle at the side. If the garment was a bit thick they had quite a difficult task to get it going. Many women only wore a brassiere for going out and a loose, unsuspecting boob getting too close to the rollers, just as they drew the garment through could give a very nasty injury.

I digress, but I have tried to set the scene as it was for my mother in Northampton in 1944. She managed to get her children back with her and the future was beginning to look bearable, though money was desperately short.

The Allies were building up the forces for the inevitable assault on Europe and the Americans descended on Northampton in strength. There were Air Bases at Heyford, Croughton, Chelveston and many other locations within a reasonable distance of the biggest town in the area. The servicemen would all go into Northampton at weekends to have a drink and meet the local ladies.

They had money and such luxuries as chocolate and stockings, which were unobtainable for the local women. They were generous and although it did not make them popular with the local men, it did with the women. Vacuee women, who liked a drink and were perhaps a little less puritan than the locals, soon began to mix with the American servicemen more and more.

I have never been able to piece together the truth about my father. My mother was a romantic and when she eventually told me anything at all, it was tinged with the comforting glow of rose coloured spectacles and more than a hint of covering her own reputation. Unfortunately, my sister, who was really the only child old enough to understand what was happening, shared the romantic traits and when she eventually told me the story, it would have been worthy of Mills and Boon.

What does seem likely to be the truth is that my father was an American serviceman from one of the local airforce bases who visited regularly and, according to one version, actually stayed at the house from the beginning of 1944 until 'D' day, 6 June 1944, when he was involved in the Normandy landings. I use the term 'according to one version' advisedly because it seems unlikely that even the US Services, who were not reputed to be as well disciplined as the English, would allow their troops to stay in a local town on a permanent basis.

Apparently, he did not return to Northampton after 'D' Day and has not been seen or heard of in the area since. My Mother would have been 3 months pregnant with me when he left. I believe he was not killed in the action so his leaving seems to have been a convenient exit for him. You might wonder why I have never traced him, with all the resources available to a senior police officer but early efforts by my sister to trace him were not successful and I, frankly, had a life of my own to lead.

I shall not refer to him again so I will explain that, with the advent of the Internet, I did make a few enquiries based upon the knowledge (perhaps) of his name and the fact that he came from Utah. I had also acquired a fragment of a torn postcard, approximately one and a half inches by one inch, showing a man I am told is my father, on a porch with a small boy behind him. Some tiny remains of writing on the back seem to point to his first name being 'Bob' like my own and an indication that he may have written it after he left Northampton for the last time.

The miracles of modern technology have allowed me to enhance the picture to full-page size and I have used it to contact the only two ex servicemen with the correct names and ages from Utah. One of these is dead and his son (also named Bob and the correct age for the boy in the photograph) insists that his father never left the US. The other is still alive but has satisfied me that it was not he.

It may be that the deceased man was my father but it is a feature of my own nature and upbringing that I really do not care enough to find out for sure. I am a very independent person and can be very determined about what I do or do not care about. My life is for my own family and if this man had wanted to know about me, he could have done so easily.

Many people have asked me why I don't go further to eliminate him or confirm my suspicion that it was him and I am not sure that I am able to set down the complex reasons why it doesn't matter that much to me. It has even been suggested that I would not be able to let it go but that is one of the odd aspects of my nature and I simply don't care enough.

One of the oddest twists to my tale involves how I came to be brought up by Mrs Pentelope and Mr Marzetti who lived the whole of their adult lives together but NOT as man and wife. Mr Marzetti and Mrs Pentelope's husband were friends who fought in the First World War together. It seems that Mr Pentelope asked Mr Marzetti to look after his wife if he did not return. Mr Pentelope was killed in the trenches and Mr Marzetti kept his solemn promise throughout his whole life. He moved in with her, in separate bedrooms and kept her until she died in 1952.

Their home was next door to the terraced house occupied by my mother. She continued with her life style of going to the local pubs with a group of friends after I was born in December 1944 and Mrs Pentelope was a convenient and willing baby sitter having been denied the opportunity to have a family of her own.

Many years later, I allowed myself to be hypnotised and regressed to those early days. There are many misapprehensions about hypnotism. The Police do not use it in Britain because of the dangers of false memories being created and I believe that to be sound logic. People are afraid of hypnotism because they fear that it 'takes away a persons will power and allows another to control them'. This is not true. Hypnotism is merely a means of taking a person into a very relaxed state, short of a dream but on the edge of sleep, where you know what is happening but are not awake enough to react. Most of us experience the feeling quite regularly just before we fall asleep and it is quite common to think of things in that state, resolve to action them the next day but not be able to remember the following morning.

Indeed, another worry people have about hypnotism is that they won't be able to come out of a trance afterwards. This is another unjustified concern as the worst that can happen is that you fall into a deep, natural and untroubled sleep, awaking refreshed afterwards.

It can, nevertheless, be a deep and sobering experience as I found when I allowed myself to be regressed. I was taken back through various years and stages of my life until I pictured myself as a three-month-old baby. I could see myself lying on a blanket by an open fire in Mrs Pentelope's house with her standing over me, with Mr Marzetti in the background. Mrs Pentelope was saying to me, "Don't worry, we'll look after you" and I could vividly see my mother walking out of the room saying, "I'm going to the pub," in a very 'Alf Garnet' accent.

This image was so real that I found myself crying and quite distressed when my hypnotist friend brought me back to full consciousness a few moments later. I truly believed that I had resurrected some deeply ingrained image of a true event. Unfortunately for the romantic side of my nature, I have since learned that I never stayed with Mrs Pentelope until I was more than a year old. So, whether the memory is correct and the timings slightly off or whether the whole thing was a figment of my imagination under hypnosis I really cannot say. I do know that sometime in my first eighteen months, my mother left me with Mrs Pentelope and Mr Marzetti whilst she went to Southend for the day.

It seems she returned late and agreed that I should stay there the night. Somehow, I never left them again. It may seem that this was a curious arrangement! Here we had a child of less than two years staying with an unmarried middle-aged couple whilst his mother, sister and two brothers lived next door. Were it the case that Bill Marzetti and Jane Pentelope were good friends with my mother it might have been understandable even if a little unconventional in those days but the fact is that they did not get on at all well.

I was not allowed to have any real contact with my family and my mother seemed to be reasonably content with the arrangement. In fact, even now, I recall that I used to call Jane and Bill, 'Mum' and 'Dad' but I did not have a name to call my mother by. I did not even know for sure that she was my mother in those early days.

I must have had some idea that she was because, one of my earliest and most abiding memories is of my first day at infant school, when Jane took me to the gate and sent me into the playground with the other children. We were rounded up by the Head Teacher who I heard call herself Mr Aper. (It was some time later that I realised she was really Miss Draper!)

Mr Aper asked us all our names for the register. Shock, horror! I had no idea what my name was. Was it Pentelope? Was it Marzetti? Or was it Thorogood – the name the somehow related people next door had? No five-year-old wants to put himself or herself into a position where they have to be singled out for an open enquiry in front of the whole school and I took a flying guess at Thorogood. I was right of course, that is the name on my Birth Certificate but I truly did not know then and was too scared to ask Jane and Bill.

None of this should lead one to think that I had a deprived or unhappy childhood. Nothing could be further from the truth. Bill and Jane made sure that I had everything I could want within the constraints of post war rationing and I was content playing with the other urchins in the street.

This was not a wealthy neighbourhood. The only family who had any money were the people who kept the local Fish and Chip shop. Their only son was very popular with us kids. He was the only one who had a bike which he would let us take turns to ride across the Racecourse (the local park) and he obviously shared his parents entrepreneurial spirit because he charged us a penny a go. Also, if we arranged to play with him after school we could almost guarantee a free bag of chips for tea. Actually I found this to be one of my first moral dilemmas. You see, he was really a little creep who none of us truly liked but we had to keep in with him if we wanted the bike and the chips.

I was eight years old. Jane had been getting old and a bit senile. She had taken to walking the streets and not remembering how to get home. Then she started to degenerate physically as well. Her bed was moved down into the 'front room' and my last memories of her were lying in the bed by the front window and looking very old and weak. One day I came home from school and found Bill there. This was unusual as he worked in a shoe factory and wouldn't normally be home until after five. He gently told me that Jane had passed away.

This did not mean much to me. I vaguely knew that it meant she would not be there any more but the impact of that was not of great significance to an eight year old boy who needed to practice his cycling skills at a penny a go and had suddenly acquired a sixpenny piece without really knowing why.

It never crossed my mind that there might be a question of where I would live then. That I was to be living with a man who had never been married and had never really shown interest in the opposite sex was way too sophisticated for me then. That it was allowed to continue now seems amazing to me and I have since discovered that my mother did broach the subject of my return home then. Bill told her that he would fight her to the death to resist it and I guess she couldn't face the thought of my history being made public so she didn't make a fight of it.

Not that there was anything to be worried about. Bill was a wonderful father to me. There was never anything improper in our relationship. He had no concept of cleanliness and my teeth had not seen a toothbrush ever. Washing was done at the kitchen sink and as there was no hot water, I don't suppose it was very thorough but that certainly mattered not one iota to us.

I was happy. Non school days were spent playing with the other kids in the street. Bill went off to work leaving the front door unlocked and when he got home, we would still be playing in the street. That seems so irresponsible and impossible now but it was the norm in those simple days.

In the evenings we would sit by the radio and listen to 'Journey into Space' with Jet Morgan, Lemme and the crew complete with the latest radio effects or 'Riders of the Range'. Then came the inevitable trek with the candle and the old newspapers into the scary darkness of the garden where the wind in our cherry tree and the crowing of Bill's cockerels were the only sounds to be heard.

How I hated those damned birds. Bill thought it was a treat for me to feed the stupid things but I was scared of them and they knew it. They would attack me if I went inside the pen and I am still terrified of anything that has wings or flutters at me today. I was so relieved when the day came that he decided to get rid of them and wrung their necks. This left the cherry tree as the sole occupant of the garden and that was much better than cockerels. Apart from the fact that you could climb it, it produced the sweetest cherries I ever tasted and all that for free in the middle of town.

The only real source of discomfort for me was what was happening next door. My uncle had returned from abroad and lived with my Mother for a time. He was a strange man. He had quite a few male friends but never any females and I believe now that he may have been homosexual though such things were never talked of openly in those days. Perhaps fortunately, he didn't like me at all and I was scared of him. I assume he disliked the shame I had brought to his sister and he wanted to be the head of the household.

My mother became engaged and soon married a man whose family were well known in the town because they sold ice cream and flowers on Northampton market. What a brave man! He took on a woman who had three children all at difficult ages (and another one next door), a brother who was a challenge for supremacy in the household and the upkeep of the house itself that they eventually bought from the dairy.

Not that I saw much of all that. I was next door and Bill would not let me have anything to do with any of them. My mother and sister used to try to send me on errands but if Bill found out there would be a real row. I was not invited to the wedding of my mother and eventual stepfather and it was then that I first began to feel the stirrings of any form of jealousy. I had no desire to hurt Bill in any way but deep inside I wanted to share part of the family next door.

Sometimes I would surreptitiously run an errand for my sister, both of us knowing that there would be trouble if Bill found out, but I was a major admirer of my big and devastatingly beautiful sister. She was six feet tall, slim and a big attraction for the American Servicemen – yes, them again. She eventually married one and he took her off to America where she made her home and stayed until she died in 1992. That was another wedding I was not invited to. Nor was I invited to the wedding of my eldest brother. These were all small, unnoticed little darts causing me internal pain. To them I was just a weird kid next door. I suppose I was a little weird. But then, I might have had some slight cause for it. I know I was, even then, the most independent child in the street, always doing what I wanted to do and not what was expected of me.

Love is a major factor in the lives of most people and I am no exception. I know the family love I had was perhaps the strangest love imaginable but I didn't realise that then. I was in love with ten-year-old

Pauline Glynn. She sat next to me in school and never noticed that I existed. One day, she fainted and Mr Ginn the teacher picked her up and carried her out of the room. How I wished I could have done that.

It is strange that impressions made at that time of life do last so long. Holidays for Bill and I consisted of either a day at Skegness or a visit to a relative of his at Irthlingborough. Where? Irthlingborough. It is a small village/town about fifteen miles from Northampton, better known now for its millionaire owned Rushden and Diamonds Football Club but then, not known for anything other than its shoe factories. But we used to stay there whenever we could and the high point of the day would always be the walk over a viaduct and back via an old bridge with perhaps a stop at a pub on the way or, at the right time of the year, a blackberrying trip in March Lane.

My most vivid recollection of this time was a Christmas when it snowed on Christmas day and we went out into the yard in the glow of the gaslights of the house. A very Dickensian picture but also an indication of the conditions they lived in.

The other treat Bill liked to give me was a Sunday morning walk to the Brittania pub just outside Northampton where he would have a pint of beer whilst I swam in the river – not something one would contemplate today. It is also odd that my mother used to make us sandwiches to take with us and, after Jane's death, she would cook our main meal every day, even though she and Bill could never agree about anything.

Indeed, this meal arrangement played a part in my first contact with the police. As he had always done, Bill used to leave the house unlocked when he went to work and my mother would go in and tidy up, leaving the meal for when he got home. One day, I arrived home from school and found some of my National Savings stamps in the hallway. When Bill arrived home I told him and he immediately went to see my mother to ask if she had moved them. Unsurprisingly, she was most indignant and said that she certainly had not and would not touch them. Closer inspection revealed that we had been burgled.

Several small items were missing from various rooms and there were signs of a search. Bill and I immediately went round to Campbell Square Police Station where we were shown into the office of a Detective Sergeant whose name I cannot now recall. Also present, however, was a young ginger haired detective named Chapman and they arranged to visit the house. Even though I have since been in charge of that police station I cannot now say where the office was located. The building has not changed greatly but I suppose that, as I was ten at the time, it is not too surprising that I have forgotten.

The two detectives came round to the house later in their long raincoats and trilby hats (almost a uniform in those days) and the impact of the words they said has stayed with me always.

Would that today's police could say the same with confidence. The Constable said, "When we catch these people, you will have to go to court to give evidence" (this was before the Criminal Justice Act allowed statements to be read out in guilty pleas). How often now that police officers say, "Well of course there is little chance of catching anyone" but these officers had no such doubts. They had justification for their confidence too because they were back within 24 hours to explain that they had caught the offenders and apologised for not having recovered the stolen items.

Of course, we lived in a simpler world where doors were left unlocked in the daytime, policemen had time to check everyone's front door at night and the detectives knew all their rogues. These two were caught by the simple expedient of going to the factory where Bill worked, checking who was not at work that day and swiftly getting an admission. The two, a lad who lived in the next street and a youth from Semilong, were duly arraigned at the Number One Magistrates Court and sentenced to two years probation. Ah well, some things never change.

I was given a shilling (5p) for giving my evidence by a very large, avuncular Sergeant and thus a lifetime ambition was set. I have no idea how the sergeant was able to give me that shilling. He could not have afforded to give it from his own pocket and I wonder how it showed up in the annual budget.

There was a sequel to this incident because I had two friends who were twins of my age and went to the same school. They were more popular than the Fish Shop owner's son because they were the only people who had a television set in the area. They lived in a flat above a very small printers shop that their Father ran in Leicester Street and we used to visit them whenever we could to see the black and white 9-inch screen TV. One night, the printers shop was broken into and who should be arrested but the lad who had broken into our house. This was his second offence and this time he went to Borstal.

I have already referred to my independent streak and this was just beginning to show as I reached the last year in Junior School. How much the following anecdote owed to the movies and how much was me I cannot say but there was a boy who lived nearby. He saw himself as the brains of the gang although I suspect that all he possessed was the innate cunning that some children have. He would always try to be smart, always have some money-making plot and his quick wit had a tendency to make him unpopular with the other kids. I was a big lad even then. I was very tall for my age and exceptionally strong though more prone to being bullied than to bully. Evidently this boy saw these traits as useful to him and would regularly try to get me involved in his plans.

In true movie bad guy style he said to me one day, "You know, with my brains and your brawn we can really do great things together." I am as proud today as I was then of my reply, which came without hesitation, "With my brains and my brawn, what do I need you for?"

I enjoyed school at that time. I was sitting next to Pauline still and Mr Ginn was my hero. Though not quite top of the class, I was always around the top three in most subjects and found I had a natural ability with English, which has always made reports and all writing a pleasure for me.

I enjoyed stories and one of the best at Military Road was the one the Headmaster used to tell. He delighted in gathering the children around him in a group seated on the floor of the hall and he would regale them with tales in a magical way, which was almost hypnotic. He said that he had been to a fortune teller who told him that he would go to teach near a castle with crenellated turrets and he would be so happy there that he would stay for the rest of his life. He said that Military Road was the happiest place he had ever been in and as he was quite old, it was obvious that he would not be going anywhere else to teach. He then explained that the 'Drill Hall' in the next street had turrets and was just like a castle to him. This was true and the turrets still stand to this day.

The only blot on my horizon was the bullying. It seems incongruous now but there was I, about the biggest kid in school, albeit slightly tubby, not lacking in intelligence and not unpopular but there were one or two who would take every opportunity to jump on my back or generally push me around. I only retaliated once in junior school. On that occasion, the most prolific bully jumped on me as I left school and I bent forward throwing him over my shoulder. I was terrified that he would get me back but he never came near me again.

I had not realised, because kids tend not to, but Bill was nearly seventy by then and his health was waning rapidly. He certainly could not exert any control or give me any guidance any more. Nor was there anyone else who could or wished to. Relations with next door continued to be a little strained and I knew they were having their own problems.

My brothers were adults, or nearly so, and were not really accepting of the authority of their stepfather although the competition for 'Head of the Household' was long over. My uncle had gone to rented accommodation and my stepfather thought he was it. What he had overlooked was the fact that Eastend women only ever deceive their menfolk into believing they run the show. 'Eastenders' fans will readily associate this concept with the Matriarchal attitude to family that exists there. My mother was no exception to this and she was always in control.

The 'Eleven Plus' exams were a breeze for me. I actually revelled in the certainty that I would pass easily and I did, though not with the highest marks. My eldest brother had gone to Northampton Grammar School, my sister to a quite poor Secondary School (St George's) and my other brother to one of the worst schools in town (Campbell Square Secondary). The choices available for me were the Grammar School, where the best students normally went, Trinity High School (then known as the Technical High School) which was for good grades but not quite as good as the Grammar School, or of course I could elect to go to Secondary school, though that was not a realistic option for anyone who passed the exam.

Even at that age, I made my own choice without consulting anyone else. I can feel you thinking that would not be possible for an eleven year old. Nevertheless, it is absolutely true. I have not always made correct or even good decisions but I have always made the decisions myself. I decided that I did not want the snobbery of Grammar School and I knew that, at Trinity, they taught a trade as well as a good education so I decided that was where I was going.

At school we were asked to take in the election form signed by a parent and it was a formality that Bill just signed where I asked him. My choice was a big mistake but mine alone.

On the day I started at Trinity, the school moved to a new building, stopped teaching trades and set its sights on becoming a second Grammar School. I had effectively got what I wanted to avoid but missed out on the best teachers and the well-established traditions of a respected Grammar School.

I made another life changing decision during the holiday leading up to the school change. I decided one day, as I was walking alone from my house to the Racecourse, that I had been bullied for the last time. New school, new lifestyle. It was a not a stray thought, it was not a long planned change nor was it a wishful dream. It was simply a decision, no matter what the cost in black eyes, bruises or whatever, the next person to try to bully me was going to find out that it was a mistake.

There were quite a few friends going to the same school so it was quite likely that the knowledge that I was available to be bullied would go with me and I consciously realised that my new resolve would be put to the test.

It was, in the first term of the first year. I was in the 'A' stream but I started to mix with the more sports-minded group in the 'B' stream at play times. One member of the group was a lad who came from a fairly rough area of town (Spencer).

He evidently decided that it would be fun to punch the big kid and run off. What he did not expect was that the big kid would chase him determinedly and could, in fact run like the wind for one his size. Neither did he expect that the big kid would savagely take his legs out from behind as he reached the gravelled part of the playground.

I was scared stiff. His face looked like he had been through a mincer. He had to go to the office for first aid and I knew they would ask him how he did it. He had to be sent home and I thought I was in deep Doo-Doo. All the other kids in the group had seen it happen and I was sure they would back him up. Also, what would happen if his mates decided to get me?

The answer was – nothing. He never told how it happened, no one tried to get me and I was suddenly a kid to be respected and looked up to. Now, this was good and bad at the same time, good, because I enjoyed the attention and my sporting prowess was suddenly in demand, bad because I switched off studying completely and lost all interest in everything except sport and meeting up with students in the 'B' stream.

The only exceptions to this were English, which I still loved, and French, which we were introduced to in that year. The reason I did well in French was, however, quite different. We were to be taught that language by the Deputy Headmaster, 'Gunner' Wright. The first time I met him was when the door of the classroom burst open and this fierce, red faced, angry looking man stormed in as if he was facing the enemy in the Second World War. 'Levez vous' he roared. Thirty-one faces looked at him blankly. 'Levez vous' he stormed, face getting redder and anger getting worse. Thirty-one faces looked at him blankly.

'Levez vous' he ranted but this time accompanied by a lifting gesture, which conveyed the meaning that he wanted us to stand up. 'Assayez vous mes enfants' he said in a slightly calmer but somehow more threatening tone, this time accompanied by a 'sit' gesture. Scared? You better believe we were scared.

I mean he was big and he was the discipline authority for the school. He wore a cape and mortarboard AND he was the one who normally gave the cane. This was a legendary activity, the way he did it. His office was quite big and had glass panels so any stray child could be seen passing or could witness the administering of the cane. I never felt it but I saw it once.

The offender was made to bend and touch his toes at one end of the room. Gunner would take the cane from his selection on the wall (no escape if one broke) and he would wind himself up at the other end of the room before charging across the room like some avenging cavalry captain swinging his sabre and bringing it down wildly on the offenders bottom. The screams would make a grown man wilt.

It was in this first year that I was introduced to the game of Rugby. I had been useless at soccer in junior school because I was simply not the right shape. Yes I was tall, but I was also very broad and built more like a truck than a racing car. I was soon selected to play for the first year team under the guidance of 'Gary' Grimshaw who was a fierce little Welshman with a determination to show that his school was going to produce better rugby players that the Grammar school.

The annual game against them was always something to behold. The rivalry was intense and there was always the possibility that violence would break out, sometimes between the players as well as the teachers! I jest not. These games were refereed by a teacher from whichever school was hosting the game, on the basis that they were all gentlemen and could be trusted not to display bias. Some joke. During one game I was involved in when the game was at the Grammar school and therefore refereed by them, 'Gary' stormed onto the pitch, incensed at some really one sided decisions and put his fists up to the referee who would have been quite happy to have a fight on the spot if it had not been for the fact that a few of us strapping 13 year olds pulled them apart.

We had a second Welsh rugby teacher named Mathews who was, or claimed to be, a forward of some standing in his younger days. His favourite cry was, "Come on you English wimps! When I was a boy I used to rr.run (yes rr run) down the pitch with eight men on my bach".

Unfortunately, my pre-occupation with rugby was costing me dear in study terms. At the end of the first year I came literally first in the A stream at English because I had a talent for it, first at French because I dare do no other and last at everything else. Yes, last, not nearly last but in the ultimate, end, can't get any lower position.

As a result, I was moved down to the 'B' stream, which actually made me happy because I was with my best friends but on reflection, shows that the school was not able to recognise or nurture what talent I had.

At home, I managed to get myself a paper round, even though I was strictly too young and I developed a work ethic, which has lasted ever since. I quite liked the money and Bill allowed me to buy a bright green and yellow Raleigh racing bike, which was the envy of all the local kids including the Fish Shop owner's son. Another little perk of the paper round was that there was a girl whose round was roughly the same as mine and I would see her regularly when she collected the papers for her Newsagent from the *Chronicle and Echo* near the market at the same time as I collected ours. My way of showing that I quite liked her was to hit her on the head with a newspaper. These advances did not impress her and I never got further than finding out that her name was Ginnie.

Bill was sinking fast. I had no idea what was wrong with him but he was in obvious pain. I occasionally found him lying in the garden in the sun and he would say he was trying to get some fresh air. He was taken to Creaton Sanatorium for a time but then returned home. For the second time in my life, I came home from school to be told that one of my 'parents' had died during the day.

By now I was thirteen but the significance of this event still did not hit me fully. I was obviously very upset and realised there were about to be some changes in my life. My mother and stepfather simply took me in. There was no discussion, nor did I expect there to be. I just moved next door. There was no problem with the accommodation because they had had a bathroom built at the back of the kitchen, including a water heater so I was able to take the small third bedroom. It did not cross my mind that I could have been regarded as an orphan until the Headmaster sent for me and asked where I would be living. This was as close as the school got to pastoral care and when I told them it was not a problem they were satisfied.

I became a very unhappy child about then and it was more by luck than judgement that I did not acquire a criminal record. Teddy boys were in fashion and I admired them. One of the most feared and dangerous amongst them was none other than the lad who I had given evidence against three years before. He now carried a bicycle chain and occasionally a gun. It was certainly an air gun but to us it was a gun and he was reputed to have shot someone in the town one night.

He had a gang who followed him slavishly and I would have loved to be in the gang. That was never going to happen, although he did seem to have forgiven me for the court case. Thank goodness that was as far as it went because they all went on to get into serious trouble.

I made friends at school who used to go to Abington Park at the other end of town and we had our own gang, although the nearest we got to being Teddy boys was when one of the lads, whose mother was a tailor, made him a draped school blazer to go with his thick crepe soled shoes. We used to gather in the park and generally cause mischief but one night when, for some unaccountable reason, I did not go to the park but instead walked the streets feeling depressed and lonely, the rest of the gang broke into the museum in the park and all got caught inside. Another night, when I was there, we moved all of the park benches and put them across a pathway which was poorly lit and in such a way that any unsuspected adult walking a dog would walk into them.

I realise now that the main source of my feeling depressed and miserable was the appearance on the scene of girls. I had lost Pauline Glyn. The last time I saw her was in the first year I was at Trinity. She went to the Girls' Grammar School, which was very close to Trinity, and our path to school had been across the racecourse.

The closest I got to telling her how much I loved her was one lunchtime as we returned to school and I said I wished she had come to Trinity instead of the single sex school. She agreed! And I thought maybe she cared for me a little bit but then I bought my bike and went a different way to school. I have never seen her from that day to this.

But girls at the park were something different. My love for Pauline was an innocent childish thing but the girls at the park were sexy. They were just beginning to experiment as were the boys and there was a great deal of fumbling and squeezing going on.

Of course, it is easy to say now that it was the permissive sixties but my recollection of the sixties was not of a permissive age at all. What was happening in the park was a whole series of sexual offences. Unbelievable though it may seem, one afternoon, I walked through a spinney which links two of the lakes and in a clearing I happened upon a girl of about thirteen who I knew vaguely. She was lying in the clearing completely naked engaged in sexual activity with no less than five boys of the same age. I don't even know if they were aware of my presence and I was too embarrassed to stay long.

There was a girl named Eileen who was spoken of as a willing partner. She too was thirteen and was said to have been with up to sixty boys although I have no doubt that was a serious exaggeration. Certainly she was kind enough to let me touch her beneath her skirt and I was still young enough to wonder what all the fuss was about.

Almost all of the girls there shared their favours with many of the boys and I have always been a little ashamed of an occasion when I rescued a girl named Gail from the unwanted attentions of a boy, only to take his place minutes later.

Whether any of them went as far as full sex I do not know. Boys always claimed successes but I definitely never enjoyed any such conquests. This was a time of experiments and not for lasting relationships but it certainly left me with the feeling that life was not worth living. I was perhaps not the best looking or most desirable lad in the gang and I don't suppose my cleanliness standards would have won too many accolades at that time. It simply was still not an important feature of life.

The school dentist told me that I would not have a tooth left in my head by the time I was twenty if I didn't start to clean them. It took me a while before I did start but if he is still out there forty years later, I have still got them!

I may not have been a happy soul at home or at school but the one exception was the rugby where I found that I was blessed with a talent and I was still the second biggest lad in the year so I made the County Schools side at second row and went on to England trials though I was not good enough for the National team.

Unfortunately for me, I stopped growing at age fourteen. My two brothers are both six feet five, my sister was six feet and my mother was almost six feet. I was five feet ten at fourteen and I am five feet ten now. I may even be fractionally shorter now because I had to change positions in the scrum and front row forwards always get their heads pushed back into their shoulders a bit!

Indeed, my little extra talent led me to play for the second team of a local club too early and quickly snuffed out any ability I had. It can be disconcerting every week to wake up on the touchline to the smell of smelling salts having been knocked senseless by some ageing, twenty stone, has-been front row forward.

Chapter 2

Following Bill's death, I was now a man of substance. He had left me everything he had including the house which was valued at the princely sum of £400 and his life savings amounting to about £1600, all virtually untouchable until I was 21. My mother, who was named as an executrix, paid someone to clear the house of all the furniture, including many items, which, even then, were of value. Several valuable 'hunter' watches, gold chains and sovereigns also disappeared and I still resent the fact that the only things I have to remember Bill by are a gold horseshoe tiepin and a few sepia photographs.

The house was let to a friend of my mother at a very reduced rate and life went on as usual for me. I did find it hard to accept paying board and lodgings to my mother out of my paper round money but, in fact, I believe this was the norm in many Eastend households. I still think that £1 per week out of £2.10s was a bit much for a boy still at school.

It was then that I made the second of my big, lifestyle decisions. I decided that, when I left school, I was going to be a businessman. I had no idea what sort of business; I just knew that I would have some sort of business. My uncle, stepfather and both brothers all worked at Pollard Bearings, a local Engineering company and my stepfather assumed that I too would leave school as soon as possible and work there. There was no shortage of jobs but I had no intention of working in a factory and I never have.

The official age to leave Trinity was, by now, sixteen but I had no interest in school, was not doing very well and my family could see no reason for me to stay on when I could be earning money. As for me, I wanted my own business, knew I would have to learn how to run it and saw that the local corner Co-op shop seemed to do a good trade so I went and asked for a job there. I left school at the Easter of my fifteenth year and started filling blue bags with sugar for £1.5s a week. I had to keep on the paper round as well to make ends meet.

I hated it from day one. It was a total drudge and after a short time I was transferred to the main Co-op in Abington Street, Northampton where I worked on the sweet counter. Not good for someone prone to put on weight and I still hated it. I was still on the edge of the Teddy Boy scene and had taken to wearing tight trousers and a longish jacket with suede shoes although I was not involved with any of the major Teddy Boy gangs that were rife at the time.

I still went to the park when I could and it was there that an event occurred which ultimately changed my whole life and set me on a completely different path. I met a girl at the park and started to talk to her. She eventually agreed to meet me in the Town Centre on a Saturday night and go from there to St Mary's Church Hall in Far Cotton where there was a dance.

Dressed to kill in the latest fashion of grey slacks, Italian style blazer and winkle-picker shoes I made my way to the town centre to meet her. I was early and waited impatiently for her to arrive. It was the style for girls to turn up late and I wasn't too worried when, half an hour after the appointed time, she wasn't there. An hour late meant I had been stood up and I crashed down into the depths of despair. She obviously wasn't coming and I had to decide what to do.

As a fifteen year old, I simply could not believe that she had turned me down in so harsh a way. Was I to wait even longer, go home or go to the dance by myself in the vain hope that she had misunderstood the meeting arrangement?

It was at that moment that Jeffrey came along. A less likely figure for my saviour could not be imagined. He was tall and thin, generally not a popular lad. He had dirty teeth and an old fashioned hairstyle. He was a wimp! However, he probably doesn't know, even now, that he became my hero that night even if it was in a convoluted and odd way.

Jeffrey was walking, as usual, alone in the town. He lived near to me and asked what I was doing. My first thought was to suggest that the one thing I didn't want was to have the company of a wimp, but then he said those immortal words, "I'm thinking of going to St Mary's dance, do you fancy going there?" Well that was the problem solved wasn't it? If she had mixed up the meeting place, I could just dump Jeffrey and if she wasn't there, I had a companion. Who was to know? Maybe we might even meet someone else and, as he was such a wimp, I would look the best choice of a pair if we met two girls.

When the bus arrived at St Mary's, we paid the entrance fee (I think it was 2s-6d) and went in. There she was, standing talking on the dance floor. My heart leapt with joy. Then it crashed down to the depths. She was with another boy. I had to speak to her so I found a moment when the boy was not around and went up to her. "What happened, I thought we were going to meet in the town centre?" I asked. "Oh, I was only kidding, I've got a boyfriend" she replied.

Tail firmly between the legs, I went back to find the only person in the room I knew – Jeffrey. When I did find him, he was talking to a large group of girls. Now, that didn't seem at all fair to me. There was Jeffrey the wimp, with this group of about eight girls and me, the guy in the blazer and Italian slacks, rejected. I had to go and join him to get myself introduced. It was easy as they were girls he knew from going to the Roadmenders club. That was a youth club in those days where they played table tennis and drank coffee. Not my scene.

One of the girls really caught my eye. She was tall, very slim with shortish hair in a current style and she seemed to smile at me. Her name was Jackie and I found out she worked at Richardson's Chemists. We spent the whole evening sitting and chatting. I couldn't dance anyway but she couldn't either because she had broken the heel of her shoe. It worked out quite well for me really. My mind began to work out how I was going to get to know her and separate her from the rest of the group. I decided the best plan would be to wait until we caught the bus back to the town centre when the dance ended at 10pm.

We joined the queue together, amazingly, just Jeffrey, the girls and me. No one else had tried to cut in all night. As we got on the bus, I had to work out the seating order so that I would end up with Jackie. No such luck. She sat down alone but before I could sit next to her, one of the other girls had done so. There was only one seat left, next to one of the other girls, Laura. I sat next to her and looked at her for the first time. She too was tall and slim with blonde hair. I was now in a dilemma because I could lose everything. It didn't occur to me that I could get off the bus when Jackie did and just ask to walk her home. That would be too daring but if I did nothing, I might not see any of them again.

I decided to take what seemed to me to be the only option; I asked Laura if I could walk her home. She said 'OK' and I started going out with her. She was a nice girl but we weren't suited at all. I joined the Roadmenders and virtually every night was spent there.

Abington Park was now only a venue for walks on a Sunday afternoon for us and my focus had changed completely. Who would have thought that, only months before, I was at risk of becoming a Teddy Boy, a rebel and maybe even on the wrong side of the law. Now I was a regular Youth club attendee and joining in with the woodwork classes, the table tennis and then meeting up with the girls for the last hour between nine and ten. Yes, that's right, we were segregated until 9 pm and even after that there were strict rules against physical contact between the sexes, except for dancing, which was allowed either to records or later, to our own group.

Although I was 'going out' with Laura, my attention was still firmly on Jackie and we all used to leave the club together to walk the first part of the journey home as a group before splitting up at Regent Square, where Jackie would go off to the left and the rest of us went right towards the town centre. In that short distance, I somehow managed to contrive to have an arm around Laura but at the same time hold hands with Jackie without poor Laura knowing. Or did she know? Because it was only three months before she told me that we were through. It was nothing dramatic. I arrived at her house on a Saturday night and she met me at the door. "I'm not coming out tonight" she said. When I asked why, she simply said, "I don't think we are really suited, we don't like the same things and it would be better if we just split up as friends."

That was another Saturday night when I wandered into town feeling really low and rejected. I didn't meet any Jeffrey that night but, by the time I returned home, I had resolved that, on the following Monday, I would ask Jackie if I could walk her home. The rest of the weekend was a blur. All I could think about was Monday night and how I would pluck up the courage to ask her.

Monday night finally arrived. I could hardly wait for nine o'clock, when we were allowed to mix with the girls. When the time came, I was first into the coffee bar and was soon joined by the group of girls including both Laura and Jackie. The hour until the club closed at ten seemed an eternity but then we were walking, as usual, to the separation point. I had not told them that we had split up until we reached Regent Square and I finally asked Jackie if I could walk her home.

She said 'Yes' and Jeffrey's unrecognised act as my saviour and life changer had, at last, been realised, three months after he had performed that unwitting act of kindness. I have never seen Jeffrey since the Roadmender days and I have never thanked him for what he did. Forty years late, I do so now.

It was only a very short walk to Jackie's house and we were there in five minutes. It was a small terraced house in Hampton Street and as we shared our first kiss outside, I looked over her shoulder to see the curtains open and her mother say, in surprise, "Our Jackie's got a boy out there". We both burst out laughing and I was taken in to meet her mother, father and younger sister, Ginnie – yes, that was the Ginnie who I had, almost three years earlier, demonstrated affection to by hitting her on the head.

From that night on, there was little doubt that Jackie and I were to become a long-term item. We instantly fell into a routine of meeting every night and every opportunity we could although, having walked to the Roadmenders together, we would then have to part until nine o'clock.

Another major change had occurred during the three months I was with Laura. My work at the Co-op was awful. I had known from day one that I did not like the boredom of working in a grocery shop and my transfer to the Central store had brought me under the close gaze of the manager of the flagship store. There was another, slightly older lad working there who had a tendency to know all the tricks to avoid work and acquire little 'perks' such as the odd packet of cigarettes or a few sweets from my counter. I knew what he was doing but did nothing about it, except to accept the occasional cigarette or sweet from him.

This must have been noticed by other assistants who obviously thought we were both stealing heavily from the shop. One day, one of the assistants, a middle aged woman, reported to the manager that I had just gone to the cigarette counter, taken a packet of Woodbines and put them in my trouser pocket.

I was immediately summoned to the manager's office where she repeated her allegation and I was instructed to turn my pockets out. This was in the era of 'The Fonz' (not the TV character but the real people he was based upon) and it was almost compulsory for teenage boys to run a comb through their slicked down hair whenever there was a possibility of a female passing, notwithstanding the fact that the said teenage boy might be serving in a food shop at the time. All I had actually done was to take a comb, which just happened to be the same shade of green as a Woodbine packet, from my pocket, run it through my hair and put it back.

I had no cigarettes of any brand and was able to prove my innocence but I decided that was the last straw and, the next week, I handed in my notice. One of the area managers saw me and asked me to stay by promising me that by the time I was 21 I would be given my own mobile shop to go round the villages and a salary of as much as £9 per week. Whether this was because of the false accusation or whether they felt there was some future for me was not clear but I had decided that I would not stay even for a promise of £9 a week in six years time.

Perhaps for the first time in my life, I found an adult exerting some influence over my decisions. My stepfather said that there was good money to be earned in the building trade and I was sent off to get myself a job. I went to several of the local builders alone, seeking any kind of work before he again took a hand and went with me to Messrs Adkins and Shaw Ltd where I was quickly signed on as an apprentice bricklayer.

This was not really in my plan but I felt that I had got to reconcile myself to gaining a trade qualification before realising my ambition to have my own business. On my first day, I was given little tasks on the site, which was in Kettering. I hated it. When they assigned me to a tradesman to be taught the rudiments of the trade, he was the most miserable man I had ever met. He was from the 'old school' who still wore a collar and tie with overalls and he believed the only way to teach someone was to tell them once and then shout at them until they learned.

That had been successful in teaching me French at school but I did not want to repeat the experience. My first ambition was to escape from him and I spent as much time as I could with the piecework bricklayers who were robust, genial men earning good wages but always ready for a joke or to play tricks on people.

I also admired the young labourers on the site, who were extremely fit and strong. There were two, both eighteen year olds, who would readily have a fight with anyone over the slightest provocation and, although somewhat afraid of them, because I was bigger than either but had not developed the physical strength they had, I was viewed as one of their peer group.

One day, whilst one of these two and myself were shovelling cement into a mixer, I swung the shovel out of time and hit him between the eyes with the sharp blade. He had to be taken to hospital and I was terrified of his reaction when he returned. I apologised as soon as I saw him but he just replied, "It's OK it was just an accident," and never mentioned it again.

On another memorable occasion, the two came into work looking as if an express train had run them down. Both had black eyes and bruises on their bruises. Both of them could barely walk but they managed to get through the day's work. When asked what had happened to them they both said they had been in a fight but would not be drawn further. We all assumed they were ashamed of having been beaten and avoided talking about it any more. It was some weeks before we discovered they had been fighting each other over some minor dispute.

Conditions on the site were basic to say the least. There were no washing facilities; the toilets were a trench dug by a JCB digger with a single plank and a small hut balanced over the top. A source of great glee was to tip the whole thing into the trench when someone was in the hut. Apprentices soon learned never to let anyone know if they were going there.

Lunch breaks would not be believed by modern builders. Bricklayers always took their large sharp trowels to lunch with them. The reason for this was that most bricklayers could throw a trowel like a throwing knife with great accuracy. Our task was to try to kill any rats that had got into the hut before the other workers arrived for lunch. I never saw anyone actually kill a rat but I certainly saw a few and the evidence of their footprints was often to be seen in the fat left in a frying pan from one day to the next.

Some of the labourers were so dirty and maleducated that they would happily eat anything left over from the day before or not wanted by the tradesmen. One in particular, whose name was Eric, used his tin mug so many times without cleaning it that someone wrote in the bottom of it the word 'poison'. On another occasion, one of the bricklayers made up some sandwiches of Kit-E-Kat cat food and told Eric he wasn't hungry. Poor Eric gladly accepted the gift and ate them with great relish. I am ashamed to say that I laughed as loud as the rest.

But building sites were dangerous places, even more then than now, and poor Eric came to a nasty end as far as that site was concerned. He was the on-site lorry driver and one day he backed it too near to a deep hole. Miraculously, he was not badly hurt but the lorry was and he was instantly fired.

I too had some narrow escapes. One day, I was carrying a concrete lintel over a plank crossing a trench. The plank gave way and I fell into the trench with the lintel on my shoulder. I managed to carry on work although I had bruised the shoulder and strained my stomach.

I was not a good first year apprentice, happier driving a dumper truck, shovelling with the labourers and avoiding my tradesman who by now hated me as much as I hated him. In that first year, apprentices did not start attending the Technical College and it amazes me that I managed to keep the job at that time. It may have had more to do with the Site Manager's love of rugby than my prowess as a bricklayer.

There was quite a lot of activity going on for me at that time and Jackie was the constant source of support, friendship and soon, love, that helped me through it all. I was still playing Rugby and training once per week. We had also decided to form a group at the Roadmenders.

Skiffle was just about dead and Rock'n'Roll was coming in but lots of lads were forming groups and hoping for fame and fortune. Most had acquired a guitar and could play the chords of F, Am, C and G7 which seemed to be all that were needed for the tunes of the day. I was no exception; the only problem being that I knew not a note of music, had no sense of rhythm and could not tune a guitar. I could not even play the chords in order unless someone told me the sequence. Fortunately, we had a lead guitarist in Julian Coulter who could play anything if he heard it once, a good drummer named Graham Waugh, Michel Karew, a bass guitarist of some talent and we were rounded off by Glenn Ward who was better than me as a rhythm guitarist. Thus we were probably the only group with two rhythm guitarists. All we needed then was a singer. We all had a try and I recall my own audition, "Got myself a crying, talking, sleeping, walking, living doll...." I warbled. "OK, that's enough," they all said and there ended my singing career.

We did find ourselves a singer, an evil looking, one eyed lad who shall remain nameless because he only lasted a short time before going off to serve Her Majesty – doing time in the Nick! Johnny Charalambou replaced him and 'Johnny and the Jetstreams' were born. Apart from my own poor efforts, they were not a bad group and after some practice before the discerning audience at the Roadmenders we moved on to a regular Friday night session at the Gayways club in Abington Street run by Ron and Jean Stanley and a regular Saturday night 'gig' at the 'Tech Dance' at St Mary's Hall in Far Cotton.

It is hard now to know how all this was fitted in, combining a still new career with Rugby, the band and a steady girlfriend but somehow, it worked. We had settled into a regular pattern of going either to the Roadmenders or a café in Abington Street, near to the Gayways called, 'The Gainsborough'. It was not quite as sophisticated as the name suggests and it was quite possible for an impoverished couple of teenagers to buy a cup of coffee each, one sticky bun to share and put threepence in the jukebox as the total fee for their evening's entertainment.

A fierce assistant named Peggy would ensure that good order was maintained and we would regularly meet up with a group of friends to ensure that the supply of threepenny pieces kept the music going. Two favourites were 'Oh Carol', by Neil Sedaka and 'Rocking Goose' by Lord Rockingham's Eleven and these would be played incessantly.

Money was a source of concern. I earned the princely sum of £1. 5s per week and could no longer do my paper round because I had to leave for work too early. Jackie earned £2. 10s. Luckily, my mother had suspended the payment of board so we could just about manage if we were very careful. I had managed to acquire a BSA Bantam motorcycle by selling my bicycle and having the balance (about £10) on hire purchase but it was such a poor machine that I spent most of my time pushing it. I had to push it while I was with Jackie anyway because I was still a learner driver.

It was during this period that my mother went to America to visit my sister who was having major problems with her husband. He had taken to drinking and mixing with the Mafia on a very small scale and the plan was that my mother would help her to resolve her problems.

As is often the case, a mother and daughter who could never see eye-to-eye when they were living in the same house had become very close when apart and my mother was quite happy to board a plane for the first time in her life to see for herself what was happening. There was one difficulty for her. Neither she nor my stepfather had enough money for the fare and they had to ask me if they could borrow it from my inheritance.

Naturally, I agreed and it was subsequently repaid to the account in full but it seemed really odd and unnatural to me to be lending money to my own mother. It was symptomatic of our situation at that time that, when my mother went, she gave me a ten-shilling note and on the journey from the Gainsborough to Jackie's house, I lost it and spent literally hours covering the ground to try and find it without success.

Soon after she had left, I noticed a strange lump in my lower groin and was extremely worried. I had no one I felt I could turn to about such an intimate problem. I did not feel I knew my stepfather well enough to discuss it with him and although Jackie and I were now very close, our relationship certainly had not gone that far. That sounds odd in these enlightened days but the liberated sixties were not that liberated.

Finally, I had to do something. The lump was getting bigger and certainly not going away. One Sunday afternoon, Jackie and I were on the Racecourse when I decided I had to tell her. I'm not sure what went through the mind of this innocent, convent-educated seventeen year old when I started to undo my trousers on a sunny afternoon in the park but she had no doubts when I was able to shyly expose this sensitive area. A visit to the doctor was needed urgently and my stepfather had to know.

The doctor quickly diagnosed a hernia, probably caused by the earlier fall into the trench with the lintel at work and I had to have an operation at the Nissen Ward at Northampton General Hospital – yes, it WAS a Nissen hut converted into a hospital ward. The usual hospital stay for such an operation was six weeks but they agreed to let me go home after two because my mother, who of course knew nothing about it, was due home.

Relations between Jackie and my mother were not wonderful. They were not improved on mothers return when the 45-rpm record she had brought me back from America was left on a chair and Jackie sat on it on her first visit. I never did get to hear Jimmie Rodgers singing 'Devil Woman'.

We did not really feel comfortable in the house and tended to spend a huge amount of time at my eldest brother's house nearby. I have no idea how they managed to tolerate us so often but they did and we have remained firm friends as well as relations ever since. One should not be left with the impression that Jackie and I were simply a perfect match and never at odds with each other. We would argue regularly and on one occasion, Jackie stormed off to the Racecourse leaving me at my brother's. When I eventually went to find her, I was unsuccessful and finally returned to my brother's to find her back there, hiding behind the settee having waited until I was out of the house before sneaking back in.

I decided that the BSA Bantam had to go and borrowed £15 from a lad at the Roadmenders to buy a BSA 250cc motorbike that was advertised at Churchills of Silverstone. Jackie and I set off on the bus one Saturday afternoon and made the deal. Then we had to get it home. The garage owner showed me how to start it up and we mounted the bike for the 12-mile journey back.

As we approached Northampton on the Towcester road, the bike started to slow down and I thought it was having trouble. It was. I hadn't realised that you had to change down a gear when going up hill. But then, with no licence, no insurance, no helmets and precious little experience of a motorbike that would actually run, it wasn't that surprising. We were lucky enough to get home without being stopped and that was good fortune indeed as we had to go to Jackie's house in the centre of town.

That motorbike was only a slight improvement on the previous one and it was not too long before we decided to move up market and buy a Lambretta scooter for the massive sum of £55 from Bert Avill in Barrack Road. I also had to get a proper driving licence and we also bought matching helmets (white ones with peaks). This really opened up new horizons for us because we used it to travel literally thousands of miles, visiting the seaside and various interesting places.

Johnny and The Jetstreams were still going from strength to strength and we had to become members of the Musicians Union for some of the bigger dates we were obtaining. If we had an important gig, we all used to go to Fraser Son and McKenzie's music shop and borrow top class equipment on approval, returning it the next day as unsuitable. One night, Gayways advertised a special attraction. The 'Terry Woods, £1000 equipment' group from London. Yes that's how they billed themselves. We were to be the back up group as usual so we all went to good old Fraser Son and McKenzie's and borrowed the most dazzling guitars they had. I recall that I had a Fender Stratocaster as used by Hank Marvin. The look on the faces of Terry Wood and his group was something to behold even if they played better than us.

The group was now becoming a problem. As we grew in confidence and the gigs were improving, it was taking more and more time. Jackie started to get a bit jealous because, as was the fashion in those days, the girls in the audience would come to the front and scream in ecstasy at us. I could still only manage C, Am, F and G7 in the wrong order and by now, the group were beginning to turn my amplifier down a bit so it did not spoil the sound too much.

I think it was a relief to all when Jackie gave me the ultimatum, "Either the group goes or I do, I'm not having all those girls screaming at you every week." The group went on to tour Germany in the footsteps of 'The Beatles' – well, the same venues anyway, until they somehow upset the local Polizie, had their equipment confiscated and were run out of town. They did stay together and I saw them, many years later, playing in a nightclub in Corby when I was a Detective Inspector. Oddly they did not invite me to join in for a session.

Of course, I had managed to get through my first year of apprenticeship and had moved on to the second year when we began to attend the Technical College. Having had, what was effectively a Grammar School education, I found that, academically if not practically, I could leave the other students standing. The most advanced Maths we did was covered in my first school year and in respect of report writing I found it less than elementary. 100% scores in all the tests were easy. This led to me receiving the award of 'The Silver Trowel'. It wasn't really silver of course and I felt a real fraud because many of the other students were better than me at laying bricks, which was, of course, what we were there for.

I still hated bricklaying. It was mind numbingly boring, it was very hard work and I could see no future in it. I still had my ambition to own my own business and this was my principal reason for staying with it. Also, I have never been able to let something go once I have started it and I was determined to complete the apprenticeship.

When I was eighteen, Jackie and I decided to buy our first car. It was a 1955, Austin A30 which we bought from an old lady who was giving up driving. It had low mileage and looked wonderful. Its 800cc engine was in good condition and I was blissfully unaware of a design fault on the A30, which was subsequently to cost me dearly.

The winter of 1962/63 was the worst since 1947 and deep snow fell the day after Boxing Day. We were building houses at Moulton and all the site workers except the foreman and me (as the one apprentice on site) were laid off. That snow remained, almost three feet deep until some time in

March. My foreman insisted that I stay on site throughout, though he had found a nice warm welcoming resident of the female persuasion to look after him through the winter.

I managed to thaw some bricks and sand in a hut and built a fireplace, complete with chimney and grate where I burned a tonne of coke in three months. It was probably the coldest, loneliest time of my life and the foreman would not even allow me to go home early because he had to have someone watching for deliveries (there were none) whilst he enjoyed himself.

I did manage to get in a few driving lessons with my brother and took the test which I failed. Several lessons with the BSM improved my chances and I retook the test, just as the weather finally broke, in April 1963. Despite reaching 32 miles per hour on a downhill slope when the examiner clapped his hands for the emergency stop, he still gave me a begrudging pass and we were now free to go where we wanted to.

Trips to Great Yarmouth, Brighton and even London became possible and we began to plan a summer holiday. We were going to sleep in the car together and what our parents would have said, had it come to pass, I cannot imagine, not to mention the practicality of sleeping in a tiny car like the A30. But it was not to be in any event.

At work, I had progressed into a fast, if not particularly accurate, bricklayer. Even though the apprenticeship was for 5 years, at eighteen I had spent as much time as I could with the pieceworkers and they would contribute to my wages. I was working with a new gang of two bricklayers and one labourer on a site at Wellingborough, where we were earning a good salary and building houses very quickly.

Sometimes, I would go to work on the company transport but, occasionally, I would use our car. On Saturday 21st July 1963, we decided to work in the morning and I therefore went in the car. We were 'topping out' a house, which entailed cutting all the bricks up to the peak of the gables, and we finished it at about 1pm. I agreed to give a lift to two of the site labourers.

We set off from the site along Northampton Road and past the Earls Barton crossroads on what is now the A4500. The road from there is a very steep incline and is three lanes wide. Following close behind was the firm's lorry and we were travelling at about 45 mph. Part way down the incline, I must have drifted slightly towards the kerb and hit a pothole where a sunken drain remained unrepaired from the previous winter.

Most people involved in road accidents say afterwards that they do not remember anything of it. I doubt if that is truly correct and it certainly was not the case for me. One colleague was in the rear seat and the other in the front passenger seat. None of us were wearing seatbelts because they were not fitted when my car was built.

I recall very clearly, the sensation of hitting the pothole, which immediately threw the car onto the pathway. The design fault with the A30 was that its wheelbase was far too narrow at just over four feet and the car became unstable on any sharp turns. I had experienced it before if I ever took a bend a little too fast but I had never experienced anything like the results of trying to get the car back on the road at 45mph.

It swerved violently towards the far kerb and I could see the hedgerow coming at me. I turned the wheel into what was really a dry skid and the car responded and stayed on the road. I had over-corrected and began to head back towards the nearside kerb. This was more than the narrow little car could take and I heard the front seat passenger shout, "Look out". I glanced towards him and saw to my horror that he was trying to open the door to get out.

Disaster struck. Just as he opened the door, the car flipped over, rolling towards me and throwing him out of the other side but up into the air. I was fully aware of the sensation of rolling over four times, twisting in the air and rolling twice more end to end. I could even remember flying upside down at one stage.

I must have passed out then because I was thrown out of the open driver's window and landed on the road. I was bleeding from a wound to my back, where the small quarter light window had caught me as I went out. Another wound on my right elbow was also bleeding heavily and I had cuts and bruises all over my body. I felt nothing and picked myself up. The car was lying, on its wheels, at right angles to the road and in the centre, completely blocking the middle lane at the bottom of the hill. I saw my rear seat passenger getting out of it and my mind would not register that I could not find my front seat passenger.

I immediately began to try to direct traffic. This was, of course, ridiculous because everything was stopped but it must have been the shock and concussion. A woman came up to me and said, "you silly bugger, you were trying to overtake." This was equally ridiculous and I was much offended at the injustice of the comment. There had been no vehicle in front of us to overtake but I suppose she was equally shocked. Certainly I never saw her again and she did not make a statement to the police.

Suddenly, I remembered my front seat passenger and looked around for him. I noticed a group of people kneeling and standing around something of the verge about twenty yards ahead of where the car had ended up. Surely this could not possibly be him because the car had gone through six somersaults after he had got out. But it was him. He had been thrown high into the air and over this massive distance by the impetus of the speed of the car combined with the catapult effect of rolling over.

The police and two ambulances arrived at that moment and my rear seat passenger and I were taken to one of them. My friend from the front seat was obviously seriously injured and he was placed gently into the other ambulance. We began the journey to Northampton General Hospital but then, unbelievably, the ambulance that he was in broke down. We all stopped and he was carefully transferred to the one we were in. This was absolutely awful. The rear seat passenger and I were both fully conscious and had to sit watching as the crew worked on our friend's massive head injuries.

Finally, we arrived at the hospital and were treated. My rear seat passenger was soon discharged but I was kept in over night. After a night of nightmares and being unable to find out any information about my other friend's condition, I woke to hear two nurses talking outside my room. "Did you lose any during the night?" one said. "Yes, I'm afraid we lost two. There was the racing driver from Silverstone and the other one from the road crash…." Her voice tailed off and I was not sure of what I had heard. It couldn't be my passenger, he couldn't be dead.

I still could get nothing from the nurses about his condition and then, finally, the traffic police arrived. They were very reasonable and prepared to spend as much time as I needed to tell the story. But I only wanted one thing. I had to know how my friend was. Very tenderly, they explained that it was indeed him who was the second patient who had died during the night.

I was distraught. I could not stop crying and these two large, official policemen were very kind and helpful. Despite my unusual life history, I had never been prepared for this. My friend had a wife and nine children, all under the age of sixteen. I could not reconcile how this could have happened to him and I was relatively unscathed.

Later that day, I was allowed to go home and was collected by my brother. I had no idea what to do next and was now, finally beginning to feel the pain of my injuries. Jackie and I had some tearful sessions as I convalesced and my eldest brother took me to see the car, which was certainly beyond repair. He also took me to the scene of the crash where, amazingly, the pothole had already been repaired. A major problem for me was that I could not get into a car without bursting into tears and I began to doubt if I would ever drive again. My brother offered to take us to Great Yarmouth for a day, in an effort to get me out of it but I spent the whole journey in the rear seat crying and unable to look up.

The car had been insured only for third party risks so, obviously, we could not replace it. The Insurance Company dealt with my friend's widow and it was a long time before I discovered how much she had been paid. Certainly not enough to compensate for the loss of a husband in her situation. The inquest was at Northampton General Hospital and, naturally, I had to attend with the rear seat passenger and face our other friend's family. Little was said and the jury returned a verdict of 'Accidental Death'. The explanation for the crash was fully accepted and I was not prosecuted even for Driving without Due Care and Attention.

Life had to go on. I returned to work with the same gang, who had all witnessed the accident and provided me with their rough sympathy and support. The rear seat passenger and I became firm friends. It was as if the shared experience had created a bond between us and we began to go out with him and his girlfriend as a foursome. By now, we were working at Rothwell and used to be collected in an open-backed landrover on Barrack Road to travel the country road to Rothwell. One day, the driver told me that they had decided they were going to get me over my continuing fear of motor vehicles. Their simple psychology was drastic but it worked. They insisted that I sit in the back and the driver would go as fast as he possibly could along the eight-mile route. I gradually went from paralysed fear to grudging acceptance to the reconciliation of my phobia.

Eventually, I bought an old van and began to drive again but it was at least a year before I was able to do so with any confidence. I subsequently began to receive hate mail, which was obviously from my dead friend's family, and this became so bad that we had to go to the police and ask their help to get it stopped. They obviously did because the mail had dried up by the following Christmas.

There was one other strange outcome some time later, which was an encounter I had in a public house in the Town centre. I was drinking with one of our labourers and he said, "I've got someone I want you to meet," and took me to a dark haired woman who was drinking at the bar. He then said, "This is XXXX's widow" and told her who I was. I was amazed that he could do such a thing and thought she might attack me but she was very pleasant and said she realised it was an accident and I could not help it. Later, when I confronted him, he explained that it was a set up and really she just wanted the chance to tell me that there were no hard feelings.

Jackie and I had got engaged just after the accident and planned to marry the following July. Well, actually, Jackie had decided we would. Every night we had fallen into a ritual as we walked home. She had a pet phrase. "Whens ya gonna marry me Honey?" which was repeated until I gave in.

Chapter 3

At this time, I had become somewhat dominated by my mother, which is surprising considering my background, but it was a combination of the events of the year, combined with the natural tendency of Eastend mothers to rule their sons. Telling her we were getting married, especially as I would be nineteen and Jackie twenty was not easy. She did not approve. What made it worse was when I announced that I wanted my house back to live in and her friend would have to find somewhere else to live.

Nevertheless, our plans went ahead and we managed to get mother's friend to leave amicably about nine months ahead of the wedding. We needed this time to modernise the house. We wanted a picture window in the kitchen (overlooking a blank wall six feet away), new doors throughout, a bathroom in the rear bedroom and the rest of the windows replacing with louvre windows.

Some real friends came to our rescue then. The main source of inspiration was Trevor Eden, a carpenter who gave us months of his time without any charge whatsoever. Iain Rivers, a gas fitter and plumber and Russ Abbott, an electrician (not a comedian) all joined in, giving their services free of charge and we actually managed to complete the work a week before the wedding.

There were some interesting experiences along the way. I had only ever seen Jackie drunk on one occasion before. That was when a friend had taken us out for the evening in his green Ford Consul with Venetian blinds in the back window, a knob on the steering wheel for making really cool turns one handed and just a generally cool machine. Jackie had not known what to drink and I suggested the only female drink I could think of, Cherry B. Half a dozen of those and she was out for the count. I had to smuggle her past her parents so she could go straight to bed without them knowing and she decided she didn't really like drinking.

Whilst we were renovating however, one of my mother's friends brought his lorry to take away the rubbish and when we had loaded it, he charged me £2 and promptly spent it buying us drinks in 'The Bat and Wickets'. I had not realised that Jackie had drunk a couple of Gin and Bitter Lemons and when we returned to the house, Trevor Eden and I were talking for about an hour before we realised she was missing. We started a search and eventually located her in the middle bedroom lying on an old mattress, fast asleep. I think she must have been tired!

The whole gas supply had to be replaced because it was in lead pipes and Iain worked for the Gas Board. He knew how to do it but we could not afford the cost of having it done officially. Iain therefore agreed to replace the meter by getting all the joints loosened off, the new equipment ready and then disconnecting the old with the gas supply still on.

To achieve this, he had to hold his breath while the cellar was filling up with gas and very quickly make the new connection. Obviously (because he is still alive) he did it, but only just before he passed out and we had to revive him and give him lots of milk to counteract the effects.

Tensions were very high and we all, except Jackie, were smoking heavily. She has never smoked and did not approve but that had no real effect on us. The only controlling factor was money and, about a week before the wedding, one evening, Terry, Iain and I clubbed together to buy a packet of five Senior Service. One each was fine but then someone had to miss out on the second round. Now, it seems so inevitable that it would be me but I did not see it that way then.

We could not agree and ended up fighting, with punches and rolling about the floor to decide who lost out. I cannot even claim that it was good- natured fighting because it wasn't. What it did achieve was to make me decide, in the cold light of day to give up smoking and I did, permanently.

My sister, who by now had changed her name from Florence to Theodora (Teddy) and had ditched her husband after finding him with a gun hidden under his pillow, came over for our wedding with her two children, Brett and Craig, who were to be our pageboys. They were a revelation. None of us knew what to expect from American children and these two were the epitome of our worst nightmares.

Brett was five and Craig was four. The younger one was all charm and smiles but very devious with it and Brett, well Brett was something else. I thought from the outset that there was something odd about him. This impression was probably created when Jackie and I babysat for them in the week before our wedding. They both flatly refused to go to bed or indeed do anything we tried to tell them to do. Jackie tried to be firm with them and this had the somewhat unexpected and unusual result of Brett simply spitting in her face.

Now, I am a fairly placid and unflappable individual but I was not that calm then. It has often been said that we have a family trait, which leads us to be outwardly calm and not prone to violent temper. Unfortunately, when that temper snaps it is potentially more violent than in people who are normally more volatile.

I absolutely saw red. I can barely recall chasing him up the stairs of my mother's house but I caught him at the top and hit him. He took off and hit the wall above his bed before sliding down in a heap. I am not proud of that. I was a very strong nineteen-year-old and he was five but I truly could not help myself. As soon as I realised what I had done, panic set in. I believed I had done him serious harm and pictured the wedding cancelled, me in prison and my sister not speaking to me again. I could not honestly say I cared about what happened to him, only the consequences.

To my amazement, he just looked up, laughed and said, "You didn't hurt me" in a very insolent manner. He never told his mother and we only admitted that they had been difficult.

On the day of the wedding, we faced the prospect of our two pageboys with some trepidation but we need not have worried. They were as well behaved as anyone could have hoped for and the ceremony went off without a hitch. Everyone was there in their finest at The Church of the Holy Sepulchre, which is a fine old building and a perfect setting for a summer wedding.

From there we went to the reception at The Friendly's Club and one of Jackie's aunts embarrassed us by getting drunk and noisy. Back at our newly refurbished house afterwards, we were both unceremoniously dumped onto the bed by my family and left to it.

Now, most people go off on honeymoon at that point but we pooled all our resources and found we were left with the princely sum of 10s 0d (50p) between us, to last us a fortnight so our honeymoon was to be spent at home. By 7pm, we were sitting wondering what we could do. We had no TV so we decided to walk to Jackie's parents' house, where the family was still having a quiet drink.

Our lives then settled into a routine of work and domestic bliss, punctuated by constant quarrels between my mother and Jackie. Mother developed a habit of coming in to see me before Jackie got home and asking for Jackie to go round to her as soon as she got in. (The houses were of course next door to each other). This was a cause of much upset, as Jackie wanted to prepare dinner and my mother invariably only wanted some trivial problem resolving. It was probably her way of making friends but it certainly did not work and it was some years before they developed any kind of understanding.

We decided to start a family and our first son Martin was born on 12th

December 1965, which was my 21st Birthday. It was also the day I completed my apprenticeship and decided that the time had come to start my own business using the inheritance, which also passed into my hands on that date.

With hindsight, I can see that I was far too inexperienced as a builder and as a businessman for such an enterprise at that age. I had no idea of estimating work, how to go out and win contracts and, most importantly, how to collect debts. If I could have realised it, there was little chance of a business as a jobbing builder being successful. There were so many trying to succeed in the same business; an estimate would have to be so low to get the work that it was impossible to make a profit.

A recession contributed to the problems because no one had the courage to have work carried out in the uncertainty about the future and, quite often, those that did couldn't pay at the end. I had employed my elder brother and my father-in-law, who was also a bricklayer but soon found I did not have enough work to keep them on and had to let them both go. This was very traumatic for one so young, having to fire two close relations who I liked a great deal but it became inevitable.

It was then brought home to me, how difficult it can be for a jobbing builder working alone. I had a roof repair job to carry out on an old terraced house and, lacking the proper equipment, I put one ladder against the side of the house with a second one resting against it up to the ridge of the roof. The first ladder was tied, through a bedroom window, to an old gas bracket and I relied on this to hold the second ladder in place.

When I climbed to the top and started up the rungs of the second ladder on the roof, carrying my tools and cement, I soon found that the bracket gave way and the ladder I was on, started to slip down the roof. I had a split second to decide whether to dive for the ridge and hold on or to try to scramble back onto the first ladder before it moved too far away from the wall. I decided to go for the latter option, as the first would have left me stranded on the roof. I managed to get back onto the ladder when the top was almost three feet away from the wall. I have never liked heights very much and when I finally got back on the ground I resolved not to take on any more roof work.

I can see now, that even faced with those difficulties, opportunities still existed for the business to be successful. One contract with an asphalting company was quite lucrative and could have been developed by someone with more acumen than I had at that time. It certainly provided me with some excitement when we were tasked to repair the pits at Silverstone circuit. The pits are located in the centre of the circuit and I had to get my heavy old builder's van across the track to start work. I was a little surprised to see an ambulance and a marshal at the entrance to the track on a Monday morning and I was even more surprised when the marshal stopped me and told me to wait at the entrance as they were testing cars.

Finally, he told me to get on the track, keep to the nearside until I was level with the pits and then carefully check my mirrors before crossing as quickly as I could. I set off at my maximum speed of about 30mph and then, just as I was about to cross over, I looked in the mirror to see a huge Vauxhall bearing down on me at about 120mph. He shot past me and I was off that track quicker than I thought possible. That was my only claim to fame as a racing driver but I can honestly say that I have driven Silverstone circuit.

Soon after this, not realising that the business was already in difficulties, we decided that it was time to move house. The squabbles between my mother and Jackie were not getting better and we felt we needed to set up anew elsewhere. We bought a new house in Beaufort Drive, New Duston. It was a three bedroomed chalet style house, which cost us £3250 with a mortgage of £2000 at £5 per week. It was a very pleasant home and we furnished it better than we should have, given the state of our finances.

This effectively solved the attempts by my mother to dominate our lives because we were too far away for interference and I was surprised how much better the relationship became. The main problem now became my enthusiasm for running the Rugby Club. I had joined the Trinity Old Boys' team because of the ties to school and the fact that they only had thirteen players and needed fifteen for a team. Together with a few close friends in the team, we started to build a viable club and I spent far more time on the task of Team Secretary than I should have, to the further detriment of the business.

Jackie became very frustrated with my attitude to the club and, on more than one occasion, she actually hid my rugby kit on a Saturday in the hope that it would stop me playing. She was mistaken in this because it just redoubled my determination to play. Playing also took my mind off the problems of the business, which was getting further into debt at the bank. Anyone who has not known the misery of a failing business and the dreaded letters from the Bank Manager cannot know how stressful it can be. It is necessary to put on a smile for the customers, try to get work and get payments in, when all you really want to do is forget the whole problem.

This came to a climax for me when an old school friend asked me to build an extension for a bathroom at his terraced house in Moore Street. I found myself putting off the start of the job by finishing small tasks elsewhere when I knew I needed to get started on the bigger contract. Eventually, he came and found me where I was working and forced me to order the materials.

I soon found that I had underestimated the costs and encountered problems with the foundations when I discovered a well, immediately beneath where a main wall was to go. Although I overcame the problem and enlisted help from friends, ex-colleagues and the client, to complete the job, I incurred even further losses and decided to get out of the business before it went bankrupt.

Our second child, Carolyn had been born on 17 June 1967. Of course, the expense of two very young children added to the burden we faced and there were some extremely hard times. I cannot now believe that, when we decided that I would have to close the business down, our car fell in need of major repairs and I actually went out and bought a brand new Vauxhall Viva. I can only think that this was some form of psychological compensator for the state I found myself in. Having gone from a position of having a house, which I owned and a substantial sum in the bank, I now had a mortgage, owed the bank several hundreds of pounds and incurred the debt of a new car.

Fortunately, the building trade began to boom and I was able to join a gang of bricklayers with one of the men I had worked with as an apprentice. It was extremely good of him to take me on, as they were already a 'standard' size gang of two tradesmen and a labourer. They were all self-employed on what became known as 'The Lump', which was later outlawed as a tax avoidance device.

My former colleague effectively led the gang and persuaded the others that we could make a team of three tradesmen and one labourer work. And so it did except that it made too much work for the labourer and the tradesmen had to take turns helping him out. Our gang leader was a very dominant character who always insisted that things had to be done his way (and he was often right) but that did not make for happy working relationships. The other tradesman soon formed a closer bond with me. Indeed, we were closer in age and tended to use newer ideas to get the work done. This was to lead to a serious, moral dilemma for me and ultimately contribute to my decision to join the police force.

After a few months, during which, I managed to recover my financial position fully, he invited Jackie and me to tea one Sunday afternoon. The purpose of the visit soon became clear. He wanted to contrive a quarrel with our leader so that we could fall out with him and split up the gang, leaving the leader and the labourer to find another tradesman while we started a new gang, using a labourer who my new partner knew.

Reluctantly, I agreed to his plan. I was tired of our leader's ways and knew that my new partner and I could earn really good pay if left to our own devices. I was, nevertheless, a little ashamed of the subterfuge and the fact that our leader was the one who had allowed me to be 'a cuckoo in his nest'.

The following day, we started work at 8am and my new partner began to instigate a dispute with our leader. This went on for about 15 minutes before I decided it was not my way of dealing with problems. I believed in meeting things head on so I walked up to our leader and just told him outright that we had decided to leave. He exploded! There was a great deal of abuse thrown around and my new partner and I walked off the site. I felt much better about dealing with it in this way even though I still felt really bad about leaving our leader in this way.

My new partner and I drove about a mile to another site, where we instantly found work and his friend joined us later the same day. I have not seen our leader since but, surprisingly, my new partner managed to get from him the money we were owed for the previous week's work. We stayed together for almost two years, working at various sites around the town including the Housing Association development at the junction of Harlestone Road and Cotswold Avenue, Northampton, where we built most of the houses.

I never really got used to the idea of the dirty deed we had carried out on our older friend and I resolved that I did not want to spend my whole life laying bricks. I had had a Grammar school education, I knew I was not unintelligent and bricklaying was the most boring, soul-destroying job I could imagine.

Finding a change of career direction was no longer quite so easy as it had been when I started work and I made a number of applications for jobs as a sales representative without success. I did get to interview several times but bricklayers were obviously not a popular choice.

One day, I went to see a football match at the County Ground, Northampton and there I met an old school friend who was on duty as a police officer. Jason Holding had been in the year above me but our interest in Rugby had brought us together. I told Jason about my situation and he asked me why I had not considered the police service as a career. I told him I would love to but could not afford to drop to the salary they earned at that time. Jason said they had recently been awarded a big pay rise and they were seeking people to 'join the thousand pounds a year men' which was the advertising slogan in use at that time.

I was then earning £80 to £100 per week but there was no holiday pay and no income if the weather was too bad to lay bricks, (which was quite often). I calculated that an average annual income was probably not more than £1400 and the police wage was enhanced by allowances. Perhaps I wasn't such a brilliant mathematician. My bricklaying career was effectively over though my partner was very unhappy with me when I told him, and he never spoke to me again after he had told me that he thought we were partners for life.

Jackie was very supportive of my decision to join the thousand pounds a year men but when I told my family they were totally incredulous and opposed to the idea. I broke it to them at a Sunday teatime gathering in my mother's house and I was quite surprised at the level of opposition, particularly as I then learned that my uncle had been a Special Constable, as had his father. Of course, this had little effect on me. I had always been independent and the decision was only being imparted to them, not introduced for discussion.

There was one last chapter in my building career. We had heard about a house for sale in Kingsley Avenue. It was a three bedroomed-terraced house with a bay front and a huge rear garden. Unfortunately, it suffered from subsidence and dry rot. The result of these two problems was that the rear elevation had sunk by about six inches, taking the roof with it and the ground floor was unsafe to walk on. I had concluded that, if it could be purchased at the right price, it could be corrected.

The plan was to remove the slates, demolish the back wall and jack up the roof to its proper height. The rear wall foundations would be replaced and the wall rebuilt. The rubble would then be used to replace the rotten wooden floor with a concrete screed. The asking price was £2500 and I made an offer of £1200. The Estate Agent laughed when I told him but I simply said. "Just put it to your client", knowing that no one would get a mortgage on such a property. I had to sell the house in New Duston to raise the capital and did so, raising £3950, which was a profit of £700 on the original purchase price. We had moved in with Jackie's parents on the basis that it would only be for a short time.

I heard nothing about my offer and my application to the police force was accepted. This meant that I would be going to the police-training centre at Ryton on Dunsmore for three months. Police officers were not allowed to own their own house until they had ten years service at that time so, when I heard, out of the blue, that my offer for the house was accepted, I could not follow it up. I was therefore left without a home but with some money in the bank again.

Chapter 4

May 9th 1969 was, for me, the beginning of a whole new world. I had no idea what to expect at the Police Training Centre at Ryton on Dunsmore but I had carefully shaved off my beard and had a very short haircut in anticipation that it would be a little like I imagined the Army to be, though I had no experience of that either. I had arranged to take a fellow new recruit with me as he had no car and I was the proud owner of an ancient Hillman Imp by this time. Unfortunately, the Hillman Imp, which had a rear-mounted engine, was a little prone to overheating. When we were about half way to the Training Centre, I noticed the light come on to indicate a problem.

I got out, lifted the bonnet and warned my colleague to stand back whilst I opened the radiator cap. What I was not aware of was the fact that he was a very curious individual who could not resist having a close look. A huge jet of boiling water shot from the radiator and soaked him from the waist down. He was badly scalded on both legs and I had no idea of how to treat him. I quickly found some sort of ointment in my case and applied it to his injuries. We decided it would then be best to carry on to the Training Centre to get better assistance, which we did.

On arrival, I was shocked to see that it was, indeed, an old Army barracks complete with parade ground. I went direct to the reception and was sent with my casualty to the first aid post where a large sergeant took charge. He patiently explained to me that ointment is not the recommended treatment for burns. In fact, I remember his carefully chosen words. "You stupid berk. Have you never learned anything in your life? Only a pillock would put something greasy on burned flesh. Don't you know it will just cook him? You'll be lucky to get through this course now. He'll probably sue you and if he doesn't, I'll make sure you learn something from this the hard way…etc., etc."

This was my introduction to the subtle ways of making learning easy at Ryton. As far as my colleague was concerned, he did not sue me but he had a very uncomfortable first five weeks after hospital treatment and, somehow, having forgotten that I did warn him to keep back, he never spoke to me again.

The regime was really quite harsh by modern standards. We were billeted in old Nissen huts and we were required to 'box' our bedding every day. For those who have not had this pleasure, it involves stripping the bed and folding the sheets and blankets into a neat box to be inspected by the sergeant. Failure to make it neat enough would result in having it thrown on the floor, having to re-do it all and then parade at reception in full uniform at 9pm for a personal inspection.

My sergeant was, in fact, a Northamptonshire officer who had a reputation as a real bully. I saw him lift a young recruit off the ground by his head for some minor infraction but this was probably because the lad came from the West Midlands Force, which was not popular with the sergeant.

Bullying was not restricted to the men either. The Drill sergeant had a nasty habit of shouting so loud and hard that his false teeth would literally fly out of his mouth. On one occasion when he did this, one of the young female recruits actually wet herself on the parade ground. I wonder what would be made of that today.

There were three intakes at the Centre and we were treated like new children at a school. The newest intake were only allowed into the Dining Hall after the others had been served, with the result that it was common to end up with no food or just what was left over.

I was surprised at how juvenile some of my colleagues were, although I was, at 24, the second oldest on the intake of 120 students. I went to bed early one night in the first week and was disturbed about an hour later by colleagues engaged in corridor sledging. Three men would run along the corridor towing a fourth on a blanket as fast as they could. They would then step aside and the person on the sledge careered on over the edge of the two steps down at the end to the great amusement of the others.

Spookily, this did not amuse a married, older, ex brickie who was trying to sleep and I asked them to desist. The threat of a broken nose seemed to help them decide to go elsewhere and although it was not my intention, it helped considerably to set me up as something of a leader in the group.

I quickly decided that I was not about to be bullied by anyone, least of all the sergeant but it was almost as if he knew and seemed to take a liking to me. In fact, he asked if I had had Military service but in fact, it was simply that I had decided that I would obey the rules provided they treated me with a little respect and it was really very easy to comply. When people asked me about the discipline, I replied that it was stricter than I expected but it was not like having to go to work, which was much harder.

At that time, Ryton was suffering from the attentions of an arsonist. The domestic staff was mostly comprised of displaced persons from the war who had stayed on in England and they were suspected. There were workers who came in for contracts, the grounds were totally insecure and, of course, there were the students although it was doubted if it was one of them because the fires had spanned a longer period than any of the intakes were there.

Some of the fires were quite serious and the management had instituted night-time patrols. Of course, this was a cheap option because the students got the job. Two would be appointed each night and would then be excused lessons until lunchtime. One of them had to man the switchboard whilst the other walked the grounds. When my turn came around, I set off on my patrol for the first hour and had only gone a short distance when I saw the glow of flames near to one of the dormitory blocks.

On running to see what it was, I found a patch of grass burning near to the female block. It was quite exciting to have an emergency on my very first lone patrol but I found that, having got it under control, calling out the sergeant and resolving the issue (We thought it was not the arsonist but a student smoking as he left the female block by a rear window) was a most satisfying experience. I kept going back all through the night to check it again and again in case someone started the fire again. I have noticed since that officers have a tendency to continue to pay attention to the scene of a crime and whether it is for curiosity or some complex instinct, I do not know but I do know that it has been known to pay off occasionally when a criminal returns to his crime for some reason.

My night patrol passed off without further excitement but I also discovered how lonely and eerie a night patrol could be. It was always to be my favourite tour of duty but one spends a great deal of time on edge, always expecting something to be waiting for you around the corner. The small night noises also seem more pronounced and suspicious and I contend that any police officer who says that he or she has not been scared at night is not telling the truth – but more of that later.

I learned to swim at the Mounts Baths in Northampton when I was eight. There were no formal lessons so the kids taught themselves and I only ever learned to do the 'crawl'. I was quite good at it and achieved the half-mile certificate as well as joining the local water polo team. It followed, logically, when I joined the police force, that I should claim on the application form that I could swim.

On the day of the first lifesaving session in Ryton's own pool (where,

The Author in Initial Police Training at Ryton-on-Dunsmore, Coventry

incidentally an instructor had drowned the previous summer) we were met by the fattest swimming instructor sergeant imaginable. In fact, I never ever saw him in the pool. His first bellowed instruction to us was, "Swimmers to me, non swimmers to the shallow end and splash about". Naturally, I went to his 'swimmers' group and he instantly selected me to dive in and swim two lengths breast stroke. No way! I could neither dive nor swim the breaststroke. My protestations met with little sympathy from the fat sergeant who told me that if I could swim I could dive AND do the breaststroke. I did my finest belly flop and somehow got to the shallow end without drowning. Once there I was able to hop and make it look like swimming until I recovered my breath enough for the return trip. The problem was that I was by then exhausted and approaching the deep end where I could not put one foot down.

The sergeant was not a very observant character but even he could see that I was in trouble about ten yards from the end. Nevertheless, there was no heroic rescue and I just had to make it alone. On dragging myself, half drowned from the pool, he just dismissed me to go to the shallow end with the other non-swimmers and none of us had another lesson. We simply went and splashed about in the shallow end three times a week.

I was determined to learn enough breaststroke to swim those two lengths and I did, though not very well. In the last week of the course, the sergeant finally spoke to the non-swimmers again and asked us if any of us wanted to try for the basic personal safety badge. I was the only taker.

The test included two lengths freestyle wearing pyjamas (no problem) two lengths on the back in pyjamas (no problem) then two lengths breast stroke in pyjamas (BIG problem but I did it) then a two minute session of keeping afloat in pyjamas followed by removing the pyjamas in the water and finally diving for a rubber brick. I won the badge and a little grudging respect from the sergeant and I still have the badge today. I don't suppose the sergeant still respects me and I certainly never respected him.

Sport was a major feature at Ryton and when the Rugby season ended (about one week into my course) we did cross country runs. One of these sticks in my memory, not because of the physical effort but because of a fellow student with whom I had made friends. He was particularly bad at running and, although I could have been in the early finishers because I was quite fit then, I stayed back talking to him about politics and we came in 144th and 145th (staff joined in as well as students for the benefit of the alert reader who will have noticed that there were only 120 students on the course). My fellow student went on to become the Chief Constable of West Yorkshire so, obviously, my views on politics helped him a great deal.

It is, or was, a popular misconception that the police are taught self defence at training school. To be fair, they are now; but the training was rudimentary to say the least in those days. A five feet nothing, ex- marine, civilian instructor used to give us the benefit of his wisdom for about two hours per week.

We were taught three holds, which were designated police hold No. 1, 2 and 3. I cannot recall which was which but I know one of them involved taking the persons right wrist, twisting it behind him, tucking it through your elbow and gripping his shoulder with your other arm to either lift him or bring him crashing to the floor depending whether he was bigger or smaller than you. The second involved bending the opponent's arm back in some excruciating manner and the third involved grasping him under the nose, avoiding his teeth, and lifting with the other hand behind his neck.

This is an interesting hold because it was designed to look like a gentle, persuasive movement to remove someone who is holding onto a railing whilst taking part in a demonstration or some other semi lawful activity. The police officer was supposed to accompany the lift with gentle words of encouragement such as, "Now, come along sir, you don't want to stay there".

What is interesting is that the recipient will be in excruciating pain in the nose and resistance is impossible. The downside is that a little too much pressure could result in the small bones in the nose breaking and going into the brain with instantly fatal results. A modern, drug crazed individual would be unlikely to feel the pain and might well resist too strongly with the undesired results, assuming he didn't manage to bite your hand off first.

It is probably significant that our instructor ended his lessons with the advice that a kick in the testicles was probably the best option when attacked by a psychopath and if you do go down, roll towards the kicks, not away from them.

We were also taught about the truncheon. Prior to the modern P24 side handled batons, police officers carried their truncheons in a special pocket down the side of the trousers (women had a tiny truncheon that fit in the handbag). Instructions were that no one was to be hit on the head unless it was unavoidable and that a report must be submitted each time it was used.

Many officers found that it was usually impossible in a fight to avoid the head and also that it was not a requirement to submit a report if the offender was hit with a black rubber torch which was also standard issue. The trouble with a truncheon was always that it was hard to get it out of the pocket, it could easily be pulled from your grasp unless you had time to wrap the handle round your wrist (there was a set procedure to achieve this if you had time) and the sad fact was that an assailant probably had a bigger piece of wood to hit you with.

Although it looks more aggressive, the side-handled baton is actually a far better weapon to prevent aggression and modern police officers are well trained in its use. Officers are now taught a progressive scale of activity in the face of an aggressor, starting from their own physical presence, through words and hand gestures such as 'Stay back' with the hands held palm outwards, to the sound of the 'racking out' of the extendable baton, to finally leg and arm strikes. They are required to qualify annually in these procedures and although there are more reported strikes with the baton, there are fewer injuries and fewer complaints. Even this is now being superseded by the advent of the OC Pepper spray, which, I am told (as I have never used it) is a far better pacifier than a baton. Not really surprising when you know that it is sprayed into the eyes and gives excruciating pain and stinging for a few minutes, though it has the disadvantage of blowing back on the user in a wind or in a car.

The training regime at Ryton-on-Dunsmore in the late sixties would not be acceptable today. Of that there is no doubt. It was based on a bullying and militaristic approach, to such an extent that they even taught traffic control to military music and the passing out ceremony included a marching parade involving drill and traffic signals combined.

Nevertheless, it was an enjoyable time in a strange way and officers who survived it came away as stronger, more mature, people. There could be no return to those easily instilled rules and instant obedience achieved in the initial course and it was noticeable that, when recruits returned for their refresher course a few months later, they would not tolerate the demands for military haircuts and bullying behaviour.

There was one final memory of the initial course for me. During my first week, when I had little idea of the rank structure or politics of the force, I encountered one of the Inspector instructors, cleaning his car outside his quarters. I had noticed that his uniform was the Northamptonshire one and thought I would stop for a chat.

He was very friendly and told me that he would be going back to the force at the end of my course. As a subject for conversation, I happened to refer to the Police College at Bramshill and asked what the requirements were to attend. His response was dismissive. He said I should just concentrate on the initial training and not worry about Bramshill. Naturally, on this advice from a senior officer, I did as he suggested and did not mention it again. This early conversation was to come back and haunt me two years later.

We received our postings in the last week at Ryton. I had made a fundamental mistake when I joined the Force. The Deputy Chief Constable had asked me where I wanted to serve. Having joined Northampton and County Constabulary as it was then called, I could be sent anywhere in the County but I had assumed that I would be at Northampton which was my hometown. I had, of course, sold my home and we were living with my Parents-in–Law, which meant that I needed a Police house.

I had told the Deputy Chief Constable that I would prefer to be at Northampton but I did not mind where I worked provided it was not Corby. He had asked me why I did not want to go to Corby and I had explained that I had never even visited the town, knew no one there and preferred not to take my family so far from their relatives. He had accepted this readily enough so it came as a great shock that (*without passing 'go' or collecting the £200*) my posting was direct to Corby. I'm less naïve now!

I took Jackie to see the place and the house we had been allocated. It looked quite reasonable as a town with pretty parks in the town centre, lots of amenities and modern houses, even if they were all Council houses and a little 'barrack block' in style. The only real disadvantage was the house we had been given. It was a Council house, which had been designated as a Police house, and it was in a run down area but we concluded that, as it was effectively free, we could put up with it.

The salary had also come as a shock. They had advertised it with the slogan,' Join the thousand pounds a year men'. What a joke that was. After superannuation and other stoppages, my first five weeks take home wages totalled £75 compared to my last week as a bricklayer, when I had received £80, a drop of over 80%. I really believed I would not be able to survive and the proceeds from the sale of our house and our savings were soon exhausted.

Money was not the only problem. We soon discovered that Corby was regarded as a punishment station. The town itself had been developed as a 'New Town' project after the Scottish steel company, Stewarts and Lloyds had opened a massive steelmaking operation there and many thousands of Scots had migrated to the area, resulting in the Town having a population that was at least 50% of Scots descent. Many of these came from the poorer areas of Glasgow and brought with them some customs that were unfamiliar in the heart of the Northamptonshire countryside. These customs included drinking, fighting and petty stealing. Anyone who upset the Chief Officers could expect to be sent there very quickly. I had not realised that saying I did not want to go there would be enough to ensure that I did. We began to discover the folly of my mistake within the first couple of weeks when we returned from shopping to find the milkman unconscious in our garden having been mugged – in the garden of a police house no less.

The stray dogs, wild kids and the prevalence of a strong Gorbals, Glasgow accent all combined to test our determination to stay. Our house had previously been allocated to the Detective Inspector, which had influenced us to take it but it was not long before it became intolerable. In addition to the poor state of the area, the house was built of concrete and was very damp and cold and I determined that we would have to get a transfer, at least to another house.

On arrival at the police station for the first time, a bald sergeant, who looked very old, had met me and he had taken me to meet my Inspector. It was the same Inspector I had met at Ryton and discussed Bramshill with.

He was still very friendly and approachable and I felt that I got on well with him. It was therefore not difficult to approach him about a house move after about three months. Although luck was not immediately on my side, within a few months, a house became available, near enough not to necessitate a change of school for the two children and in a far nicer location. There was some competition for this house but I had applied first and was successful in obtaining the move. What I did not know that this second encounter with my Inspector was to have unexpected results at the end of my two years probation.

And so I settled into the routine of police work. On my first day, which happened to be a Sunday afternoon shift, it took me only 45 minutes to get my first prisoner and learn my first lesson in the real world of policemen. We received a report of a drunk near the town's Fire Station, which was only 100 yards from the police station.

I was sent there with a more experienced colleague but I really had no difficulty in seeing that this man was drunk and incapable (not the police officer) so I just went into the routine I had been trained for and administered the caution, telling him that he was under arrest for being drunk and incapable.

Unfortunately, I had not thought it through beyond that and I then faced the difficulty of getting him to the station in the back of a Morris Minor Panda car. Those cursed cars were the bane of my life. They only had two doors and had been purchased on the basis that they were to get officers around their beat, not to carry drunken and violent prisoners.

This one wasn't violent. He just messed, wet himself and vomited in the back of the car. The lesson was that you simply did not ever find a drunk in that condition. You might have to detour miles to not find him but you definitely did not find him. My only saving grace in the eyes of the sergeant was that it was my first shift and the drunk was, after all, on the steps of Trumpton (the Fire Service).

I had only been at Corby for about a week when I received an introduction into the twists and turns of good and bad luck that make up a policeman's lot. We paraded for duty on late turn (2pm to 10pm). Parading was an exercise that had to be undertaken in your own time, at 1.45pm and you would be considered late for duty (a disciplinary offence) if you arrived after 1.45pm even though you were paid for eight hours duty. Nevertheless, it was a good opportunity to be told what had happened since the last tour of duty and to be given the assignments for the day.

On this day, all of the niceties were abandoned because three men armed with a shotgun had attacked a gamekeeper at Weldon. He had not been fired upon but had been struck heavily on the head with the gun. The three had then made off into the fields near to the village.

At that time officers were equipped with the Phillips two-piece personal radio. This primitive device consisted of a transmitter with a spring loaded aerial that could take off your nose quicker than Arkwrights till in 'Open all Hours' and a receiver which worked sometimes. There were barely enough of these to go round and as the early shift had been kept on for the search for the offenders, we were seriously short of radios.

A simple solution was found and each officer was issued with one half of the radio. A large group of us were despatched to Weldon in the van with instructions to spread out and search the fields. There was no supervisor on the van so the driver became, de facto, in charge.

We drove along the A43 past Weldon village and stopped beside a field with a wood beyond it. The driver told me to walk across the field and then go through the woods back to the farm where the incident had occurred. Naturally, as a brand new recruit, I set off as instructed. As I crossed the field, I saw the van drive off with all of my colleagues and as I reached the wood, I started to think about my assignment. There I was in a wood, totally lost with no idea how far it was to the farm or where the nearest road was, completely alone and searching for three armed men, equipped with, yes you guessed, the listening half of a radio. It would be fair to say that I suffered some slight trepidation about my situation if I should encounter them and I felt very lucky that I did not meet them or my nemesis in that wood.

After about half an hour, I emerged safely onto the Weldon to Oundle road, just in time to meet Constable John Beavis driving past in his Morris Minor Panda car. It was the latest addition to the fleet and had only a few miles on the clock. He had the speaking half of the radio so we teamed up on our own initiative. This was another piece of good fortune because I now had the best transport, communication and an experienced colleague to keep me out of trouble.

Misfortune befell us within two miles. John tried to turn in a gateway and as he did so, we heard a terrible rending noise from under the car. We got out to look but could see nothing amiss, apart from the fact that a huge rut of earth had come into contact with the sump of the car. It was still running so we carried on.

The reason we had turned round was because there was a caravan park on that road and after debating how obvious it was that the CID would have already been there, we decided that it was not so obvious and we had better check it out.

At the caravan park, a quick chat with the woman on duty at the office soon revealed that she had not been visited by the CID but she had seen three young men armed with a shotgun go into a particular caravan about an hour before and they were still there.

Using our two pieces of radio we called for some assistance and the rural Sergeant together with Constable Keith Watson from Gretton, duly arrived. This was their 'patch' and to our chagrin we were soon pushed into the background whilst they marched up to the caravan, smartly made the arrests and emerged with three prisoners and a shotgun.

The initiative we had shown was instantly forgotten in the euphoria that followed so fortune had declined to shine on us after all. In addition, the panda car promptly overheated, having lost all its oil on the journey back to the station and we were left trying to explain why the brand new Morris Minor suddenly needed a new engine.

Chapter 5

There were many things to learn, such as the fact that stray dogs brought to the police station invariably escaped within minutes of getting there. The reason for this phenomenon was that one of the Inspectors lived in the flats at the rear of the Police Station and detained dogs have a habit of howling all night.

Another trick was that, if a bicycle was reported stolen, a crime report had to be typed out by the unlucky officer receiving the report. There were no typing lessons and if there was a mistake in the report, the sergeant would use his red pen and it would have to be retyped, perhaps several times. To compound this, if the bicycle was subsequently found abandoned, the offence was reduced to 'taking a pedal cycle without consent' which was too petty to be recorded as a crime so the crime had to be cancelled.

There was therefore quite an incentive not to record a crime and if the person came to the counter to say that their bicycle was not where they had left it, the office constable would say, "Oh, you've lost your bike have you?" On receiving the affirmative reply, a lost property slip would quickly be produced and the victim informed that they would be told when the police found it for them.

This ploy worked every time until I tried it. My victim saw the thief riding her bike two days later and when she called the police they could find no record of a stolen cycle. A more experienced officer would have been more convincing about having confused the initial report but I just had to face the music although I got away with it on the basis of inexperience.

In the days before Panda cars, the public were used to the idea that the police would take a while to arrive at a fight or any disturbance but, with the mobility of the cars, which they had had for about a year when I arrived, the public expected a speedy response. What they had not known before was that the police could time their arrival to perfection to coincide with the moment when one of the protagonists was defeated – even if it meant waiting round the corner until it was over. The only exception had, of course, been the van which could arrive at the height of a fight but only if the number of officers on board was enough to be sure of winning. With the advent of the Panda car it became necessary to have radio black spots.

A skilled black spotter could tell from the tone of the controller's voice whether it was likely to be necessary to be in a black spot and not be able to hear the direction to attend. These officers could never hear the radio if a fight was in progress but the radio would miraculously recover as soon as the danger was past. I was never a black spotter but there were a few.

Sleeping standing up was another trick that some mastered. The king of the upright snooze was a character called Fingers (I've no idea why – he was not a thief). One morning when I reported for early turn, there was a real flap going on. No one had heard from Fingers since he went on foot patrol in the town centre at 2am. We were all despatched to our beats early to help the night shift search for him and I had only been out on the town centre beat for ten minutes when I found him standing in a shop doorway fast asleep. He told me that he had 'come over tired' about 4am and just closed his eyes, standing up in the doorway.

Yet another technique for avoiding work was the 'Whose prisoner is this' method. It was impossible to avoid being involved in fights at the weekend and it was inevitable that prisoners would have to be taken but some officers, only too happy to be involved in the action, fancied the paperwork somewhat less. The trick therefore was to get the prisoners to the station all at the same time so that in the busy charge room no one was quite sure who had arrested whom. The young probationer constable could then be left to be shown as the arresting officer for most or all of the prisoners.

One example of this was a Saturday evening when a huge fight broke out outside the famous 'Candle' Public House, which was opposite the Police Station. The whole shift ran out from refreshment break and began to arrest men and women involved in the fight. I do recall taking two prisoners to the station but when the dust settled and the charge sheets were completed, I found that I must have dropped off to sleep or something because I had apparently arrested at least seven people, some of whom I could not even recognise, whilst no other officer had arrested anyone. Luckily, the defence failed to spot this and all pleaded guilty at court.

Having described a few of the work avoidance techniques, it is only fair to put into perspective, how desperately short of resources the Force was. Corby had one Chief Inspector, three uniformed Inspectors, one Detective Inspector and roughly 12 sergeants including the CID. This to cover a vast rural area from the border with Market Harborough to Stamford and round almost to Kettering, together with a town which had a reputation for violence known throughout the land.

The average number of constables per shift was five or six plus perhaps two rural officers and three CID. Holidays, sickness and courses could decimate those numbers and I have a particularly vivid memory of a Sunday early turn when I had about three months service and I was met at the back door of the station at 5.45am by the sergeant who said, "Right boy, you can do the outside and I'll do the inside" which told me that I was to be the only outside officer all morning and he was the only person to run the station including the enquiry office and the telephones as well as the cells which were, unusually, but fortunately empty that day.

Police Officers now are only allowed out alone after several months of accompanied patrol but we were so desperate that I had been allowed to qualify to drive a Panda within two months of my arrival, already being in possession of a driving licence and having passed the thirty-minute driving test with the Traffic sergeant (the only driver training I was to receive until 1986) and I was then sent out on patrol alone. On this Sunday morning, I was naturally hoping that nothing difficult would happen. For example, how difficult would it be for a new probationer constable to deal with a fourteen-year-old girl who had been raped on her paper round at 6.30am on a Sunday morning? That is exactly what I was faced with that day and the only saving grace was that it was so serious that the CID had to be called out to deal with it.

However, by the time that incident happened, I had already gained sufficient experience to be trusted with the ubiquitous Morris Minor. Modern police officers are required to undertake rigorous training and spend considerable time with a 'Tutor Constable' who, in turn has received extensive training in how to teach the new student.

In 1969, a new recruit had to rely on any senior constable who was prepared to impart any scraps of knowledge whilst carrying out his own work or work avoidance. There were both ups and downs in looking after the new probationer. Swift judgements would have to be made about this newcomer.

If he was a total plonker, anyone taking him under his wing would be likely to have to work very hard, not only showing him the ropes but also re-doing his miserable mistakes and at the same time, not being in black spots because the probationer was expected to pick up lots of simple jobs – things which a more experienced officer would almost certainly 'cuff'. Cuffing was the art of making a job disappear up the cuff of ones sleeve, never to see the light of day again.

Thefts from gas and electric meters were favourite targets for the cuff. A householder would report a burglary. Miraculously, the only thing taken would be the contents of the meter (whichever one was due for collection, even the other meter would usually escape). The evidence of forced entry would usually be that the door was left open for the first time in months and only for two minutes.

The Utilities still held the householder responsible for the money, which would have to be paid back over a few months, and it was perfectly obvious who had raided the meter. Now, unless the householder was daft enough to still have a pocket full of coins – as they occasionally did – a note would be made in a book kept in the CID office. For some reason I have never fathomed, it was called the 'Barred in' book. No further action was taken unless an insurance company became involved or the Utility wanted more information. If that happened, they could be given details and even a reference number, which looked remarkably like a crime number but wasn't.

None of this was official and it was dramatically counterproductive because the effort to avoid a crime report could have been better spent detecting an easy crime and a truer picture of the level of crime would have emerged but I was soon to find that the real world was very different to that fondly imagined by the hierarchy or 'Supervision' as they are collectively known in some areas.

Of course, an experienced officer with a new probationer could not afford to perform any of these tricks because the sergeant would be watching how the probationer developed. However, if he was a good prospect and not a plonker, the scenario was completely different. Take on a good prospect and you could have a willing workhorse who would gladly do all of the crime reports, put his name on the arrest sheet and even, once he passed the thirty minute test, drive you around whilst you had a sleep on nights.

It will be noticed that I have referred only to 'he' and 'him' so far. Equality of the sexes was still years away and we had a separate 'Policewomen's Department' that dealt only with women and children and certainly did not work at night unless called out for an indecency victim. Despite this, a policewoman was inadvertently helpful to me in getting an early insight into the CID.

My very first shoplifter was a female who stole a few groceries from the local Co-op in the main street of Corby. WPC Hazel Measham was detailed to deal because it was a female but Hazel was very good at work avoidance and I was regarded as a prospect. It took her seconds to think of inviting the controller to send the new probationer along to see how it was done and an even shorter time to leave me with the prisoner, the crime report and the property to sort out.

I put the offender into a cell and decided to go back to the Co-op to get a box to put the property in for return as it was perishable (it didn't occur to me or Hazel not to take it in, in the first place). I duly collected my box and started to walk back to the police station fifty yards away, in full uniform except for the helmet which I did not bother with as it was so near.

Did you ever have one of those moments when you simply wished the ground would open and you could fall in? Or just happen to have been somewhere else? This was my first of many. A woman rushed up to me in a highly agitated state, shouting, "Officer, Officer, my five year old daughter has just pointed out the man who indecently assaulted her last week – and that's him over there." There was nowhere to hide, no escape, no one to ask for advice (I had not thought it worth taking the radio on such a mundane errand).

I vaguely remembered that we had been taught about powers of arrest on suspicion but I also knew there was some problem about indecent assault if not found committing. "Excuse me sir," I said to the sixteen year old suspect (another problem, he was a juvenile) "This lady has just pointed you out as the man who indecently assaulted her daughter last week, is that correct?"

In all our practical training at Ryton he would have told me it was a fair cop and come willingly to the police station. Needless to say he did none of that so I had to make my first truly independent arrest. I was so relieved when I got him into the charge room and was met by Detective Constable Reggie Binns who told me he was dealing with the case and my suspect really did match the description. I was even more relieved when he told me later that, even though I had acted completely unlawfully as there was no power of arrest unless found committing that offence, he had, 'coughed' (admitted the offence) and therefore I was unlikely to be challenged on my misuse of power.

The next morning, I was called to see the Chief Inspector who told me I was to be congratulated on making two arrests so quickly. He then went on to tell me that I should not have been there in the first place because I shouldn't have taken possession of the groceries, I should not have gone out without a radio, I had no power of arrest and, by the way, what was I doing outside the police station without my helmet. They were good at giving praise in those days.

I was undaunted by this and a few weeks later, on a foggy night, I was called to a house near to the rear of the police station where a woman had seen a man ' flashing' (exposing himself) at her through her rear window. She gave me a description, which matched my sixteen-year-old indecency suspect. I went straight to his house and met him just arriving home in a dishevelled state. He also admitted that offence.

The officer who took me under his wing was John Beavis who, with about three years service, was one of the seniors on the shift. I think our shared experience with the three armed offenders had convinced him that I was not a plonker. John patiently showed me about police work and he was very conscientious in those days.

He was later to become quite bitter about the police force and I suspect that was largely because his father was a Superintendent in the same force. He was a very strong character but his father's position always seemed to be like a shadow in the background. If he did something good it was shrugged off as being something his father had taught him. If it was bad, there was some sneering derision about not living up to his father and there were those who resented something the father had done and wanted to visit their revenge on the son.

We became close friends on and off duty and although there were a few who later suggested I had cultivated him because his father was a Superintendent, nothing could have been further from the truth. John never used his father's rank in any way and it certainly did not enter my thinking at all.

Chapter 6

One of the strangest sights I have ever seen occurred one Saturday afternoon, shortly after I was allowed out alone in a Panda. As usual, there were only two cars out in the whole town. I was covering the two Panda beats encompassing the Eastern half of the town and John was covering the rest. I received a call to go to the Catholic Church in Occupation Road, which was on my area and where a man was reported to be going berserk and causing damage. As I made my way there, John came up on the radio and said he would also attend to assist me.

We arrived together within two to three minutes (no blackspots or hanging back for us) and entered the church. We were met by a scene of devastation. Pews were overturned, statues broken and literature scattered throughout the main body of the church.

We both heard a loud banging noise coming from the vestry and quickly ran down the church toward it. In the vestry we found a West Indian man who was obviously the offender. I knew he must be the offender because two catholic priests were holding him down on the floor while a third was giving him a real kicking.

I was quite surprised at this because the only priests I had met until then were gentle, turn the other cheek, sort of people. But then, I hadn't worked in Corby before and, although it was not him that day, I had not met the famous Father Corbin whose methods were unorthodox to say the least. I will not name the Fathers concerned because they are all probably Bishops by now but they know who they are.

John really came into his own that day because he instantly recognised that this would be a difficult case and far beyond my capability at the time. Not least of the reasons for this was that it would have to go to Crown Court for trial. He therefore, willingly took it on and allowed me to watch as he put the file together.

No mention was ever made about the unruly Fathers even though the accused man denied the offence. His defence that it was no offence to smash up a Catholic church, as he did not recognise the religion. You will form your own view on that but I am satisfied that the poor man was completely deranged. This view was confirmed later that evening when he was found drinking the water from the toilet in his cell.

A police officer's first sergeant always makes a lasting impression and sets the standards for the future. Mine was no exception. Bill Bream was from 'the old school' with strict discipline and that curious mix of help and criticism for which army sergeants have long been famous. Whilst he would brook no argument with his decisions and could be a real pain in the neck with his attention to grammatical detail, he was always there to help and advise in times of trouble.

We struck up an immediate affinity, partly, I suspect, because I was that little older than the rest of the shift and partly because we both started at Corby on the same day, me as a new recruit and he on promotion to sergeant. His promotion had come late in his service and I believe only happened then because of an incident he was involved in as the constable at Maidwell.

He related to me that he had been quite content as a village constable, despite having passed the rigorous tests that then formed the sergeants and Inspectors exams. On one of the farms in his area, a farm labourer had gone missing, leaving all his possessions at the local bus stop. He was thought to have had an affair with the farmer's wife and there were some suspicions that he might have come to harm at the hands of that farmer. However there was no trace of a body or signs of violence so it remained a suspicious disappearance.

The Head of the CID, a Detective Chief Superintendent had been to the village and extensive enquiries had been carried out. This had proved nothing and the CID had retreated to Northampton. Bill and his own Sergeant would not leave it at that and Bill regularly visited the farmer for long 'chats'. In fact, he became so familiar with the farm that when, one day, he saw the farmer using his JCB digger to move soil and hardcore from one part of the farm to another, it struck him as odd and unnecessary.

Bill therefore sent for his Sergeant and, together, they arranged for the newly placed earth to be moved and a hole dug underneath. Several feet down, the body of the labourer was found and the farmer was subsequently convicted of murder. Bill's reward was to be promoted to Sergeant and transferred to Corby. As this was a punishment station, no one was ever quite sure how much of a reward it was but the incident absolutely typified the resolute patience with which he approached his work.

He was apparently very mild of manner until roused but it must have been very daunting for the Corby hooliganry when they discovered, on challenging this 'Clark Kent' sort of man that he was a Black Belt judo expert who could turn into a veritable Superman in the twirl of a policeman's cape.

One very special night, I had gone to a domestic incident on the infamous Exeter estate with PC Kim Jackson and the aggressive husband, who had already beaten his wife to a pulp, decided that he was tough enough to take both of us on. He was actually in the process of winding up his fist to take the first strike when Bill, who had already encountered the beaten wife in the street, entered the scene. I do not believe the aggressor knew what had hit him – well he was never 'hit' as such, he was more propelled off the floor, opening one of the internal doors with his head as he went and was in handcuffs on his way to the station before he realised that there had been some intervention in his plan.

I never actually saw Bill hit anyone; they just seemed to want to start a fight and then somehow woke up in the cells in pain from the various joints but with no bruises and no reason to complain about the polite Sergeant who had arrested them. Indeed, although it was a violent town and the police had a reputation for their tough approach, I rarely, *almost* never, saw a police officer hit someone who wasn't trying to hit him first.

Quite early in my service, my morals and approach to this aspect of the work were to be tested. There was a Constable on our shift whose name was Tony Cousins. He was accompanied on foot patrol this night by a Special Constable also called Tony Cousins (I'm sure they paired them up to confuse us all). They walked up the main street of the town (Corporation Street) and turned left into George Street.

As they did so, a well-known drunken villain who was waiting for them, hit Tony the Regular a heavy blow to the eye causing such terrible damage that we feared for his sight. Tony the Special somehow managed to call for assistance and hang on to the offender until the assistance arrived in the shape of Constable Gordon Flint (known affectionately as 'Blockhead' – not because he was stupid but because he would walk through a wall if he had to). In time-honoured fashion, Gordon managed to restrain the offender and convey his now inert form back to the police station (Gordon could pack quite a punch if the occasion demanded it!)

I was the enquiry office constable that night and it fell to me to go to the cells to check on the well being of the prisoners. Now, we had a new recruit at that time. He was from Uganda and was one of the Asians forced to leave by his namesake Idi Amin. Constable Rashkant Amin was more used to the ways of the Ugandan Police and had kindly offered to go home and fetch his Bullwhip and the red peppers to be used under the tongue to obtain a confession but the Sergeant felt that was probably going a little far.

I went to the cells and I must honestly say that it was my intention to administer a little unofficial punishment. When I got the cell door open, the prisoner, who had by now recovered consciousness, sat there expecting to be beaten up. He seemed to have it in mind that was what would have happened to him in Glasgow and he just invited me to get on with it.

I could not do it then and I never have. I knew immediately that that style of policing would never be for me and I could not respect anyone who struck a prisoner who had finished fighting. It will never be possible for the police to avoid hitting people who want to fight on the streets and it can even happen inside the police station; but it should never happen cold bloodedly when the person is under control.

On the night I faced my dilemma, I turned and walked out and as I did so I saw the Sergeant watching me. I felt that I went up in his estimation for resisting the temptation even though we thought at that time, that Tony the Regular might lose his eye. I am pleased to report that he did not lose his sight and the offender went to prison for a long time.

Fighting seemed to be an essential part of a good night out for some of the locals and it was most rare for a Friday night to pass without a really good punch-up. Usually these would occur in Corporation Street, inside or outside 'The Candle' public house, or in George Street near to the takeaways and the Clubs.

One of our regulars was Tommy Bergin who always believed he could take on half the Force and would sometimes do it just to test his theory. The only person who seemed able to calm him down was his brother Sammy but one night we were called to a club where the two of them were fighting – with each other.

Sammy was bigger and tougher than Tommy but we managed to get him handcuffed to a hefty policeman and in the back of the van, which I happened to have been selected to drive that night. The problem was, we only had one van and it was hopeless to try to get Tommy into a car. We got him handcuffed to another officer and opened the back door of the van to put him in.

If you have ever seen the cartoon about the Tasmanian Devil you will be able to picture the scene when we opened the door. Sammy and his anchor policeman were flying round the inside of the van about two feet off the floor and when the door opened they came flying out on top of Tommy and his anchor who we were trying to get in. For a few minutes it was impossible to tell which arms and legs belonged to which person.

We finally got all four, plus several more officers into the van and I drove back to the station. The van was rocking all the way like a boat in a storm and when I opened the door again at the station, the whirlwind of Tasmanian Devils came flying out again. Fortunately, the sight of the cell doors has a calming effect on most and a night behind them must be a salutary experience because they never seem quite so tough the next morning. Indeed, it is an old custody officer's trick to bail combatants out about 5.30am. Ostensibly this is to clear the decks for the morning shift but I believe it is also because the joys of an early morning walk home after a night of heavy drinking and a fight must seem like the end of the earth to the, now hung over, combatant.

Rashkant Amin deserves more of a mention than the one episode when he offered the services of the Bullwhip and red peppers. He was a most unusual and endearing character as far as I was concerned. How his command of the English language (or lack of it) allowed him into the police service is a mystery.

The Breathalyser procedure was still quite new to us. It had been around since 1967 but not tremendously used because, in the early days the statutory warnings had to be strictly followed to the letter or Magistrates Courts would be only too willing to let the offender off.

In fairness, some police officers had considerable sympathy with those who drank and drove, being regular offenders themselves. However, times were changing and Rashkant set out to get the record for the most breathalysers administered. He was regularly clocking up two or three each week.

The warning to be given precisely went something like, "I require you to blow into this bag for between ten and twenty seconds. Failure to inflate the bag will render you liable to arrest and prosecution." Rashkant could not quite handle that and his version was, "You blow in this bloody blow bag you bloody bugger." Of course no one understood what he was saying anyway and he was never once challenged on the warning.

It was quite a cultural experience when he invited my wife, the children and me to his house for tea. The first surprise was that his wife and his sister, who lived with them, were not permitted to join us for the meal but had to serve it and retreat to the kitchen. Jackie was not sure whether she should go with them but that would not be permitted either. The second was that they were vegetarian and the cauliflower curry was the most dreadful thing my kids had ever tasted. Rashkant often produced the most wonderful curries for the night shift but the vegetarian version missed the spot.

This was washed down with glasses of Wimto which, when we tasted it we realised was better known as Vimto, the slightly old fashioned children's drink. Finally we were treated to an 'Instant Delight' dessert that was supposed to be eaten chilled but could not be because they had no refrigerator at that time.

It sounds churlish to describe the occasion in this way but we did regard it as a huge compliment from someone, recently exiled from his own country with nothing. We were very proud of the children too for not saying how little they enjoyed the food.

Chapter 7

On the family front, our third child, Peter was born on 20 August 1970 and financially our situation grew even worse. We had reached a point when all our savings were gone and the monthly pay cheque only just paid off the bank overdraft. The Barclaycard, which was a recent innovation, had long since reached its limit and we were becoming desperate. This was to remain the position for a number of years and, in hindsight, I can see why some officers might have been tempted to act dishonestly.

It is an old saying that society gets the police force it deserves but despite a few sensational cases nationally, my view is that British society in those days got a far better police force than it deserved. Certainly, what is conventionally known as corruption was virtually non-existent in Northamptonshire.

The issue of what *is* corruption is not an easy one. If you believe that the acceptance of even the smallest gift by a police officer is corrupt practice then every police force and almost every officer is corrupt.

A police officer who takes a bribe to do or not to do something is quite clearly corrupt. But what if someone makes a small present to an officer for carrying out his duty properly?

For instance, if the officer detects a burglary at a crisp factory and the manager rewards him with a few packets of crisps, is that corrupt? Who can say whether the officer 'went the extra mile' in the hope that he would be rewarded? And before you settle on your final answer, what if it were not a crisp factory but a furniture warehouse and the officer was rewarded with a piece of furniture?

If you answered yes to either of these scenarios, what if an officer went to a person's home to arrest him and the person gave the officer a cup of coffee? I suggest that would not be corrupt but what if it was a glass of whisky in return for not telling his wife the reason for the arrest? Most officers I know would decline the latter but take the former as a polite gesture.

What if a night watchman was authorised to give a patrolling officer a cup of tea as an incentive to keep a police car at his premises? Most people would view the cup of tea as no more than a polite token of welcome.

I raise this issue because Corby had a number of night watchmen or security guards at that time. One in particular, at a snack food factory was authorised by the manager to give a cup of tea and a bag of nuts to any officer who visited at night and if you were fortunate enough to be assigned to that beat, once a month a bag of nuts would be forthcoming and I could, frankly see no harm in it.

The same thing happened at the crisp factory owned by Golden Wonder. There they had full time security guards and any crisps, which had passed their sell by date before they left the factory, were left for the guards to give to the police. This resulted in us receiving one bag of assorted packets of crisps per month. Avon Cosmetics security would always provide a cup of tea but, quite properly in my view, never any cosmetics.

It was a matter of disappointment to me that a few greedy officers abused those innocent gestures. One Traffic officer actually took a bag to the snack food factory and asked for some nuts for his family for Christmas. This resulted in the complete withdrawal of the offer to any police officer and precisely the same thing happened at the crisp factory.

In the context of the time, with police officers who had families being able to qualify for income support, it was a kind gesture when the owner of a footwear factory (which was later to become the maker of a world famous fashion boot) offered to let police officers buy their work shoes from his stock of rejects at cost price. How sad then, that certain officers took to buying several pairs for onward sale and a little profit. Yet another kind offer withdrawn, never to be re-instituted.

The subject of income was most interesting. Outside the force, it was a commonly held belief that police officers were well paid with many substantial allowances. It is true that we received free housing but of course, the penalty was that we were not allowed to buy our own houses for ten years. We received a 'Boot allowance' with which we had to buy our police boots and it did not cover the cost. We received a 'Typewriter allowance' of 15 shillings (75p)per month. For this, we had to buy our own typewriters and ribbons.

It was quite a daunting prospect to make the outlay necessary for a small 'Smiths Corona' portable costing about £20. Similarly, those on a 'Residential Beat' received a cycle allowance but had to supply a cycle, which had to look like a policeman's bicycle. The CID also received allowances. There was ten shillings (50p) per week allowance for what were euphemistically called 'CID expenses' – actually beer. They also had a plain-clothes allowance which failed to meet the cost of wearing their own clothes at work and finally, there was the question of overtime payment.

Uniformed officers were not paid for overtime but could get time off in lieu if they were lucky. CID officers had a most curious arrangement. The deal was, that if EVERY Detective Constable and Sergeant in the Force averaged 32 hours overtime in a month, then they all received 8 hours payment (and no time off in lieu).

The culture was such that almost all worked far more than 32 hours overtime per month. Unfortunately for them, the Deputy Chief Constable (DCC) of the day, scrutinised every claim personally and somehow, he would always find a reason why the target had been missed by the tiniest fraction. He was so good at this that the CID never qualified for overtime before 1974, but more of that later.

The DCC was a legend; he had well over 40 years service and truthfully claimed that Northampton and County Constabulary was the cheapest run force in the country. This was almost totally because of his skinflint ways. When I went to Ryton I was given one tunic which – and this is true – had the impressions of its previous owners chevrons on the sleeves and a date on the inside label with the year 1952 on it.

All other forces issued at least two new tunics so the recruit had one for best but our miserly DCC did not want to risk the waste if the recruit did not get through training. I therefore had to ensure my one second-hand tunic was always pressed for parades and of course, it could not be cleaned.

Every year, there was a ritual visit to each station by the force tailor, accompanied by the DCC, to inspect each officer's uniform and allegedly issue new if required. We all had to stand and be measured by the tailor whilst the DCC looked on. It was his habit to stand really near to the wretched officer being subjected to this procedure and if a tunic looked too big he would literally pull it in at the back saying, 'Lovely fit lad' or if it was too tight the officer would be told to lose weight or if he was in a generous mood, the tailor might let the buttons out a little, I was fortunate in this ritual because the tunic, and the second one, issued after Ryton, were both generous in cut and allowed me to put on the weight, which seemed inevitable on return from training.

The only indignity I personally had to suffer was when the tailor measured me for the first time and marked me as 'VSN'. I asked what that meant and he whispered, 'Very Short Neck'. The following year he marked the sheet, as 'NN' and I did not like to ask what it meant. I could only think that my Rugby days in the front row had diminished me from 'Very Short Neck' to 'No Neck'.

The DCC's meanness knew no bounds. He really did not like the cost of motor vehicles and ours were in a parlous state. We even had a second hand Panda car bought from Coventry City Police. It was fairly noticeable because it was the only Hillman Imp we had and it was blue and white when all of the others were the conventional Panda black and white.

The Traffic Superintendent said he believed the worst thing that ever happened to Traffic policing was when they installed heaters in patrol cars because it discouraged officers from getting out. Anyone who has ever spent a night driving an unheated car in the depths of winter will know how ridiculous that statement was.

The CID fared no better. They had the use of one grey mini van and one Austin 1100 (between thirteen constables and four sergeants) and when one of those cars failed the MOT because someone put a foot through the floor we knew they were no better off than us.

Unbelievably, the Traffic Division covering the still fairly new M1 Motorway were no better off either. They had a mixed fleet including one Humber Estate car but were so short of resources that they had to withdraw from policing the Motorway at 2am each day. The control room would ring Leicester and tell them that we were closing down so they had to cover it for us.

All this was quite amazing because the Chief Constable was a keen racing driver and sat on the Association of Chief Police Officers (ACPO) Traffic Committee. But then I do not believe he had any idea what was happening in his own force because the DCC kept such a close rein on it.

All of this was peripheral to a young probationer constable and I was having more fun than I ever had. Police work was never like 'work' to me, it was one long round of fun whether it was morning shift or nights. I love people generally and even the oddest and roughest characters fascinate me. On one of my early turns I was walking in Corby Village when I was approached by a middle aged lady who called to me in her broad Scottish accent, "Excuse me officer but can you tell me something?"

"Of course madam" said I, anxious to be of service to a member of the public.

I crossed the road to her and said, "How can I help?"

"Can you tell me?" she responded, "Why it is that gypsies never wear condoms?"

Somewhat puzzled by this question which even I suspected might be a joke, I said in a slightly embarrassed tone, "No madam, I don't know, why is it?"

"Because they've got crystal balls and they can see when they're coming," she cackled, walking merrily away and leaving me nonplussed. I had just encountered Sweaty Betty, the town's only full time prostitute and this was her customary greeting for fresh-faced young officers.

It was long said that Betty was the only full timer in town but there were quite a few enthusiastic amateurs available so poor old Betty could not charge very much. In fact I believe her rate was about three shillings and sixpence (17.5p) if she liked the punter.

Corby Old Village, where Betty plied her trade, was an interesting mix of Olde Worlde village life combined with some very rough elements, and Stocks Lane was a street almost exclusively designated to very poor homes with extremely bad parents. It was there that I had one of my memorable moments and probably deserved a commendation that was not forthcoming.

I was sent to Stocks Lane one evening because two families who lived next door to each other had left all of their children (about ten of them in ages ranging from two years to about eight) alone whilst the parents went out drinking. We were too short of resources to send more than one officer and there were no Social Services available so I was to baby-sit. The only effective way I could do this was to stand outside the two houses and make periodic checks on each house if the noise levels within got too high. The smell did help to convince me that this was the best course of action.

About 11.45pm, I was standing in the shadows outside when I heard the sound of several people talking quietly as they came down the street. I looked out and saw two men and two women (apparently the missing parents) coming towards me. The only odd thing I noticed was that they were all carrying television sets, radios and hi-fis. Now I realised that this was unusual because they didn't have a radio between the two households and I guessed they were not thinking of moving house at that time anyway. When I stepped out of the shadows, they were surprised to say the least. One of the men dropped a large TV set that was wrapped in his jacket and all four ran off up Stocks Lane.

The man who was now unencumbered made off at a rate of knots but the other three went into a builders yard where I was able to corner them and somehow hold onto then until assistance arrived. I do not know how I did this because they were not easygoing citizens and our conversation was fairly heated. I was unhappy about the time I had spent looking after their children while they were out burgling and I may have made my feelings known to them but suffice it to say that they did not try to escape.

When the Brains Dept (CID) arrived, we soon discovered the burglary at the local TV shop and one of the CID, DC Sean Smith, went with me to examine the recovered TV set with the jacket still wrapped around it. In the pocket was the Birth Certificate of the fourth man who had escaped. I had heard of similar stories with driving licences but could not believe we actually had someone's Birth Certificate. Sean and I soon arrested him and all four admitted their part in the offence. Of course, someone else had taken over the babysitting duties and the only recognition I received was to be accused of doing anything to get out of the job.

Like all towns, we had our share of odd characters that could be amusing but could equally be very dangerous. Nutty Jimmy McDougall had a nasty habit of engaging police officers in conversation and then running away to get himself chased. He once climbed a 100-foot crane in the town centre and had to be rescued by the unfortunate officer chasing him.

On another occasion he produced a knife to a Detective Sergeant which lead to the inevitable restraint in the time honoured fashion. On yet another occasion he produced a gun to an officer who did not know him and this also lead to him being restrained in the time honoured fashion, but this time the officer also received a bravery award, which those of us who knew Jimmy did not feel was appropriate. Despite the apparent danger of his strange activities, he was essentially a harmless eccentric. Perhaps his dislike of the police stemmed from years past when his antics had allegedly lead to him being escorted by police car to somewhere in Leicestershire where he was dumped to find his own way home.

There was also a young lady, a very attractive maiden, whose oddity was that she liked all police officers and could often be found walking around the streets alone at 3am. Unsuspecting officers would approach her to check that she was alright (I did say she was attractive) and they would then be amazed when she opened her coat to reveal her glamorous, naked body underneath. Most officers, like me, would be so shocked they would retreat quickly but I am told she eventually got pregnant and that the baby was born wearing a policeman's helmet.

Fred Coleman was the local town centre tramp. He lived in the open-air bus station, which was about 20 yards from the front of the police station. He liked a few drinks and had over 100 convictions for offences related to his drunkenness. In fact he was often quite sober when he committed these offences. It was just that it was cold in the town centre in winter and poor old Fred would occasionally have to smash the police station windows to get a night in the warm cell and perhaps even a few days at HMP Bedford. Indeed, he was reputed to have his own reserved cell and job there.

He was a hardy character and he would have to be very cold before he resorted to window breaking. It was quite common in winter to find him lying on the benches covered in a newspaper and a thick layer of frost.

But not all of the clientele we had to deal with were as harmless as this and, as a junior officer, I was once detailed to sit with a man who had been detained by the CID. During the night, a man had been shot in the kneecaps with a shotgun in some gangland style feud. Joe Goldwin was known to be responsible but the victim would not talk to the police despite the fact that he was almost certain to be crippled for life.

My brief was to sit with Goldwin and engage him in conversation if I could. I was not to talk about the offence but just get him chatting. Now, I like to chat and I thought that it would be a fascinating assignment.

How wrong I was. I have never encountered anyone who emitted such an air of evil. He simply sat there, unblinking and staring at me for four hours. I swear his eyes never flickered once. I soon found that football, politics, women, horseracing, in fact anything you care to mention were all OFF the agenda and the nearest he ever got to an answer was a sneer to indicate he understood that I was just a lad sent to do a man's job. He never did admit the offence and was never charged. In fact there was never any complaint made by the victim.

Joe Goldwin was to feature in my life twice more and on each occasion it was a despicable crime. Both of these were in the company of Ken and Fiona McArthur, a husband and wife team of ill repute from Glasgow. Indeed, Fiona was probably the worst member of the gang and seemed to have no moral scruples at all.

One day, I was off duty, driving along Oakley Road, when I saw a stream of police vehicles go onto the Exeter estate with blue lights flashing. I realised immediately that this was everyone on duty so, naturally, I went to see if they needed help. I was too late to assist but I discovered that two officers, including a sergeant, had gone onto the Exeter estate on patrol. They had seen Ken and Fiona McArthur with Joe Goldwin and another man, sitting outside the shops drinking. One member of the group was wanted on warrant and they had gone to make an arrest.

They could not have expected the violence that erupted about them and were badly beaten before reinforcements started to arrive. Luckily, there were some very tough officers on duty that day but the gang did not give in easily, including Fiona. In fact, she had a broken nose before she was restrained (in the time honoured fashion) and I know one officer suffered a broken hand. Serious as the incident was, it was made more so by the fact that they were trying very hard to turn the estate into a no-go area which no Police Force can ever tolerate if it is to survive.

Despite fairly substantial prison sentences, this gang were undeterred and it was only a few months after their release that they became involved in another much worse incident of violence. The 'Tally Man' is an imported phenomenon from Glasgow. These are people who lend small amounts of money and then collect the repayments at incredibly high rates of interest on a weekly basis. Obviously they are not considered by most to be objects of universal sympathy but the one who crossed Fiona McArthur deserved better than he got. He was a 'hard man' himself and used tough assistants to recover unpaid debts. Unfortunately for him, he was alone when he called on Fiona, in the middle of one of her drinking sessions with Ken and Joe Goldwin

The Tally Man suffered 106 separate blows and stab wounds all over his body and was then dumped in Willowbrook Road near to a park. The degree of injury was such that death should have been inevitable but by one of those curious chances of fate, he was still alive – just.

He started to regain consciousness and must have moved as they dumped him because he heard a voice say. 'Is he fickin daid?, then another, female voice saying, 'No he fickin isna'. He then felt a series of blows around his head as Fiona stamped on his face again and again to finish him off. He did not die but he was certain that she was trying to stamp his eyes out with her high heels.

Fortunately for Corby police, the Tally Man did give evidence and all three received sentences long enough to keep them out of our hair until they were no longer a force to be concerned with. I did however, see Joe Goldwin once more, many years later and he still looked like evil personified.

Luckily, although violence was never far from the surface, most crime was property related and the British Steel Works for which Corby was famous was not only the largest employer but also, inevitably the largest victim. It was a massive complex employing some 16,000 people and there were many opportunities for theft. These would range from the few pieces of phosphor bronze smuggled out in the car to lorry loads of expensive metals on a scale that produced some wealthy scrap dealers, at least one of whom enjoyed a spell as Mayor many years later.

The Works, as it was known, employed a large security force and could always field more staff than the uniformed police shift. We were therefore not averse to calling on their resources, borrowing vans, typewriters, torches and even men occasionally.

As professional as the security staff was, I was to find out one winter

Saturday afternoon, that they had limitations, which could almost match our own. This was not a crime scene that I was called to but a sudden death from a heart attack.

As usual, we were stretched to the limit for staff and vehicles. The van was off the road needing a new clutch and every Panda car was committed to jobs – except me. I had dealt with a few sudden deaths before and thought it would give me no trouble. I knew they had their own doctor at the works and that he had pronounced life extinct already. This would be easy. I would go there, have a cup of tea until the Co-op Funeral Service (the only funeral service in town) arrived to take the body away. Then I would just need to do the identification and a sudden death report.

Wrong again! I had forgotten that the Co-op also did weddings on Saturdays and it was the same guys who collected bodies. How difficult could this be? I knew that, before the Co-op Funeral Parlour had been there, officers used to have to take the body to the town mortuary, clean it, label it and put it in the cooler but surely, this was 1970 after all.

It soon became clear that a cup of tea was all the help I was going to get from the works security so I called on my radio for instructions. "Take the body to the mortuary" was all I got out of my controller.

"Where is it?" I asked.

"You should know, it's on your patch," he replied.

"Okay, but where?" He was in frivolous mood that day,

"It's in the dead centre of Corby," he quipped. Now, I knew it was not in the Town Centre so I said, "No it's not in the Town Centre."

This was met by howls of laughter. "Not the bloody Town Centre you daft sod, the DEAD centre, the cemetery."

"Okay," said I, "very funny, now can you get someone down here with the van so we can move it." This was not going to be fun, the cemetery was located in Rockingham Road, opposite the shopping centre and this was a Saturday afternoon.

"The van's off the road," he reminded me, helpfully.

I was now getting a bit fed up with his perky humour so I snapped, over the air, "will you get Sergeant Bream to the radio so I can get a sensible answer."

"What's the problem?" came the re-assuring voice of my mentor and leader. I explained that I was stuck at the Works with a dead body that needed transport to the mortuary and I needed some help soon because I had a whole group of security men and a doctor watching how well I would handle it.

"Well show 'em how resourceful you are then," he said.

"There's no van and nobody available to help with a little job like that, put it in the back of your Panda car and don't disturb me any more." (The last bit about not disturbing him wasn't said but it was very clear)

I could not believe he was serious. I was supposed to pick up this poor deceased man, who was likely to go into rigor mortis at any time, fold him into the back seat of a two-door Morris Minor, drive him to a busy shopping area and somehow drag him out of the car single handed, having presumably stopped off at the police station during this little tour to get the keys to the mortuary. I was then to undress him, clean him, label him and complete my report. I wondered if I was supposed to render the first aid to all the shoppers who fainted while I was dragging the corpse off the street as well.

Salvation! I remembered that the Works had its own ambulance with a full crew of security staff. Wrong again! "It's not part of our job to transport corpses to mortuaries" they quickly rejoined when I suggested it. Of course, the fact that it was beginning to get dark and the cemetery could be a little spooky may have influenced them.

My revelation that my mate on the local paper would probably think their refusal would make a good story seemed to help with their decision to give me a hand and they reluctantly helped me to load the body and even use their trolley to get it out of public view. Unfortunately, this had not endeared me to them and the inside of the mortuary was as far as they were going. If you can picture the scene, I am quite strong but this body was literally a dead weight and it was a fairly unlovely dance he and I performed to get him onto the slab and into a sitting position to be undressed. I had heard that dead bodies could often exhale a breath when bent in the middle and this one was no exception. "Uurrrgh" was all he said but it was enough for me to think I should be elsewhere than in the middle of a cemetery with a body for company.

I think he got the quickest undress and wash he ever had in his life never mind his death! And I was out of there in five minutes flat. I wonder what the officers of today would make of that.

The things those Morris Minors could be used for. Even if they did not make a good funeral cortege they made a good eraser for unwanted lines on a road on one occasion. 'Dickie' Sparrow was an unlucky constable. That happens sometimes. A perfectly normal, pleasant sort of guy just cannot put a foot right as a police officer and Dickie was one of those.

It was the middle of winter and at about 1am I had been sent to a domestic dispute on the Exeter estate. It took me quite a while to resolve because the two combatants were in their sixties and I (a twenty five year old) was trying to give them some fatherly advice. I finally persuaded them to give their marriage a thirtieth or fortieth chance and headed my Panda in the direction of the police station for refreshments about 2am.

The Morris Minor is not good in ice and when it is black ice that you haven't anticipated, it is easy to lose control. I was lucky because I only managed a couple of pirouettes in Cecil Drive before I managed to get it under control. Back at the station I reported that black ice had come down in the last hour and went for my break. I did notice that Sergeant Bream, Dickie Sparrow and Henry Henson who should have been in were not there.

The Inspector used to finish at 2am and I sat down for my sandwich alone. I had been there about five minutes when the controller called me and said I had to turn out, as Sergeant Bream wanted me in Gainsborough Road. He laughed when I reminded him about the black ice as I left but then Mick Carson, the controller or office man as they were called, used to have a funny sense of humour.

When I reached 'The Pluto' pub in Gainsborough Road, a scene of devastation met me, at least on Morris Minor scale. There were four Pandas already there and mine made a fifth or was it four and a half? One of them was just a mangled heap. It had clearly hit the barrier outside the pub and bounced off but its momentum had driven it back into the barrier once more on each of its four sides as it spun on the ice. I have never seen so much damage done to one little car by one little man as Dickie had achieved that night. He was uninjured but a gibbering wreck standing alone on the pavement.

The worst thing was that the ice had now gone from black to white and the picture was only too obvious from the marks on the road. Dickie and Henry had been racing each other to a burglar alarm on the Lincoln estate and had gone into the bends at the Pluto, neck and neck. Henry had come through it by straight lining and keeping his skid in a line when he hit the ice but Dickie was less lucky.

The procedure for Polaccs (Police Vehicle Accidents) in those days was that the Sergeant would deal with it but the Inspector had to be notified and he would not have been in bed by then so would inevitably have turned out. That did not suit Sergeant Bream's purpose at all.

Apart from the fact that the Inspector was a bit of a fussy old devil it was clear from the evidence on the road that Dickie was in the doo-doo up to the top of his helmet (which was what he would be wearing instead of a drivers cap in future). Sergeant Bream was not going to let that happen to one of his boys so the scenario had to be changed a bit.

Miraculously, no one had seen or heard the incident, but then, the people in that part of town wouldn't have admitted seeing it at five o'clock on a Friday afternoon. Somehow, a reason developed for three Panda cars to drive up and down that piece of road about fifty times in the next half hour or so and by the time the Inspector arrived there were no incriminating marks on the road.

No lies were told and a factual report was submitted which lead to poor old Dickie going to court on a 'careless driving' charge but if those marks had been visible he would still be walking the beat today.

I managed to find another use for the Morris 1000 one night in Rockingham. Netta Connelly was a venerable lady in Corby who was famous for her work with the youth of the town and she was an invaluable source of help to the police. She was certainly not an informant but if something was happening that she did not approve of, she would contact us to stop it before it happened. It was Halloween and she was holding a disco at a club but she heard some of the teenagers planning to go to the cemetery in Rockingham Castle to desecrate the gravestones and look for ghosts at midnight.

I was detailed to make sure it did not happen and I went with a Special Constable, in my Panda car to Rockingham Castle. We managed to find a place behind the graveyard where we could park the car out of sight and watch over the whole graveyard.

Just at midnight, we saw a whole group of teenagers creeping surreptitiously into the graveyard. We could see that they were already quite scared by the way they were moving so we waited until they were all in the graveyard.

A graveyard is a spooky place at midnight on any night and even more on Halloween. When an eerie blue flashing light appears from behind the gravestones accompanied by a pair of headlights and the sound of whistles blowing, the reaction of a group of teenagers is worth seeing. The whole group collectively seemed to leap about three feet in the air and take off in the direction of Corby at about thirty miles an hour. My colleague and I gave chase on foot to see them off the premises but Special Constables are renowned for their enthusiasm and he kept the chase going. I decided to return to my car but the only way to do that was through the graveyard. It is not just teenagers who find graveyards spooky at midnight and when the church bell sounded the hour my own progress was almost as rapid as the teenagers'.

Chapter 8

In my early training days at Ryton, I had discovered the joys of working nights and I referred then to the eerie feelings to be experienced in the small hours. One such occurred one night as I made my patrols alone on one of the industrial estates. It was never a comfortable place to be because the factories (including the snack foods factory) were likely targets for thieves and a lone policeman on foot would undoubtedly be in danger if he were to encounter a gang of burglars, particularly if the rudimentary, two piece radio were to fail.

There was a builder's yard on this estate, backing onto a small stream with a few overhanging trees and the infamous Exeter estate. I had left my car some distance away at about 1am and walked into the yard.

Some sixth sense told me that something was not quite as it should be and I made a very thorough check of the yard, testing all of the door handles carefully. All was secure and I could not work out what was wrong. I went and stood quietly at the back of the yard looking over the stream and the hairs on the back of my neck literally stood on end. Still I could not identify the cause of my disquiet and I stayed there for quite some time just looking all around and letting my eyes become more accustomed to the dark. Nothing stirred and eventually, I had to move on with the patrol. It felt almost as if I was being watched and I was relieved to leave the estate but still intrigued to the point where I had to keep returning to the builder's yard throughout the night. I even waited until dawn and returned in daylight but each time I found nothing although the weird feeling that something was amiss still persisted.

I went off duty with nothing to report and an uneventful night to all intents and purposes. I was on late turn the next day for some reason, with a different shift and at the 2pm briefing, the sergeant gave us details of an elderly man who had been missing since the previous day. We had barely gone out on patrol before one of the officers was called to the builder's yard where the workers had discovered the body of the old gentleman hanging from one of the trees by the stream where I had stood for so long the previous night.

The police surgeon who was called out gave his opinion that the man had been hanging there all night and I forever wondered whether some supernatural power or instinct was drawing me there to find the body. Or could it simply have been that my peripheral vision had noted something in the trees? I cannot believe it was the latter and I have never since experienced anything like the eerie feeling or had my neck hairs standing on end. The scene always remained a place I preferred not to be in thereafter.

On another memorable night shift, I found yet another use for the Morris Minor. Because of the size of the area covered from Corby, we were required to deal with quite a mix of town and rural crimes and a common rural crime was the theft of copper wire from the railway lines.

A fairly lightweight copper wire extended beside all railway lines on the familiar 'Telegraph Poles'. It was common for thieves to shin up the pole and cut the wire, pulling several hundred yards down and coiling it to take away in their car. Many of them failed to realise that the wire was all connected to an alarm system that activated as soon as it was cut. Given the time it took to get it down and coiled, the police often arrived before they could make a getaway.

On the night in question, Gerald Dickson, the rural sergeant and one of his constables, Kim Jackson, were directed to Gretton where the alarm had sounded. I was sent from Corby to provide back up and when I reached Gretton Brook Road, the sergeant came over the air to say that they were chasing a Mini Traveller from Gretton towards me and I was to block the road with my car. Now, the Morris Minor is not a big car and even though the road was not a major road there was no way for me to block it completely. I also knew that people had been killed when trying to evade roadblocks and they were not considered to be a good way of stopping an offender.

Nevertheless, I did my best and put my car sideways on, across the road with the blue light flashing. I soon saw the offender's car coming towards me followed close behind by the rural car with its lights flashing. The Mini Traveller simply shot through the gap between the hedge and me, as did the following police car. Naturally, I joined in the chase and a short way down the road, the driver of the Mini Traveller abandoned the car, leaving it and his passenger to run into a ditch. The driver ran towards me and I only had time to think, "If I stop, he will get round me and get away before I can get out but if I don't stop, I'm going to hit him", and then I hit him. He rolled up the curved bonnet and roof of my car, falling to the ground in a heap behind me. I thought I had killed him but he was up like a jackrabbit and ran into the fields.

We commenced a search but without a dog, thought it would be impossible to find him. I was worried that he might be injured because the Morris Minor might be a small car and an ineffective roadblock but I was fairly sure that it was a more than adequate block tackler and man stopper. In fact he was not badly injured at all and one of my colleagues, Alec Rose, stepped on him hiding in the field and together we made the arrest. On my return to the station my Inspector was more concerned about recording it as an accident than he was with the quality arrests we had made for what was considered to be a serious offence.

Bill Bream managed to convince him that it did not qualify as an accident and although the inspector was probably correct it was the last thing I needed. I am glad as well because it was the closest I have been to a Polacc in thirty years.

There was also a curious outcome to the incident because the Magistrates decided that the police officers involved should be formally commended for the arrests and the Chief Constable confirmed their recommendation as a matter of course. This is the only commendation I have ever received although there have been dozens of enquiries since for which I deserved some recognition and it seems ironic that the only commendation I was ever to receive was actually for running someone over with a police car.

The commendation ceremony itself was an experience not to be forgotten. I was summoned to the rural Inspector's office one day to receive it. He was a fierce, red-faced man who could frighten a probationer constable by just a glance.

I paraded at his office in full uniform complete with helmet, and smartly saluted when called in. As I stood to attention, I was a little surprised that he just kept reading his paperwork but I patiently waited until he finally looked up. "Ah Thorogood," he said, "It's a commendation, sign here," and he thrust a half sheet memo under my nose. Still at attention I scrawled my name on the paper and returned to my stiff position. He carried on with his pile of papers for three or four minutes before looking up again over his half glasses and saying, "Well, what are you waiting for?" and I was left to dismiss myself and retreat. I may not have felt that I deserved to be commended but I vowed then and there that if I were ever to be in a position to give out recognition, I would remember this day and how not to do it.

Drunks were always interesting to deal with and I never ceased to be amazed at the things they could do without hurting themselves. I arrested one man for being drunk and incapable (unconscious) in the street. He caused me no problem either in the street or in the car, apart from the obvious and familiar one of how to get him in and out of the car in that condition. At the charge room, he was equally co operative but when we started to take him to the cells, he suddenly became more aware and began to get violent.

· I remembered police hold No. 1 (the arm up the back, lock elbow and lift) but, unfortunately for him, he was not very heavy and when I lifted, he performed a somersault with the arm as a pivot and his body turned through 360 degrees before he completed the manoeuvre with a graceful nosedive to land face first on the concrete floor of the cells with me on top of him. Now, I am not tall for a policeman but I am quite heavily built and the impetus of his nosedive and my weight combined to make the face to floor contact quite an impressive spectacle.

In moments like that, young police officers often see their whole career flashing in front of their eyes and start to look for their explanations. "It was an accident, Guv" did not always impress the Complaints and Discipline Dept. I looked up to see most of my shift looking on and laughing at our circus-like activities. This did not impress me as I thought my prisoner must be dead or seriously injured but, to my amazement, he suffered not a scratch and didn't even remember the incident when I bailed him at 5.30am.

Working at Corby demanded a great deal from officers but it also gave a great deal in return. There was a remarkable turnover with people moving on and new recruits arriving constantly. The result of this was that it was possible to go from being the raw new recruit to being a senior man in an amazingly short time. I was one of the oldest members of our shift in age and so it was not too surprising that I rapidly became one of the senior members. With a little over 12 months service, I found that I was being allocated new probationers to look after and sometimes, I would be placed in charge of the van on a Friday or Saturday night with junior officers and Special Constables to look after.

On my second Christmas Eve, I was on the van with two young probationers and a Special for company. Christmas Eves were prone to becoming a little out of hand in Corby and somehow a second van had been procured. All available staff were on duty and it was busy. Sometimes, you could feel an atmosphere in the air that told you it was to be a busy night. This was not something peculiar to me and it was quite common for many of my colleagues to recognise it. I still have no idea what instinct it was that could tell us we were in for trouble but we did welcome it because there was no chance of being bored if that atmosphere was in the air.

That Christmas Eve was one such night and every vehicle and foot patrol officer was soon tied up with prisoners or incidents. My van was sent from job to job as fast as we could release ourselves from the previous one. Then we received a call to attend the British Steel Works Club in Occupation Road where a major fight was reported to be in progress.

When we arrived at the front of the club, we were met by the doormen who immediately said, "When are the rest of you coming?"

"This is it," I said, "we're all there is, how many are there fighting?"

"300", they shot back at me.

"What 300 in the club?" I asked hopefully.

"No, 300 fighting, there's about 800 in the club," came the reply I expected but did not want to hear.

My two young Regulars and one Special started to leap out of the van to go into action and I quickly dragged them back, furiously trying to think how I could hope to deal with this situation. Drawing on the 17 months experience I now had and the advice from more senior colleagues, I decided that calm, composed and unafraid were to be the watchwords.

I formed up my colleagues in a line behind me all wearing our helmets to make us look bigger and told the doormen to lead us to the room where the fight was taking place. As I instructed, when we got to the room, the doormen were to loudly announce that the police were here and that was what they did, hastily retreating when they had carried out their part of my cunning plot.

When I put my head into the room, I thought I had entered a war zone. There were bodies everywhere on the floor in various stages of unconsciousness, sitting in chairs with blood pouring from cut heads, women screaming, bottles flying overhead and, there in the middle, was one of the biggest fights I have ever seen.

The trick I was about to perform was one I had seen done some months before by big Keith Watson, the Gretton policeman. On that occasion, I was with Keith and one other on the van when we were sent to the Nags Head Pub in Corby village. Then, Keith had simply lit his pipe, put on his best 'country boy' smile and stood in the middle of the dance floor. This had resulted in the whole scene being calmed down and all violent thoughts leaving the combatants' heads without a word being said or any arrests.

The difference was, on this Christmas Eve, I didn't have Keith, I didn't smoke a pipe and perhaps most critically, Keith was about six feet four inches tall and I am only five feet ten, hence the helmets.

It worked anyway. The cry went round the room like an echo, "It's the Pollus" (Glaswegian for 'Police') and by the time it had been repeated several hundred times, I think they all thought it was an army of Polluses and not just the four of us. We advanced into the centre of the room, doing our best to imitate Keith's country boy smile and I was totally amazed to see 300 combatants diving out through the open doors and broken windows. We didn't lift a finger but in a few minutes, the only people left were the unconscious, the badly wounded, the doormen and us.

I will always remember the looks on the faces of the doormen when they saw what had happened. They were awe-struck and could not stop congratulating us on our courage and ability but of course, it was no more than a little applied psychology combined with a lot of luck. The only real disappointment that night was that a young attractive girl had been hit in the face with a glass or bottle and we had little chance of identifying the person responsible for throwing it. She suffered a really serious cut to her face which we were sure would leave her permanently scarred.

That Christmas was to be my last as a uniformed constable on a shift because I was asked soon after, to become a residential officer. These were officers whose Beat was supposed to be in the area where they lived and the Beanfield area where I then lived had become vacant. The residential section was as short of resources as the rest of the station and, like most others, I was expected to cover two Beats. My second was the Lincoln and Kingswood estates including the village of Great Oakley and developing Danesholme estate. Today, these estates are enormous and some have the most serious problems but in 1970, they were just about manageable by one officer with his cycle.

We were a close-knit section commanded by Sergeant Albert McWilliams who was the Sergeant who had met me on my first day at the station. I set out with the best of intentions, paying follow up visits to any crime scenes on my area and getting to know as many shopkeepers and residents as I could.

For someone who likes people as much as I do, this was heaven. I had an office at the front of my house and I could work from there, cycling around the beat, walking when the weather was good or even, on wet days, surreptitiously using my own car. This was strictly against the rules and I obviously received no payment for it but the area was so big it was sometimes the only way I could get around.

On Friday and Saturday nights, Residentials had to be used to supplement the van crews and although we all complained bitterly about being pulled off our beats, the truth was that it made for a welcome break and a little excitement. One night, I had gone to the police station to change my radio batteries when I heard the telephone operator receive a call from a man asking if the death penalty was still in force for murder. He was calling from Lincoln Way, which was on my beat so she asked me to speak to him. I casually asked why he wanted to know and he told me that it was more than just a point of interest as he had just murdered someone.

Naturally, my curiosity was roused at this, although we did receive our fair share of odd callers. I asked where the body was and he gave me an address in Lincoln Way. He said that it was his wife's boyfriend and that he had stabbed him in the chest. Quickly, the telephone operator sent John Beavis to have a look while I kept him on the telephone. John reported back a few minutes later that he was unable to get into the house but on looking through the letterbox, he could see blood all over the walls and floor of the hallway.

I was then sent with Gordon Flint to the callbox to try to find the caller while someone else kept him on the line. While we were still en route, John reported that he had now forced an entry and found, inside the house, the lady of the house sitting crying on the stairs and in the hallway was her boyfriend with a carving knife right through his chest.

Our caller was patiently waiting for us at a callbox not far from his home and he calmly asked us again if he would hang. We asked him why he thought that might happen and he explained that he had arrived home to find his wife with her boyfriend. The knife had been lying on a table and he had simply picked it up and stuck it into the boyfriend before turning and walking out. We arrested him on suspicion of murder and explained that there was no longer a death penalty, which seemed to be something of a relief for him.

By this time, an ambulance had arrived and the ambulance men had established that the boyfriend was not, in fact dead. The knife had punctured his lung and sliced a piece off his heart before exiting his back but he was, amazingly, still alive. They indicated that he would certainly not survive the trip to Kettering General Hospital but they were not paramedics in those days and there was no alternative to moving him.

Our prisoner was not necessarily pleased to find his victim was still alive but was a little reassured when we told him that he would not survive the night. We were wrong. He did survive and made an almost complete recovery. In fact, he went on to acquire a criminal record himself for several years before eventually dying from some unrelated cause. My first prisoner for murder (that wasn't) went on to receive a three year sentence for wounding with intent and when he was eventually released, his first task was to visit Corby police station to thank each of the officers who dealt with him during the incident.

Curiously, I made another friend as a result of arresting him during a serious incident in Lincoln Way whilst I was a Residential officer. One night, I was out on patrol on the Lincoln estate, driving my own car, when I received a call to attend the Golden Cockerel to assist other officers at a stabbing incident.

I had to park my car safely before going to the pub and as I walked into a passage between the lounge and the bar, I was confronted by the sight of two police officers who were bending to examine something on the floor. A man was behind the officers and had his arm raised to strike one of them on the head.

Wasting no time, I grabbed him by the throat and lifted him off the floor, holding him against the wall. It was then I discovered that he was about six inches taller than me and fairly strong. I was not unduly worried about this because, despite the height difference, I too was quite strong and knew I could hold him there.

What I could not do was let him down. The other officers were still fully occupied and could not help but then I heard one of the friends I had made on the estate, a local butcher, saying, "Go on Bob, down him." Which I interpreted to mean, 'lower him to the floor'.

"Bless me," I replied, "I really don't think I can." Well those may not have been the exact words, but my friendly butcher got the idea and promptly grabbed the offender's legs, lifting them high into the air and bringing him crashing down with me on top.

Gratefully, I started to drag my prisoner, who was fighting like a madman, out of the pub and towards a Panda car. I could hear the other officers, who were now able to assist, shouting, "Not the car, get him in the ambulance." I could not work out why we had to put him in the ambulance but I thought perhaps they too had realised how difficult it is to get a fighting prisoner into a Morris Minor and they had decided the ambulance would be easier.

It must be realised that all this was going on in the context of a violent and very difficult arrest and had I had time to think it through, I would have known that the Ambulance Service would never allow that to happen. But there was no time for rational thought and we managed to get him onto the bed in the ambulance and hold him down. It was only when we had him slightly quietened that the ambulance men took over and, on lifting his shirt found a major stab wound in his chest that was not bleeding because a piece of his gut had popped out through it and blocked the hole.

When my prisoner saw it he suddenly changed from being a wild and dangerous madman to a pathetic, crying and suffering patient. He gripped my hand and asked me if he was going to die. I wanted to tell him that the answer is "yes, of course you will but I don't know when" because I have little sympathy for anyone who wants to fight with me but I resisted the urge and made sympathetic noises as we transferred him direct to Kettering General Hospital.

As we went, we came to a very unofficial agreement that, as he was the injured party in the stabbing, provided he told me who had stabbed him, I would forget the arrest and fighting with me. As the clear and outright winner of the fighting, I felt I could make this generous offer, particularly as I began to think from the expressions on the ambulance men's faces and the looks they gave, combined with the speed of our journey, that his death might, after all be imminent.

I had to bend really close to his face to hear him say that it was his wife who had stabbed him over an argument they had had before he had gone to the pub. She had followed him with a knife from the kitchen, into the passage where I first saw him and simply plunged it into him. The CID were most pleased to have the information and promptly made their arrest.

My man did not die although he developed peritonitis and was in intensive care for many weeks. It transpired that he was an ex-policeman from Scotland and although I did not know why he had left the Force, I suspect it was because he was a worse villain than many of those he arrested. He was grateful to me and I was to have more dealings with him later as a prisoner and as an informant.

Not all of my criminal dealings as a Residential officer were on this level and one involving children annoying a householder almost caused me as much of a headache as the major crimes. One small part of my beat was an exclusive little estate bordered by the pathway that led to Kingswood school. One of the residents was an important journalist working for the Daily Express. He was having trouble with the kids on their way home from school, pulling up his rose canes and throwing them at his back door. Being an important journalist, he wrote to the Chief Constable to complain and I was told, in no uncertain terms, that this was my most important mission, to put a stop to it.

I was not mad on the idea but, dutifully, I hid behind a tree and waited for the little pests to come along. Sure enough, I had been there only a few minutes when a lad of about ten or twelve, came along the path and grabbed a rose cane from the garden. He was just about to throw it when I stepped out from my hiding place and grabbed him by the ear.

He immediately started to howl and cry and the important journalist

The Author as a young Police Constable having caught a youngster in the act.
He was NOT arrested.

rushed out with his camera and started snapping away at the scene. Despite my instructions to destroy the pictures he sent them to the Chief Constable on the basis that they would provide good evidence for the prosecution.

There was never going to be a prosecution because I simply took the lad home and gave him a telling off in front of his parents but, of course, we were living in a period when such a course of action was totally unofficial and I should have submitted a lengthy report for the Chief Inspector to decide that I should give him a telling off in front of his parents.

I was going on leave the next day so I had no desire to sit for hours writing a report on something so minor and which probably did not amount to an offence anyway. Unfortunately for me, when the Chief Constable saw the photographs, he thought it was quite a good piece of work and sent them to the Chief Inspector to congratulate the officer concerned.

The officer concerned was now on holiday and no one else knew about the incident. The evidence of the identity of the officer was all too plain in the pictures. I still have one of them today as a memento of yet another good piece of work that got me into trouble.

I did manage to pack a great deal into the few months I spent as a Residential officer and I regard it as being amongst the happiest times I spent in what was a very happy career anyway. One part of the fun was to avoid sergeant Albert McWilliams.

He was a good sergeant but he had a nasty habit of trying to catch his men out if he thought they were skiving at home. Now, I wouldn't say we never did that but quite often, we would actually be doing reports at home whilst having a cuppa and occasionally it was possible to book on duty as we pulled the uniform on before breakfast in the morning. We did not regard this as skiving because there was a great deal of give as well as a little take in the job.

Albert would sometimes call us on the radio and ask for a location to meet us and if I was at home, I would usually say, "Farmstead Road" or "Beanfield Avenue" as my house was at the junction of the two. That would give me five minutes to leave the house and be walking towards it from another direction when he arrived.

Unfortunately, on occasions he would already be there when he called on the radio and, more than once, I had to use my emergency exit, over the back fence, through the old people's home behind and out onto Beanfield Avenue before nonchalantly walking round the corner to keep the appointment with my leader. I think he suspected but could never be sure where I had come from.

After a few months and still within my probation period, I began to notice a distinct increase in the number of thefts from washing lines in my area. These were not the old fashioned 'pantie thefts' common among the slightly perverted members of our society but were items of male fashion clothing, mainly the latest shirts.

I began some enquiries, which were to have wide repercussions for me later in several different directions. They brought me into contact with a lad who later became a very nasty and serious criminal as he still is today. They led me to cross the path of the Regional Crime Squad's informants. They led me to meet a woman who became an ardent admirer (to my great worry) and they led me into the CID.

It began with a tip-off that there was a ring of teenagers who were responsible for these thefts and they had a good market going for the stolen property. I commenced my enquiries and one of the first people I interviewed was a fifteen-year-old boy who had never been in trouble before.

He soon told me about his part in the crimes, admitting some twenty thefts and naming associates and those to whom he had sold shirts for small sums. I believe this was the only time in his life that he has ever admitted anything without a raft of evidence being laid before him. He is the person who went on to a life of crime with serious offences ranging from rape, indecent assault and indecent exposure through to a serious assault on a police officer and several series of burglaries over a long period and wide area.

My next suspect lived in Gainsborough Road near to the Pluto pub and when I interviewed him in the presence of his mother, he soon admitted his part in the crimes. In fact his mother was very hospitable, making me coffee and chatting whilst her son made his confession.

Unfortunately it was not long after that I discovered she was watching me and making enquiries about me. She soon knew my own car number, where I lived and virtually all about me. I found this most disconcerting for several reasons. The first was that her husband was a known criminal with a history of violence, poaching and use of weapons. The second was that I felt uncomfortable, not quite knowing if her interest was a means of defending her son or whether it was some sexual interest in me! It is always flattering for a man to think that a woman finds him interesting and my sergeant, who fancied himself a bit of a ladies man, only wanted to go with me on an interview to meet her for himself but I was a happily married family man and wanted no such distractions.

This woman pursued me for several years and always seemed to be there in the background when I was on enquiries in the area, indeed, some years later when I arrived at a murder scene late one night, I noticed her in the crowd of onlookers, waving to me coquettishly.

One of my other suspects would admit nothing and his father, who was present for the interview, seemed not only to wish to support him beyond what a reasonable parent would do but also knew too much about the legal system and the police for my liking. Out of the fifteen or twenty suspects I interviewed, I finally charged six (others being cautioned for lesser parts in the crimes) and this youth, with the knowledgeable father, was the only one who pleaded not guilty. This made me all the more determined to convict him, as I knew he was one of the ringleaders and I could not stand the thought of one of the main players escaping justice while the lesser offenders were convicted.

I secured my conviction and as he left the court having been fined quite heavily, his father told me that my actions would result in him refusing to give information to the Regional Crime Squad for whom he claimed to be a major informant. I later discovered that he was indeed an informant but the Squad would not agree 'major'. He did continue to give information and was still doing so many years later when I eventually returned as the Superintendent at Corby.

This enquiry provided me with tremendous experience in putting together a complicated crime file with so many offenders, witnesses and dozens of detected crimes. In police parlance, they are known as 'roll-ups' because one simple crime 'rolls-up' into a vast matrix of detail which can swamp an inexperienced officer in paperwork and turn him into a gibbering idiot.

I recall one such file, dealt with by a colleague, which almost cost a civilian clerk his job. The officer left the file with him to record some fifty or more detected pedal cycle thefts. The clerk went for his lunch, leaving the whole file resting conveniently on top of his waste bin, which was the only free space around his desk. When he returned, the cleaners had, predictably emptied the bin and the file had gone into the solid fuel boiler with the other 'waste'. In those days of no computers or photocopiers, this meant that the file was completely lost including witness statements and confessions. Our Superintendent, who was not an easygoing soul, was somewhat upset about this and everyone was amazed that no one was sacked.

My own 'roll-up' came at a most opportune moment for me. Several CID officers were promoted and moved on to other areas, leaving vacancies at Corby. As a punishment station, no one wanted to go there voluntarily and I was approached to go into the CID with far less than two years service and therefore still a 'probationer constable'. This was previously unheard of and although it was a huge feather in my cap, it left some gaps in my experience which I had to catch up on quickly.

Chapter 9

At that time, the selection process to become a CID Aide was dependent on being noticed and thought of as a trustworthy, reliable team member with an eye for 'thief taking'. Detective Sergeant Paul Harrison was the man who picked me out and became my mentor initially. Paul Harrison was a worrier. He used to smoke cigarettes very heavily but would also take to cigars and/ or a pipe in times of stress. I have seen him with a cigarette in one hand, a pipe in the other and a cigar in the ashtray, having quite forgotten that his other stress relievers were still alight.

The other shift member was a Detective Constable of considerable ability but slightly less enthusiasm for hard work. David Bowen was a typical Rugby Club member, all bonhomie and full of tall stories. He found me a great asset because he could do all of the talking and then leave me to complete the paperwork. Nevertheless, I did not resent this because he was always there when the going got tough and an experienced hand was needed.

We were due to start work at 8am one day and I arrived at 7.45 to be greeted with relief by the uniformed shift because they had an incident in progress, which clearly needed the CID. On the Exeter estate was a wine shop, next to the local chippie. All of the shops had been built to the same design but they had gradually been altered by security needs, depending on what they sold.

The Exeter estate was the acme of notoriety in a notorious town. Sheets of reinforcing steel mesh surrounded the telephone boxes. The grocers had been burgled so many times that they had built up the front with glass bricks instead of windows and put a steel door on. One famous, true story, about the estate was the night the patrons of the lounge bar in the local pub were shocked when a man walked in with a bucket and shovel, stole the burning coal fire from the grate and walked out, without even buying a drink!

Even the chippie had had its windows broken so many times they were almost all boarded up. On this night, the wine shop had been burgled and lots of bottles of booze taken. Amazingly, two witnesses had come forward.

One was a woman who had been walking her dog late at night and had seen two men go to the front of the shop, break one of the display windows, climb in and pass the bottles out to the second man who had a pram outside. She had seen the men push the pram across the road to a flat opposite and she clearly saw that one of the men had a pronounced limp.

The second witness was a young boy who had run away from home and was sleeping in the entrance to a block of flats nearby when he too saw the limping man and his accomplice go to the flat. The uniformed staff had managed to surround the flat to ensure no one could get out and were waiting for us to arrive to get a search warrant.

Obviously, I had no more expertise or experience than them at that stage and I was desperate for my untimely colleague, David Bowen, to arrive. When he had not done so at 8.15am, I told the uniformed shift that I was going to get the warrant but actually I went to meet David who was casually walking to work.

When I explained what we had, he immediately switched into gear and we went straight to a friendly Magistrate who signed the warrant. We arrived at the flat and I knocked the door. No answer. I knocked again but still without success.

This time David applied the sensitive CID approach, 'Jean '(the name of the female flat owner) he shouted. "If you don't open the f——— door I'll kick the f——— thing off its hinges." I think she must not have heard me knocking because she soon responded to the persuasive tones of my colleague.

We entered the flat and found over 200 bottles of booze inside, hidden in the bedroom that Jean was sharing with her boyfriend. There were only the two of them there and neither had a limp. Fortunately for us, the boyfriend was the cousin of a well known local criminal nicknamed 'Limpy' who lived just around the corner in Buckfast Square so we soon had him in custody as well.

Jean gave us no problems and soon admitted handling the stolen property. She also made a statement against her boyfriend and 'Limpy' who she told us had committed the burglary. She also agreed to give evidence against them even though her evidence was of limited use as an accomplice.

The boyfriend admitted his part in the crime although he would not name his companion. We were then left with gathering the evidence against 'Limpy' who would not even admit that we were in Corby.

David had the Scenes of Crime Officer (SOCO), Pete Folwell, spend the whole day fingerprinting all of the bottles. After eight hours, they had all but despaired of finding anything other than the prints of Jean and her boyfriend when they came to the very final two bottles, which bore good prints that could easily be proved as belonging to 'Limpy'.

We had also seized his clothing and the Forensic Scientists, subsequently, were able to show that his trousers, jacket and shoes all bore particles of glass from the shop window. The discerning reader may feel that we had a fairly good case against him but, as we had come to expect, he elected trial by jury at the Crown Court and pleaded 'Not Guilty'

There could be a number of reasons for this with Corby criminals though it was a calculated risk. If convicted, they would get a heavier sentence but the chances of conviction were dramatically reduced compared to the Magistrates Court where they would almost certainly be convicted but could not get more than six months imprisonment for one offence (the maximum a Magistrates Court can impose is 12 months for multiple offences).

Another reason might be that they could delay the inevitable by electing trial and obtaining adjournments and yet another might be that it would give them time to think of an alibi. They could even be hoping that the delay would enable them to get bail and disappear to Scotland. We will dismiss the possibility that they might be innocent for the moment!

Came the day of 'Limpy's trial. We all gave our evidence without too much of a challenge, though there were the usual attacks on David Bowen and Paul Harrison about the accuracy of the records of interviews, which were not taped at that time. Even Jean stood up to cross-examination and the Forensic evidence was not challenged at all.

Then it was the turn of 'Limpy' to give his evidence. He did not have to do this because it is up to the prosecution to prove their case, not for the accused to defend himself, but he elected to give evidence on oath. He explained that, on the night in question, his baby son had awoken and needed a bottle. As a good father, he had got up to get it but found that the gas had run out. He had searched for a coin for the meter but could not find one. In desperation to quell the baby's cries, he had taken the baby in the pram out into the street to see if he could find someone with a coin for the meter.

Hence he must have been seen by the witnesses, not breaking into a shop but just looking for someone who might have a coin. Then, he noticed a light on at the house where he knew his cousin was staying with Jean. He did not want to go there because she had always hated him (which was why she gave evidence against him) but he had to get this coin for the meter so he went to the flat (which was when the witnesses saw him going there) and when he knocked on the door, it was opened by his cousin and he immediately saw all those bottles of booze in the hallway.

Concerned for his cousin he took two of the bottles and put them outside, saying, "Don't keep them here, if they are stolen the Police will think you did it" but his cousin said, "Leave them Limpy, they are mine, Jean and I stole them," and took them back inside (which is why two bottles had his prints on them). "Aha", said the Prosecuting Barrister, "What about the glass on your clothing?"

Unphased, Limpy explained that he had a broken pane of glass in his back door at his house and he had noticed a few days earlier, that the chippie (which had the same type of glass as the Off Licence) had a broken window but the remaining glass would be big enough for his door. He had therefore obtained permission from the chip shop owner to take the glass and get it cut down to fit his door. Unfortunately, on the way home, his bad leg had let him down and he had fallen in the street, breaking the glass, which had gone all over his clothing and shoes.

Some readers may feel that no jury in the land would fall for that load of garbage BUT THEY DID! I was absolutely stunned when they came back with a 'Not Guilty' verdict. Limpy came out of the dock and approached David Bowen. I thought he was going to say something nasty but he just smiled and said, "You tried to fit me up copper, there was no glass on that clothing until you put it there 'cos I was wearing my other suit when we broke into the shop."

I have no reason to think that my colleague was corrupt or that he did 'plant' evidence. Nor do I have any reason to think that this allegation was any closer to the truth than the rest of the nonsense he convinced the jury with, but I did have a chat afterwards with the usher who had escorted the jury to and from their deliberations. He told me that he had overheard part of their discussion and they were in no doubt about his guilt. They simply did not want to deprive the baby of a father if he was sent to prison.

This was also a time when TV programmes such as 'The Sweeney' were convincing the public that the police really did behave in a dishonest way and it was to become a very frustrating time for an honest cop. It seemed that everyone was only too quick to put the worst possible interpretation on anything we did. In fact, I have long had the feeling that many members of the public are not unhappy with the thought that their police are willing to 'bend' rules provided it is done in the interests of 'good' and not for reward

This may seem an odd statement at first glance but in so many conversations over the years, I have heard people intimate that they think the police are willing to hit people, twist what is said and generally act outside the law. This is usually said with a 'nudge and a wink' as if to imply that they know it goes on but it is alright.

How many times do we hear people refer to the good old days when a policeman would give youths a slap around the head or hit them with gloves or a cape? I do not know if those days ever existed outside the fiction of Dixon of Dock Green but my experience has been that such incidents were the exception rather than the rule. This is not to say that I have never seen it happen. To do so would be naïve and untrue. I do not, however, accept that it has ever happened with the frequency one might believe from TV shows.

In fact, most of those who seem to expect it of the police only think it is OK until it happens to a friend or relative of their own. I can recall a few notable exceptions to this. One was when the teenage son of a well known local criminal was arrested for some minor crime and his attitude had been so obnoxious that a colleague had simply lost his temper and slapped him about the head.

When father came to the station for the interview with his son, I met him in the foyer and he was extremely aggressive, as I had expected. "My son would not do that. You police are always harassing us for no reason etc etc". In the middle of his tirade at me he said, "If my son did do that he would get a belt round the head from me. I'm not one of those who make complaints about the police for nothing. In fact I wouldn't care if you had clouted him if he did something like that." Manna from heaven!

When we went into the interview, son quickly admitted the crime and several others but then started complaining loudly to Dad that the policeman had hit him. Dad started to respond with the anticipated shouts to speak to the Inspector until I gently reminded him of our earlier conversation and pointed out that his son had, in fact 'done something like that' several times so he could not possibly object that the policeman had done exactly what he had earlier said was alright. Amazingly, he saw the logic of that and made no complaint.

I once saw a Detective Sergeant give a thirteen year old a cuff around the head in the full view of both parents without even the slightest rebuke. Indeed, I truly believe they did not see what really happened. He had been difficult and cheeky when arrested but he also admitted his wrongdoing quite easily.

When parents arrived, he was escorted to the interview room in the presence of his parents and as they walked along the corridor, the Sergeant had his hand on the youth's shoulder and smilingly patted him on the back of the head in a friendly gesture. No one could possibly object to the sign of empathy and forgiveness for the earlier cheek.

What they failed to notice was that the gentle pats gradually got harder and harder until the youth's head was almost rattling on his shoulders. Even he did not feel able to raise an objection but he could not have failed to have a sore head later. When I mentioned this later to the Sergeant he simply smiled and said, "There's more than one way to skin a cat."

Even some police officers seemed ready to think the worst of their plain clothes colleagues and one incident, which was much more violent, actually had a reasonable explanation though two Traffic colleagues would not accept that it did. Arthur Carter was another well-known 'hard man' in the town, with a reputation for all sorts of crime including assaults on the police. He was not too bad when sober but not too many people had seen him in that condition. He could be found drunk at all hours of the day and night and on those occasions, all he wanted to do was fight. He also thought he could out fight any copper brave enough to try to arrest him. He had been proved wrong on that view many times but he was still a challenger.

At that time I worked closely with a slightly more experienced detective named Ivor Peters. Ivor Peters was undoubtedly a very tough officer who was not afraid to get close to the edge of what was permissible. He and I had just returned from lunch one day when Arthur was brought in by the two Traffic officers for a Breathalyser offence. In those days, there was no separate entrance for prisoners and the two of us detectives passed the two Traffic officers with their prisoner in the rear corridor.

Arthur knew all the CID well and as we passed he started to bait us, in fact in his version of a friendly way. This amounted to a challenge to a fair fight anywhere we wanted at any time. I tried to reason with him and help get him into the charge room where he continued to want to fight us. For some reason best known to themselves, the Traffic officers had stepped outside of the room, leaving us to look after their prisoner (perhaps they had both gone to fetch a Sergeant – or to have lunch or do some shopping or something).

Arthur decided that the odds were now in his favour and he adopted a boxing stance towards me, sparring up across the room. He punched me in the stomach. It was light blow delivered with a smile and not intended to hurt. In fact I barely noticed it but my colleague must have thought it was a hard blow delivered as an assault.

The two of them flew across the room without touching the floor and it was impossible to see who was hitting who or whose arms and legs were whose but they both ended up in a heap in a corner where there was an old-fashioned iron radiator. I wasn't sure whether I intended to help my colleague or to save Arthur but I dashed across the room to the corner, leaning over the two of them.

At that moment, I looked at Arthur and saw that he was bleeding profusely from a cut caused by one of the fins of the radiator. As I noticed this, I glanced around and saw our two colleagues coming back into the room.

The look on their faces said it all. They obviously thought we had given him an unprovoked beating and would never accept either that he had struck the first blow or that the injury was unintentional. Arthur started shouting for a Police Surgeon and the Inspector but when the doctor, who happened to be in the building, arrived a few seconds later, Arthur told him to "F—- Off". He might have thought it was another police officer but certainly, the doctor understood the term and did as he was told. The Inspector received a similar reception shortly afterwards and he too understood and complied.

Arthur finally agreed to let us put a plaster on the cut and decided that he would not make any complaint. In fact he even pleaded guilty to the drink driving offence but not one of our colleagues would believe us when we told the true story of what happened. The two Traffic colleagues had even recorded what they had seen in their pocket notebooks although they somehow omitted to include where they had gone when Arthur started to become difficult.

Another similar incident occurred soon after this and Ivor Peters and I started to get a reputation, which was not wholly deserved. We were on late shift one Sunday when a woman reported that her brother, who had been staying with her for a few weeks, had sold all of her furniture while she went to Scotland for a few days. She said that he was at the pub and would be back shortly. She added that she was very afraid of him because he could be violent. His room was upstairs and we agreed to wait up there for his return, having been told that he invariably went straight to his room on his return.

About half an hour later, he returned and, as predicted came straight upstairs to our reception committee. Also as predicted, he got violent. Unfortunately for him, we were both much bigger and fitter than him and we were not drunk. It was a simple and controlled operation for us to take him by one arm each and arrest him.

Unfortunately, getting him downstairs was neither as simple nor controlled. Ivor Peters went first, taking one resisting arm with him and I went last holding one resisting arm back. The impetus on the stairs was a little too much for me to hold back and he managed to free the arm I was holding. The effect of this was a little like a catapult and he shot past my colleague at a rate of knots to land in a bruised and battered heap at the bottom. His sister was a bit upset at this but we had made our arrest and he did not need medical treatment – at that stage.

Our next problem was to get him to the police station in our mini van (with two doors and front seats that had to be folded down to get someone in the back). We could hardly put him in the front passenger seat so he had to be folded into the back seat. This is not easy with an unresisting prisoner.

It is nearly impossible with a drunk, injured and resisting prisoner but we did it somehow. My colleague got into the driving seat and I went to put the front passenger seat down to get in myself. Unfortunately, the prisoner had left his ankle hanging out of the door on my side and when I put the seat back up, it caught his ankle in the doorjamb. Now he did need medical treatment.

It is very odd how people react to their dealings with the Police and I was very surprised that this prisoner made no complaint about his treatment and just pleaded guilty at court. When he recovered from his injuries, even though he had been very drunk at the time, he must at least have wondered how he managed to get so battered and bruised.

During this period, I came to the end of my 'probationary period'. I was not unduly concerned about being accepted as a constable because I knew I was doing well and having been accepted into the CID while still on probation there seemed little doubt that I would be accepted. I was therefore very surprised when Mick Carson, the 'Office man' from my old shift saw me one evening and suggested that I do what he did on a regular basis, which was to inspect the upstairs offices in the evenings and check the Inspector's and Superintendent's in trays.

I did so and found the confidential report submitted by my Inspector for a decision to be made on my acceptance. It seems amazing now, but these reports were not made available to the subject.

This Inspector was the same one I had first encountered at Ryton two years earlier and whom I foolishly believed was a friend and supporter of mine. In fact he had never forgotten our first encounter when I had asked him about Bramshill Police College. Nor had he forgotten my efforts to get a house move. He had reported that I was ambitious beyond my capability and that I expected to be granted things I asked for and he saw these as undesirable traits.

Obviously I could do nothing about the report because I would have been disciplined for going into the Inspector's office and looking at it so I consoled myself with the thought that at least he had recommended that I be accepted and anyway, I did not think the traits he described were that undesirable. Perhaps that was part of the arrogance he felt I was displaying. It did however teach me a valuable lesson. I would never be quite so trusting again but wasn't it sad that I learnt that lesson from a senior officer and not from criminals.

The CID are often referred to in an ironic manner as the 'Brains' department. This is so because they equally tend to refer to their uniform colleagues as 'Woodentops' or other similar derogatory names. Although, in many metropolitan areas this name calling reflected a poor relationship between the two departments, it was never so in Corby, where each relied heavily upon the other, canteen facilities were shared, the command chain involved the uniform Superintendent and the workload dictated that the degree of overlap would be great.

There was, nevertheless some resentment on occasions, particularly when a CID officer said he or she was too busy to get involved with something the uniform team was doing. Usually this claim to be busy was true and the amount of overtime worked reflected it but there were the CID equivalents of the 'Radio Blackspotters'.

Inevitably, the technique was different but the end result was the same. The Work Avoider left more for his colleagues to do. One CID officer had a technique that involved putting 12 or 13 folders in his tray, each containing papers relating to cases he had previously dealt with and on top of them would be one or two containing current cases.

Management introduced a 'Green Card' paper checking system that required all officers to maintain a record (on a green card) to show when cases were submitted and which cases were outstanding. This card had to be kept on top of the tray and was supposed to be checked each month by a Sergeant.

Fiddling the green card was the easiest thing in the world to an experienced detective and the Sergeants, who had their own heavy caseload, rarely checked anyway. Ivor Peters and I decided that we could take no more of this one officer's tricks so, when we worked a Sunday evening (which he always avoided) we would go through his tray and remove all the old files, bringing his green card up to date. We would then raise his desk onto four waste bins, put his chair on top and the now pristine tray with the empty green card on top of that.

We would then be off for two days but the first Sergeant arriving on the Monday morning could not fail to see the tray and lack of workload of this detective. We did this for three months before he finally realised who had done it but by then everyone knew what he had been up to and he had enough work to keep him busy.

His next trick was to take on a fraud enquiry. If a fraud were big enough, it would go to the Fraud Squad at Northampton but if it was slightly smaller, it was dealt with locally and this officer managed to take on a fraud that was just too small for the Squad and just complicated enough for him to be removed from other duties to concentrate on it alone. He managed to make that one case last for 18 months and when it was finally dealt with, it was no more than a variation on a scheme to defraud Mail Order Catalogues of goods by having them sent to false addresses.

Although we were busy, there was still time for jokes to be played on each other and some elaborate ruses were used. One Saturday night, Paul Harrison (my sergeant) and I went to a stabbing incident in the town, involving a young man who was taken to Kettering General Hospital with a serious stab wound to his stomach.

Stabbings in Corby were very common, but the culture of many of the ex-Glaswegians was such that few wanted to make any complaint or give evidence. We therefore used the cuffing technique described earlier to ensure that there was a record of these incidents but no crime recorded.

On this occasion, we visited the young man in hospital and received the customary warm Glaswegian greeting, "See youse fickin CIDs, ye can away and shite." Which can be translated as "Thank you for your interest but I have decided on this occasion that I do not wish to complain about my injuries?"

We gave the standard CID response to this courtesy which cannot be repeated here but may be interpreted as, "Thank you for making your position clear. We will leave now and will be at your service in the future should you need us. Indeed we may take the trouble to ask after you again soon." Having done this we returned to Corby, made a note in the 'barred in' book and went off duty. I was off the next day but Paul Harrison was again on for the 2pm – 10pm shift.

When he arrived for duty, he found the CID office empty apart from one junior officer who was on attachment. On his own office door was a notice, which read, 'Senior Investigating Officer – Detective Sergeants upstairs.' A Senior Investigating Officer (SIO) is only appointed for the most serious crimes and, in those days, was normally at least a Detective Superintendent.

Paul Harrison went back to the CID office and asked the young officer what was going on. The fully primed young officer said, "I don't know Sarge, they just told me to stay here and look after the office. There's some trouble about a guy who got stabbed last night. It wasn't booked on as a crime and they said he has died."

Paul Harrison was a worrier. He took off like a rocket, lit two cigarettes, one cigar and his pipe and shot round the station telling everybody he could find, that the man was dead. He did not stop to explain to anybody what he meant and the story went round the station like wildfire. By the time he got to the Superintendents office, he was almost into meltdown from panic and he burst into the Superintendents office shouting, "He's dead, he's dead. The bloke from last night who was stabbed, he's dead."

Now, the Superintendent had a reputation. He was called the helicopter because he was always at 10,000 feet and when he heard Paul Harrison he too, took off. Hearing this, the two Detective Sergeants who had set the whole, **untrue**, story off, decided that it had gone too far and went into the Superintendents office, just as he was calling the Chief Superintendent at Kettering to tell him that we had a murder on our hands. The two Detective Sergeants said to the Superintendent, "It's alright, don't phone the Chief, he isn't dead."

But by now, the Superintendent was so high off the ground he responded, "He is, he is dead, Paul Harrison said he's dead so he must be." In the end the two Detective Sergeants had to wrest the phone from his grasp, tell the Chief Superintendent who by now had answered the phone, that the call was a wrong number and then spend twenty difficult minutes calming Paul Harrison and the Superintendent down enough to explain that it was just a joke and no one had died, in fact, no complaint of any kind had been received.

Carpets became a feature of my early life in the CID and the first incident was to become something of a local legend. We received information that Tommy Bergin had stolen a carpet from the site of a hotel where he was working as a labourer and that the carpet was at the home of a very well known Kettering criminal.

It was early evening and, having spoken to Kettering CID, three of us went there with a search warrant for the home of this criminal. The carpet was not hard to find. In fact one would have had to be blind and incapacitated not to see it because, rolled up, it took up almost the whole of one room. It was a massive length of contractors quality, corridor carpet. Indeed, it was so long that, when we got it back to Corby Police Station, we rolled it out, right across the car park and got officers to stand every 10 feet or so, in order that the picture could give an idea of its size.

The next task was to go and arrest Tommy Bergin. I have mentioned him earlier and arresting him for theft was going to be no easier than arresting him for a drunken brawl. But now we were plain-clothes officers and had no real desire to see our own clothes ripped to pieces by the 'Tasmanian Devil' I remembered from the incident in a police van a year or so earlier. They used to say that the CID were like bananas because they were all yellow and went round in bunches but no one was going to criticise us for going six-handed to fetch Tommy.

In fact, we had to wait for him to come home from the pub, which was not a good sign and when he did come in, he gave us the standard warm Glaswegian greeting before suggesting that we might like to join him in a little light exercise or, alternatively, leave quietly without him. Neither was what we wanted and somehow, we managed to persuade him to leave the house. Luckily, his brother Sammy happened to arrive at that moment and as he was not drunk, we managed to get him to help us put Tommy in the car.

When he was in the cell, I told the sergeant that I was going in to have a word with him alone. The Sergeant thought I was absolutely mad to do this but I considered it was a bit like the advice I was once given about what to do if confronted by a lion – stare him in the eyes and make soothing noises. I had never seen it done with a lion and I had no idea whether Tommy would react favourably but then, what did I have to lose? (Answer, an awful lot).

In the cell, Tommy told me how brave and stupid he thought I was and then came a turning point. He started to tell me that coppers all thought they were tough but they had no idea how hard life was on a building site. I should say that this was not expressed in the gentle terms I have described but it was more like, "See youse fickin CIDs, youse all think youse is fickin tough but ye wouldna last a fickin day on a site."

This was, of course, my opportunity because I had worked on more building sites than he had, and when I pointed this out to him, he went through a remarkable change. Suddenly we were best buddies and it was just all the other coppers who were the problem. In fact, he kept returning, to the point of my building experience as if he could not believe it.

Having left him overnight, I decided the next day to interview him alone and in the interview room (this was long before the Police and Criminal Evidence Act and tape recording of interviews). Colleagues all thought I was daft again but he gave me no trouble and I offered him a coffee whilst I took down his statement.

In interview he would not admit stealing the carpet and we reached a point when all that was left to do was to ask him if he wished to make a statement after caution. He agreed to do so and I wrote the caution on the top of the form. I then asked him what he wanted to say and he replied, "I know f... all about it." I said, "Tommy I know that's what you are saying but what do you want me to write down on the statement?"

"I know f... all about it." He replied.

"Yes, I know that Tommy but what do you want me to put on the paper?"

"I've told you twice already, put down I know f... all about it." And that was precisely what I wrote.

Tommy was bailed to court and I was left with a roll of carpet to look after. I decided that I could not return it to its owners because there was too much dispute about who owned it (the Kettering criminal said he had bought it openly) and the sheer size of the thing was part of the evidence that it could not have been thought of as a waste off-cut. Therefore, four of us managed to get it into a spare cell where it was to wait until the case went to Northampton Crown Court.

On the day of the hearing, Paul Harrison and I were to attend and take the carpet with us in a police van in case the Judge wanted the jury to see it. I arrived early to start loading it into the van but I could not get into the cell area because the door was locked. I went to find the key but the front office staff told me the key had been missing most of the night and it was just lucky there were no prisoners.

I thought it was a bit odd but went up to the CID office to get a coffee. I poured myself a cup and went to sit at my desk while I thought about how to get to the cell and retrieve my carpet.

As I sat there, I saw Paul Harrison arrive and go to his office. Then I casually glanced at the papers on my desk and was horror-struck by what I saw. There was a note from the night duty uniform sergeant which said, "You're a crafty sod, Tommy Bergin came in about 2am with his van like you told him to, so he could take the carpet to Crown Court for you. You owe me a pint 'cause it took six of us to lift it into his van."

They say that when a rabbit sees a car bearing down on him, he just goes into a blind panic and cannot move. I think that must have happened to me because I knew it was odd that I could not get into the cell area, I certainly should have known that no police officer would hand over the main exhibit to the alleged offender and I definitely ought to have realised that there was no chance six uniform officers would have helped lift a heavy carpet for an absent CID officer.

None of that crossed my mind. I just went into Paul's office and told him what I believed had happened. Paul lit two cigarettes, one cigar and his pipe before flying off round the station telling anyone who would listen, what had happened. They left us for about half an hour before the keys to the cell area magically reappeared and we were able to retrieve the carpet, which was naturally sitting where it had always been, in the cell. We didn't get to show the jury the carpet and I never got to read out the shortest statement in the history of policing because, to our amazement Tommy pleaded guilty and got a suspended sentence.

My other 'carpet' experience was not so much funny as typical of the culture of Corby at that time though it did have its comic aspects. Weldon Caravan Park, where I had my experience with the three gunmen early in my career, was home to a few travelling carpet salesmen. They were itinerants who would go to a warehouse in Nottingham or Derby and buy cheap carpets, which they would then sell around the estates in Corby and elsewhere.

One night, one of them had his van stolen whilst he was at the pub. He had just been to replenish his stock and the van was packed to the top with carpets valued at several thousand pounds. The van was soon found empty on the car park of 'The Pluto' pub and no witnesses were forthcoming.

However, one of the Detective Sergeants had a tip off that we could find the thief and one of the carpets at an address in Corby so, armed with a warrant to search, we went to his house and recovered one brand new carpet and one very repentant thief. This was early in the evening. In his efforts to make his life easier, he kindly took us to the Exeter estate where he pointed out six houses where we would find more carpets.

We obtained six more search warrants and set to work. At each one we found at least one carpet and made an arrest. One of those arrested pointed out another house for us and we went there to execute a search warrant. By then it was 4am and the householder took a few minutes to answer the door.

When we explained what we wanted he immediately admitted that he had a Persian rug but explained that it was in his bedroom and his young wife was in the bed, naked. He wanted us to wait while she dressed but, suspecting that he was up to something, we were not prepared to do that so, as a compromise, we agreed that modesty could be preserved if she stayed in bed with the covers over her whilst we lifted the bed and removed the rug and her husband. This was done and he was suitably grateful for our consideration. She was actually highly amused and said that it was the

Celebrations by the CID at Corby about 1972

most the earth had moved for her since they had got married.

I then managed to go home for three hours sleep, having been on duty throughout the previous day and the whole night. I then had to be back on duty to interview all eight prisoners.

I decided to start with the thief who had been in custody the longest and as I took him to the interview room, he saw the custody board showing who was in the cells. On seeing which prisoners were marked against my name he said, "Why have you arrested John Huckfield?"

"Because you pointed his house to us you daft sod," I replied.

"No I didn't. I pointed out the other house in the pair of semi's," he said.

"Well, it's no problem cause we got a carpet back from his house anyway," I told him.

It then dawned on me that I needed to go and search the house he really meant and, to much hilarity in the station, I returned with another prisoner and another carpet. I think we could have chosen any ten houses at random on the Exeter estate and recovered carpet from nine of them. It is worthy of note that I worked 28 hours duty in two days, recovered thousands of pounds worth of carpet, got nine prisoners, all of whom I interviewed alone and made two new informants but I received not one single word of praise and overtime was all unpaid under the rules at that time.

Chapter 10

One of the most traumatic matters for a CID officer to deal with is a cot death and the first one I attended as a CID officer, was actually the child of the carpet thief who had pointed out where he sold his ill-gotten gains. We were called to his house one evening and the Detective Inspector took me and another officer along. A dreadful scene awaited us. The house was in a very poor area and was badly maintained. There was dirt and squalor everywhere. The parents were very young and had several other young children. The mother was completely distraught and the father was crying.

The difficulty a CID officer faces is the judgement of whether this is a homicide, something that is more common than many people realise, or whether it is just a simple, tragic mishap. Either way, the parents have to be asked some detailed questions and a post mortem examination is inevitable. The questioning must be done with the utmost tact and care to spare any further trauma and the body must be removed with as much dignity as is possible in the circumstances. These are lessons that junior detectives learn at an early stage.

Unfortunately, my Detective Inspector had not had the benefit of training for tact and dignity. Having had a cursory look in the pram where the deceased child still lay, he turned to the mother and said, "It's dead, did you kill it?" The poor woman simply dissolved into paroxysms of grief so he turned his attention to the husband with the same result. He was totally unaffected by what he had done to them and when he returned to the mother and said, "we shall have to take it away, have you got a cardboard box we can put it in?" I felt so incensed that I could have hit him. They may have been poor and living in squalor but they did not deserve to be treated in this abrupt and uncivilised way.

I did my best to retrieve the situation by ensuring that we removed the body with a little reverence in the pram top and by getting a neighbour to comfort the parents but even when the Sergeant remonstrated with him, the Detective Inspector was quite unmoved. This was probably one of the worst examples of policing I saw in my service.

On a lighter note, our senior supervisors were very hard taskmasters whose word was law and who thought that young officers needed to be roundly rebuked at least once a week, often for the slightest offence. The result of this was that young officers tended to keep as far away from anyone above the rank of Sergeant as possible.

Our Detective Chief Inspector, who was based at Kettering, was well known for his loud voice and gruff manner, so when I received a memo from a Sergeant instructing me to parade at Kettering the next morning at 5am for a major and secret operation to be led by the DCI, I simply acknowledged it and prepared for an early start.

Gordon Flint, knowing that the memo came from Tom Wilson, the same Detective Sergeant who was fond of setting up jokes, asked me if I thought the note was genuine. I was pre occupied with another case at the time and I absently replied to the effect that I had no idea. He then asked if I thought it would be a good idea to query it with the DCI. Equally absently, I said, "It's up to you." And I thought no more about it.

The next thing I realised was that he was on the telephone to the DCI asking if the order, apparently under his name, was genuine. I looked up from my work and saw that my colleague was gradually holding the instrument further and further away from his ear and I could hear the voice of our beloved leader getting louder and louder as he explained that young officers are there to obey orders not to query them with busy DCI's and if the order said to be there at 5am, he should be there at 5am. By the time he had finished he did not need the telephone because I'm sure he could have been heard from Kettering without it. Needless to say, the order was genuine and it was to lead me to my first encounter with the police use of firearms.

Today, the modern Police Force has access to numerous sophisticated weapons and is well trained in their use. That was not the case in the early seventies. It seemed that the stock of weapons was left over from World War Two, and the training relied upon those officers who had been involved in that, or any other, war.

Our task on that day was to search all of the gypsy sites in our area as part of a coordinated nationwide search for some desperate and dangerous criminals. As usual we had insufficient resources so we were split up into teams of three. The theory was that one CID officer would knock on the caravan door whilst one uniformed officer stayed at the wheel of the car and the third officer, who would be armed with either a long barrelled revolver or a .303 rifle, would stay in the car and would not produce his weapon unless fired upon.

The discerning reader will note the discrepancy in this plan as far as the CID officer was concerned. I spotted it, as I was the CID officer in the team I was with. Apart from the danger if we should encounter the dangerous criminals, many police officers know that not all gypsies are jolly characters who spend their time dancing round a camp fire and eating baked hedgehog.

They are prone to taking offence at intrusions from police officers, and tend not to have the healthy respect and fear of authority that we relied upon. CID officers, not being in uniform, were fair game, because the gypsies could always pretend they didn't know he was a police officer, and if he was apparently alone, his chances were not good. Added to that, surprisingly, some gypsies are not up and about at 5am so are not necessarily well disposed to having their door knocked by a CID officer wanting to search the caravan.

Knowing the site I was detailed to, I felt it was reasonable not to expect to find the criminals there but it was equally likely that I would not get a good reception. Nevertheless, my driver colleague and my armed colleague (on this occasion an elderly sergeant with a .38 revolver) were both happy with their instructions and obeyed them to the letter.

With trepidation, I knocked on the door and announced myself, receiving the customary warm gypsy response of, "F… off." I repeated my knocking and suddenly the door burst open. There on the step was a very upset gypsy with a huge axe in his hand. "What do you want?" he said and thinking that I definitely did not want to be scalped or split in two, I started to turn to call for my back up to get out of the car. They seemed to be reading the morning paper or something because neither made any move.

Just as I thought my life was over, the gypsy brushed past me and started to split some logs for his morning fire, nonchalantly inviting me to search his tiny caravan to my heart's content. I still do not know if he was frightened off by the threat from my two menacing colleagues but I somehow don't think so.

The whole ethos of the CID in the early seventies centred on long hours and drinking. This latter activity was allegedly to make contact with informants and generally identify criminals. In fact I rarely met an informant in a pub. I would have said 'never' but there was one notable exception.

One night, a group of us were having a drink in the bar of the notorious 'Candle' public house, when some of the local ne'er-do-wells decided to start catcalling and generally giving us a hard time. Ivor Peters, who was well known for his lack of fear and his ability to go where angels fear to tread, decided to respond. He casually walked over to the loudest criminal, took a pound note from his pocket and handed it to the criminal saying, "John, that's for the information you gave me last week. I forgot to pay you then". 'John' (not his real name) realised the position he was being put into and took the only way out he could think of. He leapt up and made a grab for Ivor. We naturally took up a defensive stance and this resulted in virtually every member of the assembled company attacking us.

Someone just had time to call for uniformed assistance before we all sank beneath the tide of sweating, swearing humanity and we were righteously pleased when the reinforcements arrived from the nearby Police Station. I recall that officers were throwing bodies out of the front door of the pub, where the Inspector, a handy boxer, would restrain them (his technique seemed to involve a right hook to the jaw). The now bemused criminal would then be escorted to the cells for the night.

I do not think that the device Ivor Peters used was either new or ethically correct but none of the participants in the fighting ever made a complaint and we counted it as a battle we had won. This was very important in those days if we were to retain the respect of the many petty criminals in the town but it did not make us popular with the uniformed colleagues who were only too well aware that the 'Brains' had to call on them as soon as the going got tough.

This, hard working, hard drinking ethos lead to many CID officer's marriages breaking up and quite a few officers were involved in affairs or wife swapping. It was impossible to avoid knowledge of what was going on but I was always determined not to get involved and I am pleased to report honestly that I never did. Nor did I get involved in too much heavy drinking because I did not enjoy drink that much and I always felt that much of it was to relieve the stress of the job. I thought it was really a coward's way of facing up to it and not really my style at all.

This did cause me to be sometimes ostracised by one clique within the department but I resolved to live with that if necessary. On one occasion, I was left as the only CID officer available for a whole night, whilst all of the others went to a party. At that time, I was still an aide and quite inexperienced.

The evening started quite well. I had a call to go to a house where a lady informed me that her 21 year old, drug addict son had been to see her and stolen a camera. I knew where he lived but was not sure how to obtain a warrant. I therefore spoke to 'Taff' Southfield, the uniformed sergeant, who was ex-CID and kindly showed me how to fill in the forms. I then made my first visit of many to a certain friendly Magistrate who granted me the warrant.

My visit to the young man's home soon resulted in the recovery of the camera, my first prisoner of the night and a half confession. I then had to leave him in the cells whilst I visited the first two of the night's burglaries.

As I left the second crime scene, I was diverted to the A6003, where a taxi driver had been robbed at knifepoint of his takings (a small sum but the knife made it a 'Robbery with violence'). I established that the driver had not seen a knife but had felt something sharp in his neck when the offender demanded that he hand over the takings. He had picked the passenger up in Shire Road, which is at the other end of the town and the offender had made off across the Beanfield School grounds.

As I noted the description of the offender, a second call came from another taxi driver who had also been robbed at knifepoint on the Kingswood estate. This time, the passenger had been picked up in Beanfield Avenue (the other end of the Beanfield school grounds) and taken to Kingswood, where he asked the driver to wait while he fetched his money. He had returned to the taxi a few minutes later, produced a knife and demanded the driver's takings (again a small sum). The description was the same as in the first robbery but this time, we could roughly identify where the offender had gone before returning with the weapon.

I knocked on a few doors and found a young woman who was prepared to say that her boyfriend, Harvey Millar, had visited her house, borrowed a knife and then left at about the time of the attack. This was my second search warrant of the night but this time with no success. I neither found Harvey or any evidence.

By the time I had circulated my suspect as wanted and visited three more burglaries it was 4am and I ended my ten hour shift with one theft (detected), five burglaries (undetected) and two robberies (potentially detectable). This was a busy night for Corby and there would normally be at least a Sergeant and two Detectives on duty but I had been forced to cope alone.

I then had to return to duty by 9am to interview my prisoner for the theft and charge him before continuing with a full day's work. About 7pm, I was informed that Harvey Millar was in hospital, having taken an overdose so, together with Paul Harrison, I went to see him. The doctors said that he was soon to be released so we arrested him and took him back to Corby Police Station.

I then prepared myself for another long night of interviews because I knew no one would admit two robberies, as the penalty was certain to be a lengthy term of imprisonment. The penalty for one robbery could be life imprisonment and trial could only be at Crown Court. I therefore had to be sure that my interviews were carefully and properly prepared.

Having psyched myself up, I began my interview with Harvey. "Tell me what you did last night" I began. "From what time?" he asked. Here we go, I thought. "From when you got home from work" I said, thinking that I would get some material to trip him up.

"Well, I had my tea, got washed and changed and then I went out and… and then I went out and robbed two taxi drivers," he replied.

He then went on to explain that he had no money so he took the first taxi and decided to rob the driver so he took out a couple of matchsticks and held them against the driver's neck, pretending that he had a knife. As he had only made three pounds, he decided to do it again but realised that he would be very lucky to get away with the matchstick trick a second time. So, having run through the school grounds, he got the second taxi to take him to near his girlfriend's house, got the knife and did the second robbery.

The only attempt Harvey made to minimise his culpability was by giving me some good information about drug dealers in the town and I did get him a small financial reward for this after he had been sentenced to three years imprisonment for his first conviction. My problem then was how to pay a reward to someone in prison and I had to open a Building Society account for him, for when he was released. Unaccountably, Harvey felt enormous enmity towards me although I had done nothing to make him feel that way and the sentence was not excessive for the enormity of the crimes.

In fact, he went on to commit a robbery at a shop in Kettering and when cornered by an unarmed police officer, he attacked the officer and fractured his skull in several places, causing the officer to suffer permanent damage and end his career. For this he received eight years and when he was released, he immediately robbed a chip shop at gunpoint and was arrested with great difficulty by one of my colleagues. I was asked to speak to him in the charge room because they were having difficulty in getting him to the cells but all he would say to me was,"Mr f…ing Thorogood, what do you f…ing want?" and then he turned his back on me and would say nothing else.

This was particularly strange because Harvey came from a good home and had parents who were both law abiding and pleasant people. He also had a brother who I will call David who did not come to the notice of the police until he was nineteen. Unfortunately, he too started his criminal career with a major crime and this was the only time I have been personally involved in a successful identification from a photofit picture.

I had attended a crime scene of a rape on a teenage girl, one night as she walked home. It was a violent attack but the girl had been able to give us a good description of the offender. She was able to assist the Scenes of Crime officers to make up a photofit picture and I had it circulated.

There were no developments for several weeks, until one day Paul Harrison was in the office, having been away on holiday. He noticed the picture and instantly said, "That's David Millar." Paul Harrison had spoken to him when we were dealing with Harvey and he was so positive that we arrested him. Like his brother David also admitted the offence, though not as readily as his brother and he too went to prison for his first offence but I have never heard of him again since his release.

In 1972, I had my first real encounter with murder. This was a crime that did not happen very often in Northamptonshire and certainly not in Corby. It was, therefore, something I relished when a colleague, Jeff Thomas and I were seconded to a murder enquiry in Northampton.

A prostitute had been found in an outhouse of a pub with her skull crushed with a hammer. The officer in charge was Detective Chief Superintendent David Somers who had recently transferred to Northamptonshire from Warwickshire. He was a very impressive man. Very stern and imposing, he had experience with major cases that had been lacking in local officers.

He led the enquiry with skill, professionalism and determination. He had no patience with fools or incompetents and officers would not lightly fail him in any way.

Jeff Thomas and I were detailed to visit the local haunts of the prostitutes, The Mitre and The Criterion and to talk to the girls. Well this may not have been the best use of our particular skills because, as I have already said, Corby was distinctly short of prostitutes and we had no idea how they talked or acted.

We sat one night at a table in the pub, thinking that we were quite unobtrusive, when one of the girls came up to us and said, "We're having a collection for the dead girl, are you two f...ers going to put something in or am I going up to Campbell Square (the local police station) to tell your governors that you two f...ers are drinking in here?" Needless to say, we contributed generously, more out of fear of the collector than the 'governors at Campbell Square'.

We found the girls to be quite normal, ordinary people but they did have a very open way of talking about their work and I recall visiting the home of one 'girl' (she was about sixty years old and about 14 stones in weight). Her name was 'Big Toni' and she happily told us that she still 'turned a few tricks' but she had to wait in dark doorways because, if the punters saw her, they would run a mile.

It was an interesting investigation and it was established that the dead girl had been blackmailing the landlord of the pub, who was one of her clients. He had lured her to the outhouse and smashed her head with a hammer, which he threw away in a nearby park. He had also taken her earnings, which she kept in her boot. He was, of course subsequently sentenced to life imprisonment.

During that year, I faced the prospect of attending a Home Office National CID Course with mixed feelings. It was an honour to be selected to attend but it was also a very costly exercise for someone with a young family. Also the prospect of being away from home for twelve weeks was somewhat daunting.

I found that I was to attend Hutton Hall, Preston for my course. This was perhaps the worst choice because it was so far distant and did not quite have the reputation of the bigger centres like The Met, West Midlands and West Yorkshire.

Jackie had to get a part time job to help us to survive because we knew that the hidden cost of the course was in the social aspects, which even formed part of the final assessment. We then had a very ancient Morris Oxford with an engine on its last legs but replacing the car was out of the question.

I had never been further north than Leicester so I asked one of my colleagues, who had previously been on a similar course at Preston, how to get there. I cannot now believe that I did not consult a map before leaving and I can only blame the volume of work but my colleague had said that you just get to Lutterworth, get on the motorway and head north until you reach Preston.

What he failed to mention was that there are two motorways with junctions at Lutterworth and the one reached first from Corby was the M1 for Leeds. In fact, I needed the M6 spur but without having looked at a map, I just got on the M1 and headed north.

It was a foggy Sunday afternoon and visibility was down to about 30 yards. After several hours, I saw signs for Leeds but none for Preston so I stopped at a service area and asked an AA patrol. He looked at me askance and politely informed me that I was about 100 miles from my destination across the Pennines. He also told me that the M62 was probably about to close because of the fog.

As it was, by then almost 5pm, when I was due to arrive at Preston, I realised I was not about to make an auspicious start to a career as a detective. There were no mobile phones then so I just had to resolve to being late and think of an excuse.

Fortunately, the M62 had not closed but the police were leading vehicles across the Pennines in convoy so I had to wait to get a 'wagon train' together before we set off. I arrived at Hutton Hall about 9pm but the weather was a ready explanation and I received a warm welcome from the staff. Until now, I have told very few people about my journey.

I soon found that the Lancashire Force and the instructors were extremely hospitable and, in the context of the time, professional in their approach. I use the expression, 'in the context of the time' because times were very different from now. The role of the detective was seen as similar to a salesman, with a confession being the equivalent of a sale. How the sale was made was irrelevant provided it was made.

Indeed we were taught to watch for 'buy signs' in the same way that salesmen are taught. In one role-play exercise, I was tasked with investigating a theft from a house and the scenario had me finding the householders' son in a compromising position with a girl. He was the suspect and I had to interview him. I was given a high mark for blackmailing him into a confession on the threat of telling his parents what I knew about him and his girlfriend. It must be remembered that it was only role-play but the fact that I was marked up for using a completely unethical method of obtaining a confession was really shameful but it was how things were done in the days when 'The Sweeney' was popular.

It is not surprising that some officers got into serious trouble and there was one night when I thought I was about to become one of them. Lancashire detectives were the only Force who granted their officers a car allowance to use their own cars for duty and the result was that the local officers all had good modern cars, while the rest of us had old worn ones.

One of our Lancashire colleagues agreed to take three of us to Blackpool for the evening in his new Ford Capri Ghia. We all had a few drinks and set off back to Preston at about 1am. This colleague decided to show us how the car would go and he wound it up to a speed of over 100 miles per hour (having consumed enough beer to be just over the limit). He was a capable driver, having previously been trained to Grade One, which is the highest grade of advanced driver but I knew we were in trouble when he overtook a Vauxhall Cavalier at that speed and I could see the uniform jacket of the driver of the 'Night Crime Car'.

They had no chance of catching us but when we arrived at the outskirts of Preston we were greeted by a roadblock just for us. I truly believed my career was over but to their shame and my eternal gratitude, the Sergeant let us go when he discovered that we were on the CID Course. Times were different then and readers can be well assured that in today's climate, a CID officer who tried that trick would be out of a job in a trice.

Motor vehicles were becoming a nuisance to me and it was not too far into the course that my Morris Oxford's engine died. In fact, I managed to limp home one Friday and spent the whole weekend finding a second hand engine at a scrap yard and getting a friendly garage to fit it before I returned to Preston on the Sunday evening.

This was a further strain on our stretched finances and I began to wonder if they would ever recover. I did survive the course and scored a creditable fifth position out of the forty or so on the course.

Some of my most abiding memories however, are of the drinking culture at the Centre, which was in the Force Headquarters complex. The bar was often open until the early hours and at least one of the instructors was an alcoholic. He took us on a formal educational visit to a local brewery and distillery one day, using the Force Bus for transport. Having been entertained to a few drinks by the management of the distillery, this instructor decided that we would stop at a pub on the way back.

Unfortunately, it was the middle of the afternoon and the landlord was having a nap when we called. He was rudely woken and persuaded to open the pub for us (outside the then permitted hours). We were all well and truly inebriated by the time we returned to the centre.

On the final weekend before the exams, I decided to stay at Hutton Hall for the weekend to study. Unfortunately, someone persuaded me to go for 'One quick half in the bar' after dinner on the Friday night. We staggered out of the bar at 5am the next day, just in time to see a drunken Detective Inspector parading three drunken Detective Sergeants around the parade ground.

There was a tradition that the final night, after the exams, would include a concert, which everyone attended. The North was well known for club entertainers and the concert included many quite well known acts and the guest of honour was a very well known and respected actor from the TV series, 'Z Cars'. I found him in a close embrace with a female detective at 3am. The most memorable highlight of the evening however was when the two senior instructors, both Detective Chief Inspectors, fell out over some minor dispute and came to blows on the dance floor. The evening ended finally when we went into breakfast at 8am.

You may be forgiven if, by now, you are forming the impression that I was part of the heavy drinking, corrupt group. In fact it was impossible to keep completely free of it. One student, who did so by locking himself in his room every night and studying, scored the highest marks on the course but was marked down badly for not socialising as it was seen as part of the detective's role. I did not then and never have really enjoyed drinking and, with the financial situation at home, I was really quite glad when it was over and I had escaped with my career intact.

If nothing else, the course showed me how the job should not be done and actually encouraged me to do it properly though that was not the result achieved by all who attended and some came to grief soon after. Indeed, for me, I believe the things I saw and learned in those early days stood me in good stead many years later when I was involved in writing the Police and Criminal Evidence Act (PACE), which made a major contribution to ridding the Force of many malpractices.

At the end of the course, I returned to Corby and became a fully qualified Detective Constable. Very soon afterwards, I became involved in my second murder investigation.

Chapter 11

One evening, in the village of Kingscliffe, which was a rural community covered by Corby Division, there was a young man named Danny Short who lived with his parents in a council house in the village. The family were devoutly religious and much respected locally.

Danny Short was courting a girl from near Polebrook and his main interest was in starting a Disco with a couple of his friends. Danny had returned home late in the evening and was told by his sister that there had been several phone calls for him from a man who wanted to organise a disco in another village. The phone rang again at about 11.45pm and this time Danny answered it. He then told his sister that he was going to meet this man about the disco. She thought it was an odd hour to be going to such a meeting but he left the house in good humour.

He spoke to a friend in the street and that friend later saw him getting into a black Austin A30, which the friend did not recognise. Just after 2.30am, Danny's father was woken by the telephone. When he answered it, a voice said that he was the man who had met Danny and had been bringing him back home from Apethorpe but his car had broken down and Danny was walking home.

Realising that it was a long walk from Apethorpe to Kingscliffe, Danny's father set off in his milk float to fetch him. Despite driving the route several times, he failed to find his son and eventually called the police.

Danny's body was found at 7am the same morning in a shallow stream at a location called the 'Second Drift' The water at that point was only about 9" deep but a post mortem revealed that he had drowned. It also revealed scratches on his elbows and knees consistent with having been held down in the water. His jacket was found inside out about 50 yards downstream.

This was clearly a major crime and the Detective Chief Superintendent was called from Northampton. David Somers had been promoted to Assistant Chief Constable and his place taken by Harold Evans who was a very personable man and someone I have liked and respected for many years since. He was, however, a more traditional thinker than David Somers.

The enquiry was complicated from the outset by the remoteness of Kingscliffe, the insular manner of the villagers and the lack of experience of such an enquiry in the Force. Kingscliffe had far more than its share of strange people and it is those people who evoke the most vivid memories. The enquiry itself made little progress. Most of the detectives had to come from Kettering or Corby, which meant a 40 or 50 mile round trip each day. The Incident room was initially set up in an old Ex-Army Lorry the Force had bought for £50 and it then transferred to a room above a stable that was used as the local Conservative Club.

Meals were taken at the local pub and they were so good that officers tended to find reasons to stay longer than they should. Only two typists were used and this meant that statements were produced too slowly and one of the senior officers spent all his time devising theories about what may have happened. This resulted in many of us being sent on wild goose chases because of his latest theory. One such was the theory that there was a homosexual link with discos in East Anglia and we spent many hours following up leads in Gainsborough and Scunthorpe, based on little more than a wild guess.

The strangeness of many of our witnesses did not help. We were often distracted by discovering quite serious crimes, which had to be investigated.

'Rubberlips' was a local man who was known to have a preference for small boys and we discovered that he had been paying too much attention to a relative of Danny's, a boy of 12. I was sent with Paul Harrison to interview this boy but when we arrived at his house, his parents were just leaving to play Bingo in Stamford. They just told us to talk to the boy as much as we wanted and he could sign his statement when they returned. They felt it was alright because his older brother was in the house anyway.

Unable to delay the enquiry, Paul Harrison and I interviewed the boy for several hours before he finally admitted that Rubberlips had been regularly and seriously sexually assaulting him. I completed his statement and obtained the parent's signature on their return. They were not even slightly perturbed by the fact that their son had been subjected to the assaults, or the interview, only by the fact that they had failed to win at Bingo.

'Rubberlips' was subsequently charged and months later, I was subjected to another career threatening moment at Leicester Crown Court. The boy had retracted his statement and alleged that the big policeman who took the statement had bullied him. I had not been involved in the arrest of 'Rubberlips' so was not in court. The Judge therefore sent for me and I was collected by a Traffic Car and whisked to Leicester. On my arrival, no officers were allowed to speak to me and the Usher escorted me straight into the well of the court. I was told to stand there and the boy was returned to the witness stand where he was asked only, "Is that the Officer?"

"Yes" he replied and was released.

I was then directed to the witness box to await questions. Prosecuting Counsel stood and looked at me directly before saying, "No questions, wait there officer." Defence Counsel stood and I waited for the onslaught with baited breath. When he looked up and said, "No questions from the defence." I was elated.

The Judge had no questions either and I was released. How I could have explained that interview without the parents, I have no idea. It was quite wrong although it had seemed the only course of action at the time. It is also true that my questioning was robust to say the least. I suspect I had let what I saw as 'Justice' get in the way of the law.

I was amazed two days later when I heard that the Judge had allowed the case to go to the jury, who had quickly found 'Rubberlips' guilty, even without the boy's statement and the Judge had sent him to prison for a year. This may not sound like a long sentence but I firmly believe that the Judge had taken a pragmatic view, decided he was guilty and administered a sentence that was long enough to hurt but unlikely to attract an appeal. In fact, he did appeal and it was upheld but by the time it was heard, he had tasted the joys of a sex offender in prison.

Another distraction was the rumour we heard about someone nicknamed 'Porky'. We were led to believe that he did not get this nickname because he was overweight. It had more to do with his sexual preferences. (They did have some very pretty pigs in Kingscliffe).

It fell to me to bring him in for interview and although he would not admit having made love to pigs, he was quite proud of his exploits with two human male friends, with whom he admitted to forming a circle in the fields at night (and I do not mean crop circles, which had not been invented then).

Amazingly, the two friends were just as happy to tell me about it but there is a 'statute of limitations' on such offences and none of them was prosecuted. The only sequel to this story was that, one night, when we were all driving back to Corby in convoy, we rounded a bend just before midnight and were confronted by a huge pig being chased down the road by a farmer in 'Wellies'. I'm sure there was a reasonable explanation but four CID cars almost went into the ditch because of the raucous laughter coming from within.

Phil Roberts was another local married man of about thirty who liked girls under fourteen. He would admit nothing and was quite a strong character. The evidence against him was good because the girls involved all voluntarily gave statements. One day, I was partnered with Nick Ronson, an experienced detective from Northampton and we were told to go and have a chat with Phil Roberts at his home. His powerfully built wife was stood in the kitchen while we chatted to him and, unknown to either of them, we could see her listening at the door.

My partner had a reputation as one of the best storytellers and talkers in the Force and I was a willing accomplice as my colleague weaved a story calculated to at least upset the marital harmony.

"I know I cannot impose my religious beliefs on everybody," Nick Ronson began, "I am the Force Padre and I know that not everybody can live up to my principles but I truly believe that it is important for a man to tell the truth, at least to his wife even if he can't be brave enough to tell it to the Police. Now I know there is something you are not telling your wife, isn't there? You should tell her what you have been doing." At this, which I had not been told to expect, I joined in by saying to Nick, "Listen, that isn't fair, just because you are the Padre and you believe it so strongly you can't expect others to feel the same way and it isn't likely that Phil is going to tell his wife the sort of things we know he has done." I had no idea whether Nick Ronson held strong beliefs and I certainly had never heard of a Force Padre but he kept it going for nearly half an hour before suddenly apologising for taking so much time, and getting up to leave.

We had barely left the front door when we heard the beginning of an enormous quarrel coming from inside. Phil's wife had heard every word, including his failure to deny that there was something he had not told her. The last sound we heard was that of pots and pans flying through the air. My partner was kind enough to tell me then that he was not in fact a 'Padre' nor was he religious, he just thought it might provoke some sort of admission from his victim. Phil Roberts eventually served three years in prison for his crimes.

One Saturday, another detective and I were detailed to do house-to-house enquires at all the houses in Blatherwycke, which is a tiny hamlet between Kingscliffe and Bulwick. We did this with comparative ease until we reached the largest house in the hamlet, which was owned by the Dowager Lady Brookes. We arrived there about 7pm and I knocked on the door, to be greeted by a middle-aged man wearing evening dress. I introduced myself and before I could say why I was there, he turned and shouted, "Mother, Mother, there's a character here from the Police."

I was somewhat taken aback by this, never having thought of myself as a 'character' before. However, before I could react, he had gone into the depths of the house to be replaced by an elderly, regal lady who introduced herself as Lady Brookes.

She explained that they were just about to have dinner and asked me to call back another day. I agreed to this but when I did return and listed the members of the household, there was no male on the list. I asked Lady Brookes about this and she explained that her son had been visiting but was not a regular visitor and had not been there at the time of the murder.

This seemed perfectly reasonable to me and I left him off the list. Imagine my chagrin when, a week later, he emerged as a possible suspect and I got the biggest rocket I had ever suffered until then. I definitely learned something from that although he was later eliminated from the enquiry.

The Detective Chief Superintendent also suffered at the hands of Lady Brookes because she telephoned him one day and told him to visit her one evening and bring an Ordnance Survey map with him. He dutifully did so and spent several hours with her whilst she assured him that she was a 'Diviner' and could tell him, with twigs, where the murderer was (the murderer – not the body).

There was a great deal of inter-breeding in Kingscliffe and the result was that many people were related and some had such defects as no eyelids so they would give one some very odd looks. The combination of the difficulties I have outlined, the introverted nature of many of the inhabitants, together with the natural reluctance of some isolated communities to talk about their business finally led to the enquiry coming to an unsatisfactory end and it remains undetected to this day although, as with all major enquiries, it was reviewed every few years throughout the rest of my service.

Chapter 12

I returned to Corby three months later to find that no one had even looked at the crimes in my tray and I had a great deal to do on mundane enquiries, including a minor fraud that I had begun just before the murder. It was a comparatively simple matter of a shoe shop manager who had been stealing the takings and covering up his thefts by falsifying the accounts. Unfortunately, he had then left suddenly and gone to Birmingham to live.

I managed to get enough evidence for my case and was left with the one remaining task to go and interview the suspect. I was amazed that one of my colleagues volunteered to accompany me for what was to be an evening job. I was so surprised because it was often difficult to find volunteers to assist with any job and one that would involve considerable overtime and an evening away from home was the least likely to attract help.

When we arrived in Birmingham, the task was fairly simple. An immediate confession was extracted from the repentant suspect and he was told that the facts would be reported. My colleague then informed me that we were going to visit a pub in the centre of Birmingham because he had to see someone there. This pub was obviously a police 'watering hole' because it was full of Crime Squad and CID officers.

My volunteer partner expressed surprise when two attractive female officers walked in and joined us. It transpired that one of them had been on a course with him and she said how pleased she was to see him because her car was 'playing up'. I knew that he had no knowledge of cars so I realised this was just an excuse to leave me (and the other girl) alone. Indeed the whole meeting was a 'set-up' and they were absent for nearly an hour, leaving me to entertain a young lady in whom I had no interest whatsoever. In fact, she had no interest in me either so it was a fairly strained and embarrassing hour.

In one of life's amazing coincidences, fifteen years later, I went into a restaurant with my wife and found my old colleague's paramour working behind the bar and what is more, my old colleague was also sitting, dining in the restaurant. I had told Jackie about the incident at the time, partly because we had no secrets and partly because I was angry about being set up. She was shocked because we knew the colleague and his wife socially and neither of us had realised that he was the type to stray, although we had been to several wild parties at their house.

The incident had left me with a feeling that the West Midlands Police had some problems with their officers because there had been so many drinking in the pub and they certainly stayed far beyond normal opening hours. I was to have my view of them reinforced when I had to visit a Young Offenders Institute in the Birmingham area later that year. I had to interview a detainee about a burglary in Corby, which he readily admitted. Unfortunately he also told me that he was due in court the following morning in Walsall for robbery and the officer in the case wanted to have all offences dealt with at the same time.

I therefore agreed to meet the officer at his tiny, back street station in Walsall on my way back home. We agreed that we would prepare the file there and then so that it too could be dealt with. I felt this was a wonderful arrangement because it meant that I would not have the file lying around for days, as I was so busy.

When I arrived at the station, I found that it was a converted terraced house with a small front office and the staff consisted of one constable, one detective and one typist. The detective invited me to make myself a cup of tea whilst he attended to another job after I had briefly told him the nature of the confession I had gained. I began to get restless when he had been gone for over half an hour but then he returned and I said, "We really have to get a move on with this file now because I have got to get back to Corby."

He simply laughed and handed me a sheaf of papers. I examined them and found that he had used the time he was away from me, with the typist to prepare the whole completed file for court. I would have been overjoyed by this except that he had not had access to my pocket note book. He could therefore have no way of knowing what had been said between the offender and me and the detective had concocted a complete statement for me to sign, purporting to give a verbatim account of the interview. In fact, it was remarkably close to the truth but I did not feel able to let him get away with such a blatant piece of 'verballing' (putting words into an offenders mouth) and I had to insist we rewrite the statement before I would sign it.

It was about then that the man who had suffered the stab wound to the stomach in my early days of service, reappeared in my life. Although he was an ex-police officer from Scotland, he had settled firmly into the criminal society of Corby and when a man from the infamous Exeter estate was thought to have indecently assaulted his eight year old daughter, he and his wife went round to the house, armed with an iron bar, broke in and attacked the man before smashing up the interior of the house.

The uniformed officers arrived on the scene but the offender and his wife (the same wife who had stabbed him two years before) had already left. When I arrived, I soon found them within a few hundred yards and again he was covered in his own blood.

This time it was from an injury to his hand, caused when he smashed the victim's television set with the iron bar. I arrested them both for aggravated burglary and when we got them to the police station, I took the wife's coat from her and found a huge piece of glass from the TV set in the pocket.

I left it there for the policewoman who was to do the formal search, to find and I was amazed when I had to point it out to her before she 'found' it. She accused me of 'planting' the glass and this was the reason she had failed to 'find' it. I was being falsely accused of inventing evidence, and it was nonsense. I would have had no reason to do it because both husband and wife were happily admitting having been there and were quite proud of what they had done. In any event, no dishonest police officer wishing to 'plant' evidence would have used a huge piece of glass like that.

It was interesting though, that the Forensic Science laboratory also failed to 'find' it until I telephoned them and pointed out where it was. I received a rather sheepish apology from the scientist who had also thought that it was 'planted' evidence and wanted no part of such dishonesty. I gave him a piece of my mind but I knew that the effect of TV programmes was rapidly leading the public to believe that all police officers were prepared to falsify evidence. This has done the Police Service one of the largest disservices imaginable.

It would be untrue to say that no police officer ever falsified evidence but it was far less common than the great British public believed. Why anyone would want to risk their careers and possible imprisonment with no other incentive than seeing someone convicted of a crime they may or may not have committed defeats me and always has. Contrary to popular belief, police officers have never received any kind of reward for the number of convictions they gain or for any spectacular wins at court. Of course the ambitious officer always wants to gain a conviction but anyone who has faced a skilled Barrister at Crown Court knows that it is very difficult to fool him or her.

Indeed, it was in the same case that I faced a really experienced Barrister, normally quite friendly to the police, but on this occasion on the side of the defence. He put me through an hour of cross-examination before challenging the accuracy of my notes. I said that they were very accurate and he asked me when I had made them. I told him that it was immediately after the interview.

He then praised my memory if I could remember word for word what had taken place in an hour-long interview. I said that I do have a very good memory, to which he replied, "Oh good officer, in that case, perhaps you will just tell me word for word, what your answer was to my first question an hour ago?"

I did actually remember that first answer though I doubt if I could have remembered the second and he just smiled as if to say, 'point made.' This lesson did teach me to remember in the future, that the answer to such a question should be that the notes were made to the best of my memory, as soon as possible after the interview and were not necessarily verbatim. This, of course opens up the challenge to the precise words of a confession but this was infinitely better than trying to claim that police officers could achieve the superhuman feat of memory required to make verbatim notes.

It also made me think how silly it was, not to tape record interviews for the protection of the police officer rather than the criminal and, of course the Police and Criminal Evidence Act (which I had a hand in writing) introduced such a measure. It is now standard practice for all interviews to be recorded and in some cases to be video taped as well.

My ex-police suspect and his wife were both convicted of Aggravated Burglary, which carries a maximum of life imprisonment but, after all our work and the trauma of the trial, the Judge completely wrecked the case in his summing-up. He had ruled a piece of interview inadmissible for some reason but had left it in his own notes and read it out during the summing-up.

The defence Barrister stood up to object then thought better of it, probably on the basis that it would make excellent grounds for an appeal. The Judge saw him rise to his feet, realised what he had done and stopped reading out the interview. However, he then took what he no doubt saw as his best way out and subsequently passed a sentence of imprisonment on both the man and his wife but he suspended both sentences, thereby making it unlikely that they would appeal.

The man did eventually have to serve his sentence because he was later caught inside a shop he was breaking into and he assaulted the police officer who caught him. It was quite a serious assault and he received a heavy sentence, enhanced by the suspended sentence for my case.

However, before he received that sentence, I was to have one more set of dealings with him. I was on duty one night when I received a phone call from him asking to meet me to give me some information. I was to go alone to a phone box in a particularly quiet street just before midnight.

There was no way I would actually do that. I remembered only too well that he was a very big strong man and I had no idea why he would feel any reason to give me information unless it was because of our first dealings after he had been stabbed. I also considered the possibility that he might have gained some information about some crime of which he disapproved and that I was the only person he knew well enough to talk to although I could not rule out the possibility that he held some grudge against me and wanted to do me harm. I decided I could not pass it up but I arranged with two CID colleagues to be nearby in the shadows in case something should go wrong. I also remembered to warn the uniformed officers to keep away from that area at that moment.

I waited and the man appeared near to the phone box. He saw me and began walking towards me with a big grin on his face. I began to think I had it wrong and he was coming to get me for some imagined wrong. Just as he got within speaking distance, a Panda car drew into the street. He looked at me, the grin faded and he gave me a gesture that indicated that he thought I had set up an ambush for him. My defence that I had not arranged the car went unheeded and he walked quickly away.

I was furious. I had put my confidence in the uniformed officers to keep away and I could only assume that curiosity had overcome them. When I rejoined my CID colleagues, we went back to the police station to complain to the Inspector, only to find that it was him who had wanted to know what was going on and could not keep away.

I then had to wait to see if the man would contact me again. It was about a month later that he phoned again. Again at midnight but this time he just said, "I'm at Greenhill Rise shops (a very public area) Come and see me urgently."

Ivor Peters and I went there as quickly as we could and I saw him near to the shops. This time, he was unconscious, or appeared to be. I was still unsure if he was just trying to get me alone so we went up to him together.

He was indeed unconscious having taken an overdose of prescribed drugs so we called an ambulance and he was taken to hospital. It is just possible that I had saved his life for a second time but he was not grateful and refused to talk to me when I visited him in hospital. I therefore never did find out why he wanted to talk to me on the previous occasion and I never saw him again after he received his sentence.

He was one of the brighter criminals I dealt with but they were not all so clever and I was not above a bit of trickery if the occasion demanded it so I was beginning to develop a reputation with some of the criminals. Two of these are worthy of mention.

The first was a huge man from Glasgow, who had a name for violence but not for thoughtful academia. He was arrested for burglary at a house on the Exeter estate, by the uniformed night shift. I interviewed him the next day in the cells and managed to get him to admit the offence by my friendly and considerate approach (and the promise of bail).

The next day, whilst on bail, he was arrested for theft and I managed to persuade him that it was nowhere near as serious as the burglary so he might as well admit the theft as well. He did so but was less amused when he realised it was an offence on bail and he would not get bail again.

He was livid with me and thought I had tricked him, which, in a sense, I suppose I had but I felt he needed to be in prison. He never really contended that he was not guilty but he really objected to his confessions, particularly as they were on consecutive days. The only worrying thing for me was that, when he was sentenced, to a fairly short term of imprisonment, he threatened that he would come after me and my family when he was released.

Fortunately for me, his attention span was only marginally longer than that of a goldfish and by the time he was released, he had forgotten me. In fact I was to meet him again some years later, when I was the Superintendent at Corby and he did not even remember who I was.

The other case in which my reputation was enhanced related to a petty criminal I had dealt with several times and who had always admitted his crimes to me. His nickname was 'Snotty' because of his unfortunate habit of failing to blow his nose.

One night, when he was drunk, he had thrown a milk bottle at Ben Moisey, one of our Traffic officers who was off duty and at home. Ben, who did not have a particularly high opinion of the CID and had much longer experience than I, had gone out to see what the noise was and when the bottle was thrown, had tried to arrest the offender, only to receive a punch in the face for his trouble.

Ben was very upset, not only because of the injury but more because it happened outside his home. He had therefore spent a lot of time going through photo albums and making enquiries to identify his attacker.

Finally he saw a picture of 'Snotty' and instantly recognised him as the person who had punched him. I think this was quite impressive because I have never been very good at identifying people from photos but Ben was absolutely sure and had gone out and arrested him on that basis.

He then set about interviewing Snotty alone but then his troubles started. I have the greatest respect for dedicated Traffic officers but interviewing is not necessarily their greatest forte. After about six hours, Ben had tried everything he could think of but he could not get a confession, without which he had no case.

Finally, he reluctantly asked one of the Detective Sergeants for some help with the interview. This must have cost his pride a great deal because he considered himself one of the best thief takers on the Traffic department and indeed, he was.

The Detective Sergeant said, "Oh, it's old Snotty, go and ask Bob Thorogood, he can always get a cough out of him." This was even worse for Ben because he had been on the same shift as me from when I started as a probationer and obviously felt he had much more experience than me. Nevertheless, he saw me in the office and said, "Look Bob, the DS told me to ask you to come and speak to this prisoner. I've been at him for six hours so there's not much chance of a cough now, but will you come and see him anyway?"

He told me the circumstances and I agreed to go in to see him. I asked Ben to let me see him alone to begin with and I went into the interview room. I said, "Hello Snotty, you know me don't you?"

"Yes Mr Thorogood," he replied.

"Now I know what you've done and you know what you've done don't you?"

"Yes Mr Thorogood," he replied.

"So you know and I know that sooner or later you are going to have to confess it to me don't you?"

"Yes Mr Thorogood," he replied.

"So are you ready to tell the other officer now?"

"Yes Mr Thorogood," he replied and I was able to go to Ben, one and half minutes after I had entered the room and tell him that his prisoner was ready to make a statement. To say he was taken aback would be an understatement.

This is not to suggest that I was a master interviewer. I was not and I certainly knew many officers who were better at it than me. Some seemed to have a natural way and an ability to keep talking even when they were completely out of ammunition. My success with Snotty was about trust, my knowledge of him, some advantage from not wearing a uniform and a little homespun psychology.

By 1973, I was becoming one of the more experienced detectives at Corby, which is quite incredible when one considers that I had only been a police officer for four years but it was not because of any great magic on my part but more a feature of life at a punishment station where people moved on as quickly as they could.

The daily round of interviews with petty criminals arrested by the uniformed night shift was beginning to pall and I began to set my sights on eventual promotion, though, in those days it was likely to be quite a few years before I could hope to achieve the rank of sergeant. My work partner, Ivor Peters, who was also my next-door neighbour, and I had studied together at every available opportunity and we had both passed the Sergeant's examination with almost identical marks. This was not the result of any cheating by us. It was simply that we had studied the same things and came up with similar answers. We then decided to study together again for the Inspector's examination, which we did that year (an officer could then take the Inspectors without having been promoted to Sergeant, which they cannot now do).

Again we both passed with very similar marks and were now forcing our way into consideration having both exams behind us and being experienced CID officers. I had also inadvertently come to the notice of the new Chief Constable. He had paid an unannounced visit to Corby and when he entered the CID office, I was the only person there doing a crime file.

He had come to the Force upon the untimely death of the previous Chief, who had been killed in his racing car whilst pursuing his hobby of Sports Car racing. I never did meet the previous Chief Constable face to face. The miserly DCC had interviewed me on appointment and the only time I had been in the presence of the Chief Constable was when I was on security duty at Barnwell Manor for the wedding of the Duke of Gloucester. Even then, I only saw him from the back and at a distance.

The new Chief Constable had an uncanny knack of remembering the name of anyone he met and he had not only met me but he had also had a long conversation with me by virtue of my colleagues having all escaped upon his approach.

Early in 1974, it was decided to introduce CID Admin sergeants throughout the Force. This was to improve the paperwork and relieve busy operational officers of some of that burden. This decision resulted in eight promotions and other circumstances, such as retirements, created a further eleven vacancies.

These factors combined to lead me, with eighteen other fresh-faced colleagues, including Ivor Peters to Force Headquarters for promotion. I was staggered to have been selected with less than five years service and I was certainly the youngest in service and possibly in age at the promotion ceremony. This was held in the gymnasium at Headquarters, each having first been spoken to by the Chief in private to be told how we were to behave and that we were now on probation in the rank of sergeant for one year. In his own inimitable style, he had us paraded at attention and went round all nineteen, shaking hands and congratulating us by name. That was, of itself, quite a feat to remember nineteen names accurately but he did it without hesitation.

Chapter 13

I was told that I would become the CID Admin Sergeant at Kettering on 1st April 1974. This entailed a house move and I was told to report to the Admin Chief Superintendent at Headquarters to be allocated a house. I had never met this man before and he knew nothing about me. He told me to go to Kettering and collect the keys to a house on a fairly poor Council estate. This was without opportunity to talk to Jackie or for her to even see the house.

I instantly bristled. Who did he think he was to allocate me a house without consultation or even a chance to see it first? I told him that I would go and look at it with my wife to see if it was suitable. He quickly replied, "You can go and see it but it will be suitable. You need a house and that is a house so get the keys and get moved in".

The man was a product of all the worst parts of the police force under the DCC and I doubt if his arrogance ever allowed a moment of compassion for a lowly Sergeant. My reaction was that I was not about to be bullied by this uncaring individual so I set about getting a change to my accommodation arrangements. First, I took Jackie to see the house in question to make sure I would not be cutting off my nose to spite my face. It was, as I had feared, a poor house in a poor area with only a low fence separating us from next-door's Alsatian dog. As we had a collie bitch at the time, this would have been awful.

I then went to see the Divisional Chief Superintendent who I knew to be a pleasant, easygoing man and who was already my commander because he covered both Kettering and Corby. He soon told me that there were at least half a dozen houses empty in Kettering and we could have our pick. He gave us all of the keys and told me to come back when I had selected one.

The house we selected was quite large and had a big garden with a shed. What we did not know at the time was that it also had mice.

When the day of the move from Corby came, my old car chose that moment to give up the ghost. I was therefore left with a new and demanding job, a new house that needed decorating and no transport to get to work. Fortunately, one of my new colleagues in Kettering CID introduced me to a local car dealer and he found me a reasonably modern, cheap car. This set up a friendship between the car dealer and me that was to last for quite a few years.

But settling into life in Kettering CID was another matter. There is less than ten miles between the two towns but the difference in culture makes them feel as if they are worlds apart. The people of Kettering did not generally like those from Corby and vice versa.

The style of policing in those days was totally different too. I did not have to face street policing for the first two years there, because I was office bound and facing constant mountains of paperwork that kept me in the office from 8am often until 10 or 11 pm. But I soon became aware that policing was different.

In Corby, I was used to knowing where I stood with the criminals. I could expect a fight if I did not get them off the street quickly enough but generally they were not very keen to do battle with someone of my build unless they were enough of them to make them brave. This was strangely reassuring because we tended not to get into friendly conversations with the criminals and they seemed to have an understanding that, once arrested, they would usually have to admit the crime and would not, therefore give us too much trouble in interview.

This did not work in Kettering where the criminals and the CID seemed to be on the friendliest of terms but the criminals would rarely admit the crime and they could turn from friendly to fighting in seconds. I never did become comfortable with this type of interaction but I did subsequently get into some interesting situations when I eventually went operational.

However, before that, I had to get through my office time. We were still living in the days of 'Roneo' stencils instead of photocopiers. This meant that every document for the Crown Court was first typed as a statement by a typist. When the person elected trial by jury, it had to be retyped onto a 'skin', which was an ink-impregnated sheet between two sheets of paper. When typed, the skin would then be placed on a drum and, by winding a handle, up to about twenty copies could be made before the skin was exhausted and if more were needed, a second skin would have to be typed. This was incredibly wasteful in time and paper but there was no other alternative available.

One Friday night, I had been so busy with Crown Court files that I was still working at midnight. The only other member of the CID still about the office was the Detective Inspector and when a report came in of a robbery at a petrol station, he decided that we would attend. On arrival, we found the male attendant in a very shaky state but uninjured. He said that a man had come into the petrol station, threatened him with a large knife and had stolen about £100, which was a great deal of money then. We set about having enquiries made and interviewing the attendant for a description and so on. Having satisfied ourselves, we had him taken home and the description circulated.

This was to be an early lesson to me that it is too easy to get out of touch with reality when you do nothing but paperwork. It also taught me that the first suspect at many crimes is often the apparent victim. It was much to my chagrin, but more to that of the Detective Inspector, that the operational CID officers who took over the case the next day, took less than an hour to get an admission from the attendant that he had stolen the money and it was in his sock when we had spoken to him.

I mention this incident only because of the benefit I gained from it. I have always been alert to all possibilities since then, even if it did make me more cynical and sometimes disbelieving, when I should have believed a witness.

My time in the office eventually came to an end but it was an invaluable time for me because it taught me to be very thorough in checking papers and to be infinitely patient when checking evidence. I believe that I owed my subsequent rise through the ranks due, in no small part, to the time I spent there. This was supplemented by the senior CID officers I encountered there, who could spot a spelling error at fifty paces and were known to return files because there was too large a gap between the end of the report and the signature or, on one notable occasion, because the staples had not been Sellotaped over to prevent the reader catching their fingers on them.

Along came my first week of nights as an operational Detective Sergeant. It was to prove quite an eventful time. On the first night, I received a request from the day shift, to find a certain criminal and arrest him for handling stolen goods (a large quantity of silverware)

I spoke to the three members of my shift and asked them if they knew where we might find the person. "Oh yes," replied Alan Burton, the most senior Constable, "He'll be drinking in 'The Talbot' about nine o'clock".

"Right," I replied, "Let's go down there, walk in, see if he's there, grab him and get out." This was the approach we would have had to take at a Corby Pub and I assumed it was how to do it in Kettering.

"Oh no," counselled Alan. "We just go in, have a drink and if he's there, I'll go and have a word with him quietly, then we meet him outside."

I could not believe this approach, which I saw as soft but, as it was my first night, I thought I had better go with his advice. Just the two of us went to the pub and we ordered a drink at the bar. I asked Alan if our quarry was there and he indicated that the man was in a group of about ten tough looking characters.

I said, "OK smartarse, how do we get him, and ourselves, out of here in one piece?"

He calmly replied, "Like I told you, when he goes to the toilet, I'll go out and speak to him." This duly happened a few minutes later and both returned to the bar, Alan Burton to me and the suspect to his group.

I was becoming seriously nervous by then and asked Alan what had happened. "No problem," he replied, "we just wait till he's finished his drink and then we'll go."

A few seconds later, the barman handed us both a second drink and let us know that it was courtesy of our suspect. I could not believe the attitude of both police and suspect. Nevertheless, some ten minutes later, our suspect moved towards the door and, as I prepared to dive on him, he turned to us and said, "Come on then, are you two bastards coming, or what." And so we returned to the police station with our suspect in custody, nobody hurt and no problems.

He never did admit the crime and the next day, between interviews he used a pen he had been allowed to keep to write a spoof 'stop press' entry on the local paper that he had been given to read. The headline was 'Innocent Man Wrongly Arrested'. And the text of his 'article' was, 'Today, Kettering Police have had to apologise to a local Silversmith, after having arrested him wrongly on suspicion of handling stolen silver, when they had no evidence against him.'

I was amazed at the good-natured joking, the reference to being a Silversmith (which he certainly was not, except for the stolen kind he had been arrested for) and friendly attitude towards us that I had never experienced at Corby. I later developed quite a friendly relationship with this man and even had him repair my flat roof at home (his actual trade).

In fact I had met this man before, while I was a Detective Constable at Corby. I should have remembered the relationship that Kettering Detectives had with their criminal clients because of the incident. Some expensive equipment had been stolen from a building site and the site owners told us that they were sure it had been taken by two flat roofers who claimed they were owed money. These two were my 'Silversmith', and a tough criminal who later went into selling cars.

I was working with another Detective Sergeant, Damien Jones, who was a very good detective, a top interviewer and a brilliant thief taker.

When I told him about the allegation, he said that he knew these two from his Kettering days and we had no chance of recovering the property unless we 'had a quiet chat' with them and got the company to accept that there would be no charges if the property was recovered.

I spoke to the site owners and they were quite happy provided they got their property back. My Sergeant contacted the pair and arranged to meet them in 'The Teapot Café' in Lindsay Street, Kettering. When we arrived, they were waiting for us. Damien told them that they could either return the items or 'be nicked' and although they absolutely denied stealing the property, they asked if the case would be forgotten if, somehow, they managed to get it back.

This was what we wanted so we parted on the understanding that the property would miraculously turn up in the next few days. It didn't!

After a week, the site owners started to make waves about their missing property and I told Damien the position. He was very angry and immediately rang 'The Silversmith'. The response he got set him back on his heels. "You haven't been into your garage lately have you?"

In a state of some surprise, Damien went to his home in Kettering and found the missing property in his own garage. Imagine the cheek of that! They had managed to open his garage door without damaging it, placed the stolen property in there and closed it again.

An example of the opposite type of behaviour came soon afterwards however. In connection with the silverware case, a group of well-known local criminals with a reputation for their tough behaviour were arrested for burglary at an antique dealer's home, which also served as his shop.

I had very little to do with the case as it was being dealt with by the Crime Squad. The only thing I did was to speak briefly to two of the gang in the cells to extract some small piece of routine information. For some reason best known to them, the gang took a dislike to me and one of them even made a preposterous allegation that I had stolen his leather jacket. This caused me no concern at all as I had never even seen the jacket in question and was confident that they had either confused me with someone else or were making the story up.

They were subsequently released on bail to await trial at the Crown Court and that was when my troubles started. They seemed to be there at every turn I made. I was even challenged to a fight in a pub when I had gone there on duty with some colleagues. Obviously, I was not going to get involved in such a no-win situation. If I accepted the challenge, a hundred witnesses were available to see me starting a brawl in the pub and if I lost, I could do nothing further about it for the same reason. I was left with the only alternative of walking away, which was something I did not enjoy.

Shortly after, another member of the gang went to the Police Station and asked to see me at midnight. I was on duty and went to see him at the enquiry counter only to be met by a barrage of abuse and another challenge to a fight. Again I could do nothing but walk away. I tried to ask why they felt they had some grudge against me in particular but could get no sensible answer. They just seemed to think that I had, in some unspecified way, 'fitted them up' (falsely created evidence against them). This was totally without foundation and outrageous, particularly as the evidence was overwhelming and I had so little contact with their case.

My relief from this situation came when they all appeared in court and were sentenced to lengthy terms of imprisonment. The shortest sentence was five years, of which the offender had to serve three years. When he was released he was one of the few hardened criminals I have ever known who completely rejected the criminal lifestyle on his release and never got into trouble again. In fact, I saw him some years later and he was very friendly, apologising for the behaviour of the gang against me.

Although I was not an operational Detective Sergeant for very long, I did come into contact with violent death during that period and it was in the most horrific circumstances imaginable. A very pretty ten-year-old girl who lived in Northampton was invited to a party at her friend's house. The friend lived in the next street, which backed onto her own home. To reach her house, the girl had to walk from her home, to the end of the street and turn right. She then had to pass an open piece of ground and turn right again into the next street.

The piece of ground in between consisted of a deep dip with a small lane and garages in the centre, accessed from the far end. Because it was a short distance and it was early evening, the parents of the girl allowed her to walk to her friend's house alone. She was wearing a red cape with a hood and this later led the news media to refer to her as 'Little Red Riding Hood'.

It was when the friend's parents rang to ask where she was, that her mother and father began to worry. She should have arrived within five minutes of leaving home and when she was half an hour late, they called the police.

The first officer on the scene was a fairly new probationer officer who had joined the Force after a short service officer career in the Navy. He was very inexperienced as a Police officer but no amount of training or experience could have prepared him for what he faced that Saturday evening.

The parents were already planning to start searching and the young officer joined them. The obvious place to begin searching was the area of open ground by the garages and, having called for support, the officer went with the girl's mother and father to the small lane leading to the garages. It was the parents who noticed that there was smoke coming from a derelict garage and went to investigate.

There was what appeared to be a bundle of rags burning in the centre of the floor, and an old broom handle standing in the middle of the flames. Closer inspection revealed a sight that would cause them all nightmares for the rest of their lives. The 'bundle of rags' was the body of the little girl who had been sexually assaulted, murdered and her body desecrated with the broom handle before being set on fire.

A major crime enquiry was soon in progress and officers, including me, were sent from all over the Force area. As a Detective Sergeant, I was given a team of officers to carry out enquiries in the area and, because of the trauma he had suffered, the young police officer who had been first on the scene was allowed to stay with the enquiry and was allocated to my team. I soon discovered that wherever he went, he seemed to be taking an almost perverse pride in having been the first on the scene and would begin all his conversations with, "I was the first officer on the scene."

I pointed out to him that it was a bit of a dubious honour to have been first on the scene of such a wicked crime and suggested he might like to change his introductory speech. He thanked me and said he would. I was therefore staggered to hear him saying to the next person he spoke to, "I had the dubious honour of being the first on the scene."

One of the first enquiries I was involved in was to interview a young paperboy who had passed the piece of open ground at the relevant time and had seen a young girl in a red cape and hood fighting with a man. He had gone straight to his home, about 50 yards away and told his mother. She looked out and could see nothing so she dismissed it as a minor family problem. How she could live with herself when she discovered that she might have prevented the murder, I will never know.

At the end of that day, the enquiry was no further forward and we were beginning to wonder just how difficult it was going to be, particularly with the inevitable media pressure that would follow. The following day, in an apparently unrelated incident, a local scoutmaster happened to meet a former member of his troop in Northampton. This person, now a grown man, asked the former scoutmaster for money and they went off together in his car. They went to Salcey forest, possibly for a homosexual encounter, when suddenly, the young man violently attacked the scoutmaster and beat

Family photo with Mother, StepFather, Martin, Peter, wife Jackie and the Author.
Carolyn (inset) took the photo!

him about the head with a blunt object before throwing him down a well in the forest.

The scoutmaster asked him why he was doing this and the young man replied that he had already killed a girl so it could not get any worse. He then left the scoutmaster in the well to die.

Fortunately the scoutmaster did not die and managed to get out of the well and get help. When he told the police what had happened it became easy to link the two enquiries and to put the suspect in the area of the girl's murder at the relevant time. He had been to a house not too far from the scene, where he had taken drugs before leaving to walk to his home, a route that would take him past the piece of ground.

He was traced to a flat on the third floor of a block in Kings Heath, Northampton, and officers went to the front door. He took the only other way out of the flat and climbed up onto the roof where he began to hurl tiles and a TV aerial at the officers who were gathering below. The Fire Brigade were called to help to get him down.

Whilst this siege was developing, and amid all of the mayhem, an amusing incident occurred. An old lady came out of an adjacent flat and when she saw detectives outside, she told them she could not get a picture on her TV. One of the officers said, "It's alright me duck. We've got a man on the roof trying to fix it now." Never realising that she was having her leg pulled, she went happily back inside to await the completion of the 'repairs'.

Eventually, Ivor Peters, who had also been seconded to the enquiry, volunteered to go up onto the roof to try to negotiate with the suspect but as he did so, the suspect backed away along the ridge of the roof. The officer tried to edge nearer to him and somehow the suspect managed to fall off the edge of the ridge, landing – luckily for him but not for society – on his feet. The only damage he suffered was two Potts Fractures of the ankles, a particularly painful fracture which, rumour had it, in his case was not helped by two nurses at the hospital (already aware of the reason he was in custody) who felt they had to manipulate the ankles to confirm the diagnosis. No one has ever suggested that he was pushed off the roof or that the nurses acted anything other than professionally but there was little sympathy for the suspect anywhere.

He soon admitted the murder and the attempted murder of the scoutmaster and was subsequently sentenced to life imprisonment with a recommendation that he serve at least twenty-five years. That time has now elapsed and he is free. I had occasion to speak to the father of the little girl when the offender was due to be released in order to warn them about the possible media interest and I discovered that he had never recovered from the events and his life had been ruined. Although I am not an advocate of an automatic death penalty for murder, for reasons I will return to later, I have never understood how society can justify allowing a person who has committed such a foul crime, to live, let alone walk free.

Chapter 14

Quite surprisingly, for someone who had experienced detective work, I still retained an affinity for uniform work, and in 1976, I was offered a post as an Acting Uniform Inspector. There was little obvious reward for this because it meant no extra salary, indeed a small drop in take-home pay, which was already desperately low, and also that someone else would have to take on my detective duties. As well as that, I would have to return to the dreaded shift work, with quick 'changeovers' twice each month, when we ended one shift at 10pm and started the next at 6am the following morning. But worst of all, in the eyes of my detective colleagues, I was to become a 'woodentop'.

It was, however, a major honour to be asked in view of my length of service as I still had less than eight years in the job and as an Inspector I was to be called 'Sir' for the first time. From the outset, I thoroughly enjoyed this time. I had two Sergeants and a shift of about six officers with varying lengths of service. It was a joy to work with them and pass on the experience I had gained in the CID, as well as seeing a completely different aspect of Police work.

My one and only real dread was the breathalyser procedure. As Kettering was the home of the General Hospital, it fell to the Inspector on duty there to carry out the breath test procedure at the hospital following accidents where drink was suspected. This was completely different from the procedure on the street and involved a complex but precise format to be followed and required the Inspector to have a detailed knowledge of the Drink/Drive legislation. I had never really mastered that as a constable and now I was to become the fount of knowledge for my shift who all knew I had spent most of my time with the CID, who they thought were all heavy drinkers and prone to breach this legislation anyway.

I studied the law until I was dizzy and still could not distinguish the finer points of distinction about when one could or could not demand a breath test. Deep down, I had no affinity with this aspect of law and could never really accept that it was as important as catching burglars.

Consolation was in the shape of Rhonda Powell, my female patrol Sergeant who was to become a very dear friend. I decided that, when my first hospital test came along, I would take her with me and rely on her to see me through the procedure.

Sure enough, within the first week, I received the dreaded call to attend the hospital to administer a breath test. I immediately called the Sergeant and told her that I wanted to take her with me to carry out the procedure. "Oh good" she replied, "I'm so glad 'cause I've never done one of those." On the way, I confided in her that I hadn't either and we had to rely on guess work and our combined limited knowledge to get through. But get through we did, and I managed to get away without a single challenge to my actions in the whole time I was Acting Inspector. That in itself was interesting because 'Acting' jobs usually lasted for a month or so but this one was destined to last for fifteen months and I never did return to the Sergeant's role.

As a family, we were desperately short of money and my first hurdle was to acquire a pair of black leather shoes to go with the uniform. I could not afford shop prices and in desperation, I asked a CID colleague if he had any contacts for rejects from one of the many shoe factories in Kettering at that time. Sure enough, he took me along to one of the larger factories (CID officers could usually find a contact for anything in those days). Unfortunately, the only cheap rejects they had available in black were quite fashionable, pointed toe, high heeled shoes with a pattern and these were for sale at only 50p to me but there was nothing else. I had to take them or look really out of place in my CID suede loafers.

They were slightly uncomfortable but I wore them anyway. On the first day I did so, a 6am to 2pm shift, we received a call just after 6am to the effect that a prisoner had escaped from Wellingborough Prison and was known to be on foot in the fields between Kettering and Wellingborough. I therefore sent most of my shift to begin the search.

I collected the duty CID officer (co-incidentally the same one who had helped me to get my shoes) and we went to one of the main roads that the escapee was likely to head for. We had just arrived when we saw him coming towards us over the fields.

He saw us at the same time and turned tail to run off back the way he had come. There was no way we were going to let him escape having spotted him so the CID colleague and I jumped over a gate into the field – straight into a 6" deep pool of mud and cows droppings. We still ran after the escapee, through the fields and hedges until the CID colleague, a fitter man than I, caught him and together we took him back to the station to receive the congratulations of our colleagues and for me to examine the remains of my new shoes. One heel had gone and both shoes were scratched, wet and plastered in mud.

Normally, if clothing is damaged in this sort of pursuit, the officer can be reimbursed but I could hardly claim for a 50p pair of rejects without having to explain how I had come by them and it would have been dishonest to claim for more than I had paid so I had to take the pain of 'writing them off' and buying a new pair from a shop.

When I had been a Detective Sergeant, there had been some overtime and I had managed to buy a bigger car from my friend the car dealer but now, with no overtime for a Uniform Inspector, I could not afford to run a car at all so I had to lay it up in the garage and start cycling to work. In fact, this did me a favour because I lost weight and got much fitter. I also used to go out on foot patrol when the paperwork was done and, with my previous experience, my paperwork was always done in the first hour of a shift so I was able to spend many happy hours either on foot patrol or out in a car with the officers. This endeared me to them as well as making me fitter.

I was also able to see some of the jokes they got up to at night. There was a young policewoman on the shift who had two notable features – no, not those! She insisted that she should not be subjected to any special protection so, even though she was petrified, she would not accept being paired up with another officer even at night. Those were not the days of equal opportunities, indeed, it was not long after the introduction of night duties for women. Unaccompanied patrols by women were therefore still unusual and she never knew that I often assigned someone to keep an eye on her during the night.

This was quite fortunate because she was also very naive and often got into difficult or dangerous situations. Either that or she would get lost or lose her car keys when on mobile patrol.

Her other endearing feature was her love of birds. Wild birds, tame birds, any kind of birds, she loved them all and would not see a bird in trouble. One night, when she was out on town centre patrol, a motorist approached her about 3am. He told her that he had accidentally hit an owl while driving along the road. He believed it was dead and had put it in the car and now wanted to know what to do with it. A quick examination appeared to reveal that it was not dead but seriously injured.

Now, owls are not classified as protected species and there was no procedure for calling out a vet or the RSPCA for injured owls in those days. Aware of this, the policewoman thought that if she sent the motorist to the Police Station, the enquiry officer would take pity on the bird and find some way to save it. I think she pictured it in a cosy nest in the boiler room of the Police Station and officers feeding it dead mice or whatever it is they eat.

Unfortunately, when the motorist got to the Police Station, the dazed, but now fighting fit and angry owl made him surrender his car and dash into the Station to report, not that he wished to deliver an injured bird, but that he wished to be rescued from it. Rhonda, who was made of tougher stuff, went out to the car, opened the door and shooed the bird on its way back to its favourite tree. However, when the policewoman came back into the Station for her 4am cuppa, she was greeted by the sight of one of the male officers busily wiping blood off the end of his truncheon and the enquiry office constable just in the process of asking him where the blood had come from. The officer, a giant of a man who was known to have a very direct manner in dealing with things, replied that he had just come into the rear yard of the Police Station and heard a terrible fluttering noise coming from one of the dustbins so he had lifted the lid and found an injured owl in there so he had quickly despatched it with his truncheon.

Whilst the policewoman stood in shocked horror, the enquiry office constable explained to him that some idiot motorist had brought an injured owl into the station, having been told by some idiot police officer that we could deal with injured owls. There was no procedure for that so he (the office constable) had given it one good hit with his truncheon and dumped it into the bin, thinking it was dead. He apologised to the other officer for not having achieved a clean kill but the other officer said it was OK because he felt fairly sure it was dead now.

In her shock and guilt, the policewoman did not stop to think that, not only are most police officers far too soft hearted to kill a bird in cold blood, but that the office constable could only remember what a truncheon was for from others reminding him, it had been so long since he carried one in anger. She screamed at them that they should be ashamed of themselves and they would not get away with such a cruel thing. She then dashed up the stairs to my office to make a formal report about the incident to me.

Knowing in advance, that the owl was fit and well and living in the park and having authorised the illicit use of a red ink stamp pad as fake blood on the end of a truncheon, I told her that, if she wished to report her colleagues, she would have to go and fetch the evidence from the dustbin and submit it with her report.

Slowly, it began to dawn on her that she was the victim, not the owl, and although she did not forgive any of us easily, she never brought another owl to the station. Incidentally, she did go on to become a good and valued police officer in time.

During this period, my good friend Rhonda, the female Sergeant, who was also a good friend of my wife and certainly not a person to engage in improper relationships, became an object of hatred by my daughter who was about eight years old. Carolyn had heard me telling my wife about the nights the Sergeant and I had spent together (actually, on patrol) and she had got it into her mind that we were having an affair.

So strong was her hatred of this threat to our marital bliss that my very possessive little girl would not allow the Sergeant's name to be mentioned in the house.

In my work, although I did not realise it, I was growing in stature and maturity and I had become accepted by the other Inspectors as one of them even though I was still only 'Acting'. My skills and experience were put to the test one morning when I arrived to commence a 6am to 2pm shift. The night shift Inspector, who was prone to taking half an hour of my time on handover, had to get away very quickly on this day and barely had time to tell me what had happened during the night.

He said that a CID officer was still on duty from the previous night and would brief me on an incident that had occurred. I went to speak to the officer, an old friend, who told me an horrific story. It transpired that a man, well known as a very violent offender, had gone to a Public House where his separated wife was the previous evening. He had dragged her screaming from the pub, across a stream and to her house where he had forced her to strip naked and tied her to a chair.

He had then injected her with 'Warfarin' a rat poison, expecting to kill her, but not realising that it would take a massive dose to kill her and that Warfarin is actually used to thin the blood of heart patients. He had then left her tied in the bedroom and she had managed to escape, leap from the bedroom window and run naked to her parents' home nearby.

This man undoubtedly inspired a great deal of fear in those he came into contact with and some police officers were afraid to deal with him because of his reputation. Some officers had been dispatched to the house and found that the man had barricaded himself in the house. He had smashed a water tank in the bedroom with a hammer, with which he had armed himself.

Water was running down the stairs. He set fire to the curtains and began to throw lighted bags of sugar at the approaching officers. Despite radio calls, no supervisor had arrived at the scene so the duty Detective and a Traffic crew took charge and decided to rush the bedroom where the man had, by then injected himself with Warfarin and was in danger of being overcome by the flames and smoke from the curtains.

As they got to the top of the stairs and approached the bedroom door, the man opened it and attacked them with the raised hammer. One Traffic

Officer put up his hand to ward off a blow aimed at his head and suffered a broken arm. At that moment, the Inspector had arrived at the scene and together with his officers, they overpowered the man and brought him crashing to the ground.

They had managed to get him to the cells after a huge fight but he refused to allow the Police Surgeon to examine him or to be taken to hospital and he had threatened the officers that if they tried to lock the cell door he would attack anyone who later tried to get him out. They had therefore left him in the cell with the door open and several officers stood outside to prevent him from leaving.

To say that I was shocked at this situation would be an understatement. There is no way anyone can be allowed to dominate the police in this way and certainly not when he is in custody. This was one occasion when I felt as an Acting Inspector, that I was in danger of being 'out of my depth'.

I therefore felt I had to report it to my Superintendent who quickly agreed with me and advised me to get the man charged with the attempted murder of his wife and of a Police Officer, get the cell door locked and arrange an urgent Court so that he could be remanded to a prison hospital for treatment for the Warfarin.

The detective and I went to the cell and I read the charges over to him and explained that he was now under a different regime and that his cell was about to be locked (I also advised him to get used to it because it was going to be home for him for a few years). I would not say he was co operative and he had to be handcuffed in court but we did get him under control and I do hope he got used to the cell because he did go to prison for a long time.

A supervisor was subsequently disciplined for failing to attend the scene and the officers who acted decisively were commended for their bravery. For me, I felt a certain satisfaction at having corrected a poor operation and I learned a great deal about when to call for support. I also felt that I learned a little about the role of the Superintendent to be there with advice and support but still leave the task to those in charge.

Some months later the same colleague again informed me at 6am changeover that he had to leave urgently but there was a prisoner in the cells who wished to make a complaint and I would have to deal with it. I decided to do the morning briefing before going to find out what it was about but as I went down the stairs from my office, the enquiry office constable informed me that there was a witness to the complaint waiting outside in the street. It transpired that he had been there since he came in to make the complaint at 2am and was still waiting to be seen.

I went and fetched him inside, reassured him that I would be dealing with the complaint immediately and elicited some details from him. He told me that he had been with his friend (who was now in the cells) just before 2am. They had left a nightclub a little the worse for drink and were trying to find a taxi when they had been approached by a constable accompanied by an Inspector.

The Constable had, with malice aforethought but no warning, suddenly attacked his friend and laid him out in the street before arresting him and dragging him the 100 yards or so to the Police Station. On further probing, I established that they had not simply been standing quietly waiting for a taxi and there had been some unfriendly words exchanged between the friend and the constable, who were known to each other.

Now, I knew the constable concerned by reputation and I suspected that the truth lie somewhere in between the version(s) I had just heard and a legitimate arrest for a 'Breach of the Peace'. The constable concerned had gone off duty by then so I could not get his version so I went to see the prisoner in the cells. I wasn't sure if I was at the scene of a road accident or in a butchers shop! Whatever he had really done I could see no reason why he had been battered so badly.

My first reaction was to get him to hospital and it was then that I learned that he had not even seen a Police Surgeon. By the time I had arranged for him to be taken to hospital and he had been treated and discharged, I was able to contact Complaints and Discipline Dept and someone had been dispatched to deal with the matter as a serious assault by a police officer in the presence of the Inspector.

I had no more personal dealings with the case but I was very surprised to find that the Constable was not suspended from duty, particularly when I heard the explanation he had given. He said that he had previously arrested the man a number of times for violence and dishonesty and the man had publicly sworn to get even with him. As he had approached with the Inspector by his side, he realised that the man was very drunk and immediately began to abuse the police.

Then suddenly, without warning, the man had run at the constable, got to within 3 feet of him and then threw himself backwards onto the pavement and repeatedly banged his head on the floor. The constable had arrested him for his own safety and as he took his prisoner to the Station, the man had said, "I've finally got you, my mate will back me up and your Inspector must have thought you punched me to make me go down like that."

Where the truth lay, I'll never know. Preposterous as it sounds, I have known people go to amazing lengths to get at a Police officer, and the Inspector later said that it really did happen as the constable said, but I must confess that I doubted it. The end result was that the man was not 'Bound Over' (one is not 'convicted' of a Breach of the Peace) and the Constable was not convicted of the disciplinary charges.

One reason for my doubts about the truth of the Constable's version was that I knew of another incident he had been involved in. One evening, an incident had occurred involving a whole double-decker busload of football supporters who were suspected of being involved in a theft in the town. An enterprising Traffic Crew had arrested the whole busload (about 50 in total) and they were mostly detained at Kettering. Unfortunately, there were insufficient cells for all and about 16 suspects were being held in the exercise yard.

They were a noisy lot, which was not that surprising as it was quite a cold night and anyone who has been drunk and outside at 3am will know it feels even colder than it actually is. Our hero was detailed to look after the prisoners and they were annoying him with the noise.

Just after 3am, he went upstairs to the canteen, just above the exercise yard, filled a bucket with water and threw it all over the prisoners in the yard, immediately ushering them inside and assuring them that it had suddenly started to rain. This was another escapade he managed to get away with and, incredibly, I do not believe he was ever dealt with for any major disciplinary matters, despite always living on the edge.

Chapter 15

Kettering was a strange place to work in those days. There was a mixture of indiscipline, funny incidents and difficult cases. The Station made the headlines of the 'News of the World' on one occasion.

There was a female member of the Civilian Staff (I dare not be more specific) who claimed to have 'had' every rank of the Police Force except the Chief Constable. Some, she claimed to have 'had' in the lift between the ground and third floors. She cheated on her claim because she claimed one officer who served as a Chief Superintendent, Assistant Chief Constable and Deputy Chief Constable but that apart, she proved to be telling the truth and it all happened at Kettering Police Station.

You may rest assured that she could not claim me in any rank and I was not even aware that it was going on until the story broke in the newspaper, although I did occasionally cover part of her shift. I did hear that she had gone out for her 45 minute break at 2am when I was on duty and in that time she had apparently met a man outside a nightclub and made love with him in the back of his car outside the Police Station. Perhaps naively, I did not believe it at the time.

I had to give it some credence however, when after the story was published, a number of officers including a Chief Inspector, were all disciplined for their part in it.

One funny incident was when a member of the public brought a pair of handcuffs into the station early one morning, having found them at the top of a slide in the local pleasure park. They were marked with the owner's collar number and they transpired to belong to a very fiery, red faced, middle-aged sergeant who was totally nonplussed when asked to explain what he had been doing at the top of the slide in the night. I still wonder what the member of the public was doing up there at 6am to find them!

During my fifteen months as Acting Inspector, the only thing to mar my enjoyment was the fact that other people kept being promoted into the job I was doing and I would be moved on to continue acting in another post. I should not have objected because I was really very young in service even to be considered for such positions, but that did not make it feel much better and I have recently been reminded that the Police Federation actually took up the issue on my behalf with the Chief Constable.

Nevertheless, I continued with the acting roles and after a year, I was asked to take on the role of Acting Detective Inspector at Kettering for three months. I had been in this job for only about one week when I became involved in a really serious murder enquiry, for the first time at this level.

It occurred because a young man had been going with a young teacher and she had decided that she did not love him and did not want to see him again. He was unable to accept this and, as it transpired, it had clearly upset the balance of his mind.

The teacher lived with her widowed mother in a small bungalow in Kettering and on this particular Friday afternoon, the mother was at home alone and her daughter was at work. The ex-boyfriend called at the house and was invited in by the mother. He then began to talk about his love for the woman's daughter and, we believe, she told him that she knew it was definitely over and that he should leave the daughter to get on with her life.

At this, the ex-boyfriend pulled three neckties from his pocket and used one of them to strangle the mother to death. Death by strangulation is not as clean as it is sometimes depicted in the movies. It can be bloody and it is certainly horrible. The tongue protrudes, the eyes bulge out of their sockets and the blood can come from the nose, eyes or even the throat. No doubt, this was too much for a young man who, judging from the number of neckties, intended to kill mother, daughter and then himself. Whatever was then going through his mind, he wrapped the body in the lounge carpet and waited for the daughter to arrive from work.

This she duly did, but, seeing him in the house, she asked where her mother was. He told her that the mother had gone to the local shop and left him to wait for the daughter by himself. This reply made her begin to worry and she said that she was going to the shop to find her mother. He said he would go with her and they walked the few yards to the shop where they were told that the mother had not been in that day.

They therefore returned to the house and the daughter was, by now, beginning to have a very bad feeling about the whole situation. She was on her guard and although she did go into the house, she left the front door open. On entering, she saw the rolled up carpet in the lounge for the first time and immediately began screaming and asking him what he had done to her mother. At this, he snatched her car keys, ran out of the house and jumped into her car and drove away. The daughter ran to a neighbour and asked him to phone the Police.

It later became one of the lighter moments of the case that the call to Kettering Police Station was passed to the local Bobby who just happened to be cycling past the street at that very moment and the witnesses were staggered that, having reported a possible murder, the Police response was a Bobby on a bike and not only that, but he got there in thirty seconds after the call!

The officer went into the house and made the gruesome discovery of the mother's body wrapped in the carpet with all the gory symptoms described but with her head wrapped tightly in a plastic bag, presumably to hide the horrible sight or possibly to ensure that she was, in fact, dead.

At that moment, the door bell rang and there stood the ex-boyfriend who explained to the Officer that he had murdered his ex-girlfriend's mother and when the ex-girlfriend saw what he had done, he decided to kill himself by ramming her car into a parked car further up the street. He had driven at full speed into the parked car, writing off both vehicles but he himself emerged without a scratch. He had then decided to give himself up for murder. Thus it was that the local Bobby with his bike had to call for transport as he could hardly take a murderer in whilst pushing that as well.

I was at Corby, as I was covering both towns that weekend, and hurriedly returned to Kettering and went to the scene. This was 1978 and murder was still a very rare crime in Northamptonshire so the Detective Chief Superintendent came out accompanied by no less a personage than the Chief Constable. These two worthies and their entourage promptly walked straight into the house, potentially destroying forensic evidence and generally getting in the way of those officers who really did need to be there. It fell to me to ask them to leave and they slowly and reluctantly went back to the Station.

The case was to be dealt with by Detective Chief Inspector Barry Hartson and I was deputed to sit with the victim's daughter to calm her down and eventually get a statement from her. Rhonda Powell accompanied me and together we spent many hours just talking and talking until we finally got the whole story from her.

By then it was well after midnight so I returned to the Station to find that the suspect had given his version of events and was now bedded down in the cell with a permanent guard because of the obvious suicide risk, having tried once with the car.

After a few short hours sleep, I went back to where the daughter was staying with the neighbour who had called the Police initially and I set about the painstaking task of taking the written statement. Meanwhile, I was aware that the suspect had been charged with murder and put before a

Magistrate's Court so that he could be remanded in custody and be given the proper supervision in prison.

Shortly after 1.30pm, just as I had finished the statement and built a really close relationship with the daughter, I was called to return urgently to the Station. There, Detective Chief Inspector Hartson briefed me that I now had the most difficult job to undertake.

The suspect had been remanded in custody and had been accompanied to HMP Bedford by Police Officers who took with them the red edged form that has to accompany any prisoner who is a risk either of escape, suicide or violence. This prisoner fitted all categories. On arrival at the prison, he had been taken to the prison hospital and issued with pyjamas. As soon as the warders turned their backs, he had tied the pyjamas round his neck and to the bed head. He had then simply slid down until he strangled himself. Within twenty minutes of his arrival at prison, he had achieved what the police had been desperate to prevent for twenty-four hours – he was dead.

I was to break this news to the ex-girlfriend and I truly believed that it could be enough to drive her out of her mind. I therefore took with me a very close friend, the Police Surgeon. I decided to take her out of the house to tell her so I told her I wanted to take her for walk around the block. She readily agreed although I could see she was wondering why I wanted to do this.

I had arranged for the Police Surgeon to be close by just in case. As the two of us walked up the street, I put my arm around her shoulders and said that I had the most dreadful news I had to break to her. When I told her, she just began to cry quietly and asked to go back to the house. In fact she took it remarkably well and declined any medical help. I have had some hard messages to deliver in my time but that was undoubtedly the worst.

I felt so sorry for her. In one day, she had lost her mother, I believe she had been within an ace of being murdered herself and then discovered that her ex-boyfriend was dead too. This was one case in which the Police had acted properly throughout. Although the Prison Service suffered some criticism at the subsequent inquest, there was no formal inquiry into their incompetence. I never heard from the daughter again but I was given to understand that she did recover fully and went on to rebuild her life later.

Chapter 16

In 1978, there were no such things as formal promotion boards and the Chief Constable, advised by his senior officers, carried out selection for promotion. Thus it was that early in that year, after almost 15 months of Acting, I was summoned to the Chief Superintendent's office, where the Chief Constable himself greeted me. He informed me that a vacancy had arisen for a Detective Inspector at Corby and that I had been selected for permanent promotion to the post if I wanted it.

There always seemed to have to be a little 'but' when junior officers were given something in those days, and the 'but' in my case was that I was the only officer with detective experience and to have passed the promotion examination to Inspector (this was not quite true but who cared anyway). He went on to remind me how difficult it would be for me to go back to Corby and be in overall command of a CID office that still contained many officers who had previously been my supervisors.

He was right about that. At least two of the Sergeants had been there when I had started as a junior detective and some of the detective constables had shown me the ropes in those early days. What is more, I still had only eight years service in the Force and the office had been led by Damien Jones, a charismatic Detective Inspector who had just been promoted to Chief Inspector. Indeed, the office was known as 'Jonah's gang' and I knew I had a difficult act to follow.

I immediately determined that they were just going to have to get used to a new style of leadership and anyone who felt they could not get used to it would have to go. Some did. My style was totally different from my predecessor and although I have always had the greatest respect for his ability as a detective, I did not necessarily agree with his management style. For me, there would be no favourites and I was never much of a drinker personally so I would not be getting involved with any of the wild parties or excessive drinking that were fairly common at that time.

The responsibility was enormous and I was on a steep learning curve but my administrative experience was to stand me in good stead. All crime files had to be checked by the Detective Inspector and returned for amendment. In addition, there were about thirty members of staff, including the administrative personnel, and a requirement to cover Kettering and even Wellingborough if their own Detective Inspector was absent for any reason.

I was able to console myself with the thought that there had only been one murder case in Corby in the previous ten years, albeit a triple murder so I was not likely to be unfortunate enough to have one to deal with before I had settled in – or was I? I had been there about two months and was just getting used to command and dealing with my Sergeants who felt they could do the job as well as I (and of course they could but I had the 'pips' on my shoulder).

As usual, on a Friday night at the end of a particularly busy week I had so much paperwork to do that I had started work at 8am and worked through with just a sandwich until midnight. I realised that the words on the paper were now starting to spin in front of my eyes so I finally put my pen down. As I did so, I heard the sound of running feet in the corridor and called out to the duty Detective Sergeant to find out what was going on. "We've got a body" he replied. I soon ascertained that the body of a nineteen-year-old female with stab wounds had been found in an alley on the Lincoln estate.

We went together to the scene and it was there, just as we arrived, that I saw the woman who had pursued me with interest some years before. She just stood smiling and giving me a little wave. I had more important things on my mind.

An ambulance was at the scene and a Police Surgeon was already there. The girl was lying in the back of the ambulance where the staff had been trying to save her. In fact, she took her final breath just as I stepped into the ambulance.

It was quickly obvious that she had suffered a number of stab wounds to the neck and chest and the surgeon pronounced life extinct. Uniformed colleagues had begun to seal off the area and were making preliminary enquiries amongst passers by, of whom there were quite a few.

One neighbour, whose house overlooked the scene, said he thought that she had been to call at the house opposite his but he could not be certain. He also thought he had seen the householder from that house trying to give her mouth-to-mouth resuscitation – definitely trying to help rather than harm her. But he was not present and there was no answer at the door of the house in question.

I gave instructions for the house to be entered immediately on the basis of my experience with the recent Kettering case and fearing that, if the offender was inside, he might attempt suicide. A search of the premises revealed that there was no one there and no obvious signs of a fight.

By this time, the Detective Chief Superintendent was on his way from Northampton and all available detectives were being called out for what looked like it could develop into a long running enquiry. Leaving officers to guard the scene, with strict instructions that NO ONE other than Scenes of Crime Officers were to enter, and detectives carrying out immediate door-to-door enquiries, I returned to the Station to set up an incident room.

This was the parade room on the ground floor and, as we were long before the days of computers, tables with various sets of forms and cards had to be laid out. It is interesting that the modern system involving the Home Office Large Major Enquiry System (HOLMES) requires far more staff to input and analyse data than the old paper system ever did. Of course HOLMES is far more efficient and likely to produce results if the enquiry really is large but I know many officers even today who would prefer to use a version of the paper system if the enquiry appears to be localised.

By the time the incident room was set up, we had identified the deceased as a young woman from a good background who had lived with her parents in one of the better districts of the town. I therefore went with the Duty Detective Sergeant to break the bad news to her parents.

On entering the house, I noticed several religious artefacts in the lounge, as well as photographs of the dead girl in happier times. I therefore decided to bring God into my method of breaking the news and this seemed to help the parents. When we left, the Sergeant said he had not realised my religious beliefs were so strong and I had to explain that they were not but I just felt it was the best way to break the news. He was quite surprised because I had convinced him that I must be a devout Christian.

By the time we returned to the Station, it had reached 2.30am and I was walking along the ground floor corridor when I encountered two of my Detective Sergeants just leaving the Station together. I enquired where they were going and they informed me that information had just come in to the effect that the culprit was a girl and they believed they knew where she was.

I had already decided that this was going to be my case (albeit under the supervision of the Detective Chief Superintendent) and there was no way I was going to allow the two to go out and make an arrest without me. So I went with them. When we reached the address in question, the female occupant, who was not the person we were looking for, invited us in. This woman was quite co-operative but not forthcoming with information.

I was glad I had gone with the Sergeants because I did not feel they were pursuing the enquiry at the house with enough vigour and I began to push hard for information. I was considering arresting the woman on suspicion of involvement in the murder and I instructed the two Sergeants to search the house.

They soon encountered a man in one of the bedrooms and he was a well-known local criminal. At the thought of being arrested he took me to one side and told me that the girl we were seeking had been there but, once cleaned up, she had gone to her brother's address, which he gave me. In return, neither he nor the woman at the house was arrested and we set off to find the culprit. At 5am, we knocked on the door of her brother's house. We were allowed in without protest and in the lounge I arrested the girl for murder.

When I cautioned her she immediately admitted that she was responsible for stabbing the dead girl and we took her to the Police Station. It is very difficult to maintain an air of suitable gravitas when, inside, you feel elated that a possibly difficult enquiry has come to a rapid and successful outcome from our point of view. This was particularly so in this case because I was feeling very mixed emotions. I was glad we had our murderer but sad that she was only just seventeen years old and it was clear that two young lives had been wasted.

Having got the suspect 'booked in' to custody and offered her the opportunity to consult with a solicitor, which she declined, I commenced an interview with her to get her early comments. There were no tape recording facilities then and we had to do major interviews either by remembering everything that was said and writing it down afterwards with all the accompanying dangers of lapses of memory or accusations of making the interview up, or taking contemporaneous notes.

I decided that, in a case as serious as this, it would have to be 'contemp notes' as they came to be known. Unfortunately, this was a most cumbersome method of interviewing, with one talking and the other interviewer writing down the question and answer. In fact it gives the suspect almost too much time to think of the answer and results in a very stilted interview.

Nevertheless, a female detective officer, DC Linda Armson, and I did just that and obtained a written version of what had taken place. The story was that the suspect, while she was still only sixteen, had gone to live with her 24-year-old boyfriend, Rab Smith, at the house we had first broken into. Unfortunately, he was something of a Romeo (he later became known to the National Press as 'Romeo Rab') and was seeing the deceased regularly on Friday nights. He would leave his young girlfriend at the house, meet up with the older girl and they would get drunk before going to a friend's flat where they had the use of a bed for lovemaking until late evening when he would return to the younger girl who had to have his supper ready – obviously he was an honourable young man!

On the fateful night, he had followed the usual pattern but when they got to the friend's flat and climbed into bed, he was not able to fulfil the expectations of his number two girlfriend and when she fell into a drunken sleep, he got up feeling hungry and went home to girlfriend number one for his supper of mince, potatoes and peas – I remember that because the plate was still on the floor with the half eaten meal congealing on it.

He had only been home a few minutes when there was a knock at the front door and being such an honourable man, he sent the girlfriend to answer it (just before midnight). It was girlfriend number two, who had awoken at the friend's flat, realised that boyfriend was missing and decided that he must have gone home. She called at the house to see if he was coming out to play again! It was her misfortune that girlfriend number one did not appreciate another girl knocking at her door and asking, "Is Rab Smith coming out again tonight?" – After she had cooked him a meal as well!

Girlfriend number one turned, walked into the kitchen, fetched a large carving knife, returned to the front door and plunged the knife into the neck of the other girl. She told us that it had been one blow only and that it had gone into the girl's back

This clearly was not the complete truth but at that stage, I only wanted to note down exactly what she said, even though I realised that there was a huge difference in likely charges if it really were one blow. The crime of Murder requires 'malice aforethought' which, effectively, means some sort of premeditated act. If this case really had involved one blow with the knife it could have been interpreted as Manslaughter on the basis of the obvious provocation although the fetching of the knife from the kitchen was likely to amount to premeditation. It was also a concern that we would have to prove that there was not a second assailant who had administered the fatal wounds. As unlikely as that may sound, it was only necessary for the defence to show an element of doubt for her to escape conviction.

I therefore attended the post mortem examination carried out by the Forensic Pathologist at Kettering General Hospital later that morning. I sometimes read with alarm, fiction novels when 'The Police Surgeon' carries out post mortem examinations. The concept is ridiculous. A Police

Surgeon is usually a General Practitioner who works privately for the Police and will normally have gained a qualification in Medical Jurisprudence. He or she will, thereby be qualified to administer drugs to prisoners, carry out vital examinations on live victims and suspects and certify 'life extinct'. As important as those functions are, they are many removes away from the work of the Forensic Pathologist. There are remarkably few of these rare creatures in the country and it is not surprising. There is far more lucrative work available to doctors with such high qualifications. Also the work is stressful by its nature and the hours are most unsociable.

However, Senior Police Officers would find their task impossible without them. It is they who are called out to the scene of a murder to apply their skills and knowledge to the investigation. It is they who will try to establish the time of death although any good Pathologist will tell you that the time of death occurred between when the deceased was last seen alive and when he was found dead. Any attempt to get closer than that will involve a great deal of guesswork. Certainly, body temperature is a very poor guide and where a body has lain for a long time, an entomologist would probably be a better adviser.

People often ask why the police attend post mortem examinations when the Pathologist does all the work. The actual reason is that it is the Senior Investigating Officer (SIO) who is responsible for ALL aspects of the investigation and while he will rely immensely on the skills of the Pathologist it is really the SIO who dictates what leads are followed and he should tell the Pathologist what he wants him to look for specifically. In practice, of course, the Pathologist knows this, and wants no direction. It is more common than many believe, when a pathologist will conclude that he cannot give a precise cause of death and that is the SIO's nightmare because it can easily lose an otherwise strong murder case.

In the case in question, the cause of death was unlikely to be difficult to define. What we needed to know was how many stab wounds there were and which of them were fatal. The pathologist soon established that there were six wounds on the body, two of which were deep penetrating wounds and four which were superficial. The two deep ones were one in the back, just below the neck and one in the front of the chest, which appeared as a wound about 1" wide, slightly below the collar bone.

The first wound was consistent with our suspect's story that she had rushed at the victim, raised the knife above her head and struck downwards behind the victim's neck. Her story fell apart with the claim that this was the only blow she struck. The evidence began to point to a frenzied attack with all six blows being struck in the same manner but landing in slightly different locations, the superficial ones striking bone and not entering deep into the body.

The Pathologist advised me that he felt the one at the back of the neck had only penetrated about two inches and was not likely to have been fatal. This meant the one at the front must have been far deeper and was critical to the cause of death. It was probably the last blow struck but this could not be proved conclusively.

No post mortem is pretty but this was to be a most gruesome affair. It was still necessary to remove the skull to prove there was no inherent disease or sub-dural haemorrhage. This is the part that has always set my teeth on edge, when the pathologist strips the skin back from the face, taking the hair and peeling it back to expose the skull before the technician uses his 'Black and Decker' circular saw to cut through the bone to allow the pathologist to examine and weigh the brain. It is a very precise operation because the technician must not cause fresh damage in exposing it.

They also have to take samples of eye fluid and I find this particularly horrible, even though I know the deceased cannot feel it. The thought of the needle entering the eyeball is something I can manage without seeing again. I fully understand why the fictional 'Morse' does not like to look at dead bodies, although, if he were real he would get used to it.

The pathologist, having established that the brain was normal, made a scalpel cut across the chest above the wound and down either side to the waist. He then took a plastic 12" ruler and cut it to the approximate shape of the knife he thought would have made the frontal wound. The next step, and the goriest, was to insert the ruler gently into the wound and trace its path into the body but removing layers of flesh to show the precise path with photos to prove that he was not making a new wound. This was a long, testing and laborious task but absolutely vital. The ribs had to be removed as the path of the wound went deeper into the chest until all of the ribs had been removed and the lungs heart and intestines were exposed.

Although it is most distasteful to describe, the interior of the human body resembles nothing more than a huge amount of liver and sausages. This was the thought that struck me as I watched. Maybe it was just my defensive reaction to what I was witnessing. I was too engrossed, not to say too tired, to have any other reaction than to be struck by this incongruous similarity.

When the ruler was inserted to its full depth, it became quite clear that the original knife wound had penetrated the heart and death was inevitable within a very few minutes. The overall depth of the wound exceeded six inches and was in a downward direction from a right-handed person standing in front of the deceased. There were only a few, minor defensive injuries to the hands to indicate a very limited resistance.

At the conclusion of the post mortem, I had to return to Corby to re-interview my suspect who still declined to have a solicitor despite strong persuasion on my part. In fact, I felt it would be to our advantage as well as her own, to have a solicitor there because I was anxious not to leave open the possibility of later accusations of improper questioning by me.

In the absence of a legal adviser, I again conducted the interview by contemporaneous notes, with the inevitable stilting of the interview. Our suspect made no real attempt to evade the facts and she agreed that she had struck up to six blows with the knife and that the last one was deeper and in the front.

By the time she had been charged with Murder and I had presented the remand case to the magistrates, it was nearly 5pm on Saturday. The discerning mathematician will have noted that, by then, I had worked 32 hours without a break and without a proper meal.

The ten-mile journey home to Kettering was one I should not have attempted and by the time I arrived home, I was almost asleep at the wheel of my car. I had telephoned my wife to tell her I was on the way and when I pulled onto the drive she opened the front door and said, "You must be absolutely shattered. I have got a meal ready for you. I thought as you have worked so hard, I would get you your favourite – liver and sausages!!" I burst into almost hysterical laughter and tried to explain why it was possibly not my favourite food any more but it would have made little difference whatever it was, because the last thing I recall was sitting at the table and falling forward, fast asleep. Jackie must have helped me to bed but I really cannot recall getting there at all.

The next thing I knew was at about 11.30pm when she had to wake me because there was a telephone call for me from the Station and they would not accept 'No' for an answer. It was the Duty Inspector who wanted to tell me that they had been called back to the house where the Detective Sergeants and I had gone and gained the information that led to the arrest.

The householder, knowing that the suspect had been charged, now wanted to clear herself of involvement and had called to say that her waste bin in her kitchen contained clumps of bloodstained hair that she had cut off the suspect when she first arrived there, because she could not get the blood out of it – a clear indication of how much blood there had been and that it had sprayed upwards. Strangely unamused, I suggested that the Inspector might like to consider dealing with it himself and leave the evidence for me to sort out in the morning. It did not enter his thoughts that I might have had a fairly long day.

Completion of a murder file is still a long and arduous task now but in 1978, it was a nightmare because there was no computer to assist with finding the correct documents. They all had to be retyped as 'Roneo skins', corrected and assembled as a file for the Director of Public Prosecutions (DPP). This was only the first step because it would then be checked personally by the Detective Chief Superintendent, who would undoubtedly find some fault if only to prove that he had read it. It would then be corrected again. The DPP would want some changes to emphasize points he wished to highlight in the case and then it would have to be reconstructed as a 'Committal File' for the Magistrates to send to Crown Court.

After Committal, there would be copies to the Probation Service, Crown Court for the Judge, Prosecuting Solicitors and the Defence. After any 'Notice of Alibi' was received there would be more work to be carried out and then the marshalling of witnesses for the Crown Court.

I will therefore jump ahead of my story by one whole year, which is the time it took to get this murder case to trial at Birmingham Crown Court. I was about to see the national press in a whole new light. I had received no formal media training at that time but experience with the local newspapers had given me a fairly rosy view of their behaviour. Luckily I was certainly not naïve by this time.

The first approach I received was on day one of the trial when representatives of a certain newspaper asked me for advance details of what was going to emerge during the trial. They had found out already that it was likely to be a juicy scandal with the older man running two teenage girlfriends, living with one who was only, by one year, old enough for him to avoid a charge of sexual assault and then one girl kills the other in a 'crime passionel'.

Disclosing what I knew could have cost me my career and the reporters would have merely gone on to the next story laughing about the simple country bumpkins. I just told them to sit in court and they would hear what had happened. It is a well known fact that police officers may develop a degree of trust with local reporters who will be round for another story the next day but a national is unlikely ever to need the officer again.

The next approach was when one of them sidled up to me on the court steps and asked if I could help him with a little problem. He said that they had been unable to get any photographs of the deceased and needed one for their story. He said that he could make sure the Police appeared in a good light and I could look forward to a substantial cash reward if I could provide a picture. I would not be at risk because he would never reveal his sources. Apart from the fact that I am an honourable man and had never before (or since) been offered a bribe, he must have taken me for a fool. To think that even a dishonest cop would put his career on the line for £50 or £100 was madness.

One might have expected me to lose my temper or arrest him but I did neither. I simply said, "Yes, I do have some photographs of the deceased, but I doubt if even your newspaper would dare to print them." I was, of course alluding to the post mortem photos and I went on to explain that to him. He just turned away and I did not see him again.

The third issue with the press was at the conclusion of the trial when it emerged that one of the Sunday papers had paid the boyfriend an enormous sum, thought to be in five figures, for his story. I would like to say that he got his moral 'comeuppance' for that, but he did not. He did have to move away from Corby for a few years because there was a great deal of ill feeling towards him in the town but he certainly had enough money to move comfortably and he did eventually return to the town.

The very distinguished and well-known barrister for the defence gave me quite a hard time in the witness box but there was nothing he could use against me and the Judge referred to the quality of the written contemporaneous notes of interview. The prosecution barrister was equally well known and distinguished and the case was very ably put to the Jury, who duly returned a verdict of 'Guilty of Murder'. As I had foreseen, the alternatives were Manslaughter, Grievous Bodily Harm or Not Guilty. I had little doubt that it would fall between Murder and Manslaughter and I was not surprised that it was the former.

The combination of the pause to fetch the knife from the kitchen and the number of blows was enough to convince the properly advised Jury that this amounted to malice aforethought and, therefore, Murder was the proper verdict. On any other charge, after a finding of guilt, the Judge has to listen to mitigation and antecedent history before passing sentence. In a Murder case, however, there is only one penalty and that is 'Life' (or in the case of an under 18, 'Detention during Her Majesty's Pleasure').

It came as something of a shock for me and the only other colleague still there at the end of the trial when, on hearing the Jury's verdict, the Judge simply said, "You have been found guilty of murder. There is only one penalty known to the law and that is, in your case, detention during Her Majesty's Pleasure. Take her down."

As we listened to this barely adult girl screaming as she was dragged from the dock of this magnificent old Court and taken 'down the steps' literally, to the cells below, I was forced to think that, had this been a few years ago and had she been the age she was now when she committed the crime as opposed to when she was convicted, she would have been sentenced to hang and the warders would have been taking her away to her doom.

I had to accept that the victim had been doomed by this girl's actions, but I felt most strongly that she did not deserve what would have been in those earlier years, the death penalty or even life imprisonment. My colleague and I felt quite shaken by the experience and had to stop for a coffee to settle us before driving home. In fact, her life had already been ruined whilst on remand in HMP Holloway, where she had been subjected to the advances of lesbian wardresses and prisoners.

She subsequently appealed against her conviction and I had to attend the Central Criminal Court where three elderly Judges made the two distinguished barristers look like small boys being told off by schoolmasters as they argued the case either way. The Appeal Court Judges told them brusquely to allow them the respect of knowing that they had read all of the papers in the case and knew it as well as the barristers. Their judgement was short and pointed. 'Appeal Dismissed'. The case was clear-cut, the Jury were properly advised by the Trial Judge and there was no reason to interfere with the original verdict.

Thus my first prisoner for a murder case that I dealt with as the SIO stayed in a Young Offenders Institution and then an adult prison for twelve years before being released on lifelong parole. Hardly the unreasonably short sentence that most members of the public believe murderers are subject to.

Chapter 17

I have said that there had only been one murder case in the previous ten years at Corby. In the four years I spent as a Detective Inspector I was involved in a total of six homicide cases. The first two I have already described and I soon after became involved in one that was a debacle from beginning to end. I am not proud of my part in it, although my own shortcomings were far less significant than those of others.

It was 3am on a wet, foggy, winter's Monday morning when I received a phone call at home. As I fought my way up from the depths of sleep, I listened to the Corby Controller telling me that a body had been found at a house in one of the rougher areas of the town. As usual, I had had a very hard week and had been looking forward to a couple of days off. I, therefore, felt reluctant to leave my warm bed but knew I had to. "I'll be there in a few minutes", I told the Controller. "I don't think so," she replied, "the fog is so thick it will take you an hour to get here, even if you manage to find your way."

She was right. It was a foul night and it did take me almost an hour to get there. When I did so, I was alarmed to find no officer on guard outside the house. I called out and went inside where I found the officer, with the Duty uniformed Inspector (an ex CID Sergeant) in the lounge with the gas fire on, smoking cigarettes. I asked why they were smoking inside a crime scene and indeed why they were in the house at all. The Inspector told me that he had told the constable to step inside because it was so cold out and they were just having a quick smoke before going out again. I asked if the gas fire had been turned up so high when they arrived and they told me that they had put it on to keep warm.

I should have taken more direct disciplinary action there and then but I can only think that I must have been so shocked at this dereliction of duty that I just stood, open mouthed and did nothing. I did get them outside before asking what had happened and I received the explanation that the deceased was the lady of the house and she had been found naked in the kitchen, by her husband, with a ligature round her neck.

They said that he had told them he went to bed quite early but his wife, who suffered from asthma, had stayed up because she could not breathe properly. She had told him, sometime before midnight, that she was going to the post-box to post a letter. He had heard this and then fallen asleep. He had then awoken about 2am and realised that she was not in bed. He got up to go and check on her and found her lying in the kitchen. He noticed that the back door was open and there were wet footmarks on the kitchen floor, leading from the body to the door. He had then phoned his mother who, in turn called the police.

The officer now standing guard had arrived at the scene and, not believing the husband's story, had arrested him on suspicion of Murder. The husband had immediately suffered an epileptic fit and had been taken, under guard, to Kettering General Hospital where he remained.

I went into the kitchen and it was there that I made my most grave error. I saw the wet footprints on the floor but, for whatever reason, whether it was because of the hour, or because of the worry about the things that had gone wrong already, I did not think to get a photographer immediately to photograph them and by the time I did think to do so, they had dried out and could not be seen. I did note that the ligature, which was wound quite tightly round her neck and appeared to be the cause of death, was also wrapped very loosely round her wrists and ankles but it appeared that she could easily have slipped out of the ties.

This hour, from 4am to 5am, was absolutely critical in the investigation, and the lack of any successful outcome to this may have been lost at that point. The Detective Chief Superintendent and Detective Chief Inspector had both arrived and the DCS took charge. I had got the Scenes of Crime Officers out by then and they were given specific instructions by the DCS. I was amazed, at 7.30am, when they both returned to the Station to say they had finished their examination.

In a more recent Murder case, I had SOCOs and forensic scientists on the scene for five days before I was satisfied that they had indeed 'finished'. Even for those days, two and a half hours was definitely insufficient to complete what they should have done and the DCS sent them back immediately to start again. Unfortunately, 'starting again' was not an option because their first cursory examination had disturbed the whole scene. Thus, much valuable evidence was lost, including my 'footprints'.

At the hospital, the doctors had given the opinion that the husband had not had an epileptic fit and other small pieces of evidence began to point very strongly to him as the culprit. When released by the hospital, he was brought back to the Station and detained but by then, he had his story solidly together and was adamant that he had heard nothing, no screams, no shouts, no banging, in fact nothing at all after she had said she was going to the post-box.

He then alleged that a few small, cheap items had been stolen from the house, presumably by the 'robber' turned murderer. He continued to stick to his story throughout five days of questioning. Such a length of detention would not be possible now but there were no legal limits at the time.

The main reason we kept him so long was that the Forensic Laboratory had found traces of, what transpired to be, his semen in his wife's mouth. He continued to deny that they had engaged in any sexual activity that night. Our very strong suspicion was that they had been involved in sex games, including bondage and oral sex and somehow it had gone wrong, perhaps by having the neck tied too tightly.

We, obviously, had to cover all possible leads and a great deal of time was spent searching for the 'missing' property, interviewing known burglars and following up every possible piece of information. None of these was to provide any positive results and the husband was released on 'Delay Charge Bail' to reappear at the Station later. This was subsequently cancelled and no one has ever been charged with anything arising out of the incident. The letter he claimed she had gone to post was recovered from the letterbox but of course, it could have been put there at any time after the last collection on the Sunday so it proved nothing.

I learned a great deal about how to, and how not to, deal with a major enquiry in the early stages, and so did the Force as a whole. We had really been fairly amateurish in our approach until then and this was in no small part due to the fact that there had been so few murders in our county. But as the number of such serious crimes increased, so did our professionalism and I can say with certainty, that we became as good a Major Incident Team as any in the country in due course.

I was to put the lessons I had gained from that enquiry to good use three more times in the period I was a Detective Inspector. But before that another incident was to test me to the full.

In the week leading up to the trial of the murder case involving the girl who stabbed her rival, I had finished the preparation work for the trial and decided to take a couple of much needed days off. I had barely relaxed, when I received a phone call from the Sub Divisional Commander. He told me that here had been a terrible murder in Kettering, involving three West Indian youths who had come up from London to rob an old lady. In the course of the robbery, they had killed the lady and, although they had been arrested, the Detective Chief Inspector, who was dealing with the murder of the woman who had been found naked in her kitchen, had been called away to deal with the second murder. I was therefore required to return to duty to continue dealing with the naked lady enquiry.

With not much enthusiasm, I went in to supervise the progress of the enquiry. I was there until 9.30pm and went home to face the disappointment of my family for having lost my short holiday.

I had been home only an hour, when I received another call from the Kettering Sub Divisional Commander. He asked me to turn out for a serious enquiry and, despite my protestations that I was on holiday but had worked all day anyway, he still instructed me to attend the Station forthwith.

On arrival at Kettering Police Station, he explained to me that he knew about my work situation and the fact that my murder case was due to start but this was a very serious internal enquiry that could not wait and I had been specifically required to deal with it by Barry Hartson, the Detective Chief Inspector. I arranged for Alan Burton, who was by now, a very capable Detective Sergeant from my own staff at Corby to be called in to assist me and then began to elicit the facts of the incident.

It transpired that on one of the estates in Corby, there was a woman who was very friendly and well disposed towards the police. She worked at a local factory where they made jeans and she had agreed to get pairs of jeans at a discount price for police officers whom she knew. The local officers also used her house as a 'Tea spot' where they could go for a quiet sit down and a cup of tea for a few minutes.

A police woman, who was not on that beat, had asked one of her male colleagues, the local Beat Officer, to arrange for the woman to get her a pair of jeans. The policewoman was on duty during that morning and so was the local Beat Officer. He had called at the 'Tea spot' and found that the jeans had been delivered so he used his radio to inform the Policewoman that 'the parcel' was ready for collection.

She decided to ask for some time off, which was granted and she then drove to the woman's house in her own car, en route to Northampton, where she was due to meet her boyfriend (also a Police Officer) when he finished work for the day. When she arrived at the house, the woman gave her the jeans and invited her in for coffee, which she accepted. They sat and talked for a while, the Beat Officer having already been there for over an hour.

During the conversation, the woman invited the two officers to sample some wine she had and this they did. The sampling must have gone on for some time because the woman then invited them to stay for a sandwich and further wine tasting.

After several hours, the policewoman decided that it was time she left for Northampton or her boyfriend would have finished work and would be wondering where she was. At this, the woman pointed out that the policewoman was in no fit state to drive because of the amount of drink she had consumed. She offered to let the policewoman use a bedroom to have a lie down for an hour, in the hope that she would then be sober enough to drive. This was agreed upon and the Policewoman went upstairs leaving the beat officer, still talking and sampling the wine, at least four hours after his arrival, even though he was still on duty and had avoided at least one job by saying that he was committed to an enquiry.

Some time later, the policewoman's boyfriend telephoned (he had evidently been contacted by his girlfriend and she had said where she was). He wanted to tell her that he was about to finish duty and let her know where he would be when she got to Northampton.

The beat officer, on hearing the woman take the message, said that he would go upstairs and pass the message to the Policewoman who must be asleep because of the length of time she had been upstairs. It was from this point that the story began to differ. We had only the Policewoman's account, which was that she had gone to the bedroom and, being unable to sleep with her clothes on, had undressed and lay in the bed. She said that she suddenly awoke to find the beat officer in the bed with her, undressed, on top of her and attempting to have sex with her. She pushed him away and told him to get out, which he did. She then got dressed and ran downstairs, where she got in her car and drove to her lodgings in Corby to tell a female colleague that she had been raped. She did not know what had happened to the beat officer after that, but we established that he had returned to the Station about 4pm and immediately booked off duty to go home to Kettering.

By the time the policewoman and her colleague had gone to the Station and made the complaint of rape, it was already well into the evening and it was thus that I was called out so late. At that time it was Police policy to interrogate alleged rape victims before taking any other action, on the basis that rape was the easiest crime to allege and one of the most difficult to disprove. Aided by a woman Inspector, I therefore began to question the policewoman, while Alan Burton went to gather evidence at the house. He soon returned, having found the policewoman's panties in the bed.

Meanwhile, my interrogation was going nowhere. I found the whole story almost beyond belief. How on earth could two responsible officers have engaged in a drinking session for several hours when one of them was on duty and both knew they would have to drive afterwards? How could the beat officer have stayed there all of his shift? Why on earth did the policewoman go to bed in the house of a woman she had met for the first time that day? Why did the beat officer, a well respected married man, decide to get into bed with her?

It seemed too preposterous to be believable but the policewoman would not be shaken from her story. Her boyfriend had also arrived at the Station and I had to warn him about his behaviour, even though I did feel some sympathy for the position he found himself in.

By the time we had obtained a statement and gathered what evidence we could, it was 4.30am and I decided to go to the beat officer's home and arrest him. We arrived there at 5am and woke him from the bed he was sharing with his wife. I gave him a moment to explain to her why he was being arrested but I certainly did not leave him alone after the lessons I had previously learned. I treated him like any other suspect except that he was not placed in a cell initially but we carried out a preliminary interview and he was quite open in giving his version of events.

He agreed with everything up to when he went upstairs to deliver the message to the policewoman and even then he did not differ that much. The only change was that he said he had opened the bedroom door and seen the policewoman lying on the bed, the sheets having possibly come off as she turned. He said, however that she had then opened her eyes, looked at him and said, "Come on, XXX, get in here with me." This was an offer he could not refuse in his inebriated state and he had undressed and got into bed with her. Because of the drink he was not able to perform the sexual act and it was then that she had suddenly sat up and shouted at him to get out.

This was going to be a difficult case to proceed with. Rape cases had to go to the DPP and he would be looking for corroboration, early complaint and witnesses, if such a case were going to be placed before a court. There was an early complaint although not to the woman at the house. There was no contest about the fact that an attempt to have intercourse took place but the woman, in whose house the incident occurred, was a very poor witness.

The bizarre nature of the case also made it difficult to proceed because juries were then unlikely to believe that a police officer would do such a thing. However, it was clear that what evidence there was, would need to be pursued as far as possible.

I decided that the courtesy of not putting a police officer in the cells could no longer be sustained and he was detained pending our enquiries. Following a further lengthy interview and a formal statement in which he did not change his story at all, I contacted the Deputy Chief Constable (the

Discipline Authority for the Force) and obtained his agreement to suspend the officer from duty before releasing him on bail.

The effect of being suspended is that the officer is required to hand in his warrant card and uniform and he is not permitted to enter a Police Station without the permission of the Investigating Officer. Most suspended officers find it a very stressful condition to be in and this one was no exception.

The policewoman was obviously allowed to continue on duty because she had done nothing that could be proved against the Discipline Code except perhaps 'Bringing the Force into Disrepute' by encouraging the Beat Officer to obtain the jeans and to be off his beat for hours.

Having gathered all of the evidence as a DPP file, I felt that it was unlikely that the case would go to court in the absence of any independent reliable witnesses but I also could not see how the Force could allow the officer ever to resume his career having shown such flagrant disregard for discipline and carrying out such an act of misconduct with a colleague.

In the event, the situation resolved itself because, while we were waiting for the DPP's decision, the officer went to the lodgings of the policewoman to beg her to withdraw her complaint. She and her colleague/flatmate were so frightened by his attitude that they called the local Duty Inspector.

By the time he arrived the officer had left the scene but a short search found him nearby, in his car, completely drunk. He was breathalysed and found to be way over the legal limit. He was not prosecuted for rape but he was for the drunken driving and this, combined with several discipline charges, led to him being dismissed.

The policewoman continued with her career for some years but only she can know how badly she was affected by the whole experience. I have seen the man quite recently and he does not appear to have any ill feeling towards either me personally or the Police Service. He had no reason to feel aggrieved but that often does not prevent offenders resenting the punishment they receive.

Chapter 18

During my time as a Detective Inspector, I was to face a moral dilemma that was to test my maturity and decide exactly where I stood in relation to the enforcement of the law. It was also to lead to the only disciplinary charge I have had to face. I have been the subject of many complaints, as have most detectives and indeed most police officers. This one however was to become a blot on my career record.

The Police Service as a whole suffered very badly from such TV dramas as 'The Sweeney', 'Starsky and Hutch' and the like. The public was gradually coming to the view that the image of 'Dixon of Dock Green' was becoming tarnished by the misconduct of detectives.

Of course, 'Dixon' was no more real than Regan in 'The Sweeney' and the 'Dixon' image was every bit as false as the more violent characters but quite a few officers began to convince themselves that some of the more doubtful methods shown in TV programmes were the way to act. For many years, the concept of a villain receiving 'a bit of instant justice' had been acceptable to the public at large and which of us has not heard the older generation referring to being caught scrumping and receiving a 'smack round the ear 'from the local copper?

Before 1964, when the Police Act of that year introduced a method of complaining against the police, there had been no way to do so and the police could act almost with impunity if they so desired. However, by the late 1970's, the world had changed and those police officers who chose to break the law by hitting suspects were so far out of step with society that they were becoming dinosaurs, although not yet extinct. These facts need to be kept firmly in mind when judging the incident I refer to.

An elderly man, who had very little money, had been for a quiet drink in his local and was walking homeward late one evening, when he was attacked, without mercy, by a young man who robbed him of 50p and in so doing beat him almost to death with a broom handle. The old gent spent some weeks in intensive care before he did finally recover but died of natural causes before we were able to trace his attacker.

Despite a very careful and protracted enquiry, we were getting absolutely nowhere when an informant contacted one of the officers and named the attacker. He also told us where the broom handle had been dumped and that the attacker had arrived home with blood on his trousers on the night in question.

The broom handle had been placed in a street drain and, unsurprisingly, it was no longer there. Nevertheless, I felt that the information was good enough to justify an arrest although insufficient at that time for a conviction. The suspect was duly arrested one morning and interviewed. He denied all knowledge of the attack and at the end of that working day, we were still no further forward. I then decided that I would have him detained overnight and re-interviewed the next day by an officer who had previously dealt with him and might have the best chance of obtaining a confession.

I then went off duty and thought no more about the case until the next day. The following morning, after the officer had been to interview the suspect, I was approached by a Detective Sergeant who told me that the suspect had admitted the offence and was now making a statement under caution. Unfortunately, his statement would include the fact that two detectives had attacked him in his cell at 1am.

There had, indeed, been two detectives on duty during the night and the description quickly told me that there must be some truth in the allegation, at least insofar as they had visited him in his cell. I was told that he had no marks that showed but my duty was clear. If I became aware of such an allegation, I must call a doctor, notify the Complaints and Discipline Department and commence a criminal enquiry as an allegation of Assault Occasioning Actual Bodily Harm.

My dilemma was that I knew that the second I did any of that, the case against the suspect, who had virtually killed an old man for 50p, would be dropped no matter what admissions he made. I also knew that if I made any attempt to cover up the allegation in any way, I could lay myself personally open to discipline and possibly criminal charges. I was well aware of the arguments, often propounded, about the penalty society pays if the police break the law and how it is better for one guilty person to escape process than allow the police to act improperly etc. etc.

I was also only too well aware of the penalty the officers concerned and myself might pay if I let it go. Thoughts in my mind were about whether it was morally right that two otherwise good officers should go to prison for a minor assault on a base criminal with no conscience, whilst he walked free, having committed such a terrible attack. Neither did I lose sight of the fact that he could just be innocent and confessing because he was afraid of another beating. This last fear was soon dispelled because he knew facts that only the attacker could have known and enquiries had produced a relative of his who made a statement confirming that he had arrived home covered in blood on the night in question.

I can only tell you now what I did and what the outcome was, and leave you to decide what action you would have taken. I decided to see him myself and see if he really did want to make a complaint. When I saw him, there were indeed no marks on him and, after a fairly long conversation with me, he agreed that he did not wish to make any complaint about the officers who visited him during the night. He then made a written statement to that effect. I asked him whether the incident had in fact occurred and he said that it did not and that he had only said that it did to explain why he was now confessing to his crime. I checked that he still wished to admit the crime and he agreed that he did.

I charged him with robbery and Assault Occasioning Grievous Bodily Harm, both of which can carry a life sentence. I then saw the two officers concerned and received their explanation that they had been out on patrol when one had said to the other that he thought they could get an admission if they had a little chat with him even though they had nothing to do with the case.

Even if they had not assaulted him, their actions were outrageous in interfering with someone else's case, especially one as difficult as this. Deep down, I did not believe them anyway. My honest thoughts were that they had been for a drink, returned to the Station buoyed up and felt they could walk on water.

I knew there was no doubt that when the suspect realised how serious his position was, he would resurrect his allegation and it would definitely be aired at Crown Court. I warned the two officers to be prepared to be called to give evidence and be sure that they told the truth at Court. I doubted whether they would escape some sort of censure but I resolved that if we were all still employed after the case, they were going to hear some strong words from me.

The months before the case came to trial seemed to drag with pressure building on all of us. This crystallised when the suspect did indeed make his allegation through his solicitor and this time produced evidence from a prisoner in another cell who claimed to have seen the two officers going into his cell and then heard the sound of banging coming from the cell although he did not actually see any assault.

Finally, the trial began at Northampton Crown Court. It lasted for several days and the two officers were put through the mill at length. I was not called to give evidence but sat through the whole trial with great trepidation. At last the Jury were sent to consider their verdict. I thought this was some achievement that we had got as far as the jury. I had feared that the Judge would say that the evidence was unreliable and throw the case out.

After about an hour, the Jury sent a message to the Judge that they had a question to ask. What could the question be? Was it about officers assaulting prisoners? No, in the event, they wanted to know why it was that the suspect had not been charged with Murder if the old man was dead. The Judge explained that he had died of natural causes unconnected to the attack and they must consider their verdict based upon the charges brought.

It was encouraging for me to think that they had in mind that he could be convicted of Murder and they duly returned the verdicts of 'Guilty' of Robbery and Assault Occasioning GBH. He was sentenced to five years in prison and the Judge made no comment about the investigation.

Shortly afterwards, the two officers were served with notice that they were being investigated for assaulting the prisoner and I was given notice that I would be investigated for failing to investigate properly the original allegation. The final outcome was that the evidence was insufficient to discipline the two but they were 'Given Advice' by their Chief Superintendent, transferred to another Station and taken off the CID. I was given a 'Reprimand' by the Chief Superintendent and some strong words of advice, which I said I would take heed of. Whether I would in the same circumstances and if the same attitudes prevailed, I do not know.

It is not an over dramatisation to say that sudden death is never very far away from the work of a Detective Inspector and it can come in many forms. Perhaps the most common is the 'cot death', which does happen with alarming regularity. They are so common that, unless there is something really suspicious, a Detective Sergeant may well deal with them from beginning to end. I was to encounter two, within a few months that certainly did not fall into the 'straightforward' category.

The first was a report from the ambulance service, late one night. They had been called to a house on the Shire Lodge estate, where the ambulance crew had found a deceased child, a few months old and they were not happy with the story being told by the mother. They also felt that there were some injuries emerging on the child's body.

It was a three-storey house with the entrance on the ground floor, living accommodation in the middle and sleeping at the top. The mother said that she and her husband had quarrelled and he had gone out for a drink. The baby had been crying all the time and she had tried to get it to sleep several times without success. She had finally left it and gone downstairs where she also had a drink.

Husband had returned and they had made up their quarrel and she decided to check the baby before going to bed because it had gone quiet. It was then she found the child in the cot, cold and unmoving.

One of the first things a detective will look for will be oddities in the relationship of the parents and this was an odd one. The husband was well into his sixties and the wife was about thirty. He seemed less than interested in what was going on and just keen to get to bed. She was very distraught and seemed on the edge of breaking down – but what was the root cause of that? It is perfectly natural that she should be so upset but was it because she had harmed the child? Was it because she knew her husband had and dare not say? Or was it simply because her baby had died suddenly?

The Post Mortem soon revealed that it was not solely the last explanation. The baby had died from head injuries with a combination of the usual bruising associated with a head injury and the sub-dural haemorrhage that can happen when the head is snapped back or forth suddenly (as in car crashes) or shaking in young children.

So who was responsible? Certainly the mother recounted a part of the evening when her husband had been alone with the child and she had, by her own admission, been alone with the baby while it was screaming but, of course, the screaming could have been because of injuries suffered earlier.

The husband continued to express his desire to get some sleep because he had to get to work and was quite happy to leave us interviewing his wife. Her background soon emerged as being complicated and from an abusive childhood herself.

I had experienced before and have done so again since, older men who, confronted with life shattering experiences, simply retreat into the mundane. Many times I have found myself suspecting elderly men of having killed their wives because their behaviour is not consistent with having just lost their partner of many years, only to find that they were really as distraught as one would expect. But it is this phenomenon of retreat into the ordinary that they use to cover their emotions.

In this case, it was just so. Intensive questioning of the mother and some enquiries with a regular babysitter showed that the mother had a drink problem and could not cope with the baby, which had come along later in life than she would have wished. She confessed to me that she had lost her temper with the baby because it would not stop crying and she had lifted the child out of the cot and thrown it against the wall.

Because of the circumstances, the Crown Prosecution Service (CPS) later reduced the Murder charge to one of Infanticide and we duly went to trial at Northampton Crown Court. I was amazed that the Trial Judge made mistakes in his summing up in spite of the fact that there had been no complications with the evidence and no challenge to the police witnesses whatsoever. He then misdirected the jury, demonstrably realised what he had done and then decided that, because of the mistakes and the circumstances of the family, the jury should be directed to return a verdict of 'Not Guilty'.

The Jury has no choice in this decision: it is one taken by the Judge but the effect is that the person, having been found 'Not Guilty' cannot be retried for the same matter. Thus she walked free. I confess that I cannot recall precisely what his mistakes were in the summing up and direction but the fault was certainly all with the Judge. After consultation with me but against my advice, the CPS decided against a complaint to the Lord Chancellor. I suppose they feared the wrath of not only this but also other judges if they did so.

I saw the woman some months later and she had left her husband and was living with a somewhat disreputable boyfriend on a rough estate. She was drinking heavily and still seemed on the verge of a breakdown. I then went to see the husband and he was living a happier, normal life as if nothing had happened.

The second infant death involved a young girl, who was living with her parents and had become pregnant by a boyfriend. She had managed to keep her pregnancy from her parents and had not visited a doctor.

One Sunday night, she went into labour and gave birth in the bathroom after her parents had gone to bed. She had taken the child into her bedroom but, knowing nothing about how to care for it and still trying to keep it from her parents, had put it into her wardrobe where it quickly died.

Her parents must have heard something, because they went into her room during the night and found her with blood on her sheets. They called an ambulance and the crew, instantly realising what they were dealing with, soon found the dead baby girl in the wardrobe.

The main issue for us was to be whether the child had ever drawn breath because this would indicate whether the baby was stillborn or if we were dealing with some form of homicide. It would not be Murder but could have been Infanticide or Manslaughter. Infanticide is committed when a mother takes the life of her own child whilst suffering from post natal depression or the effects of lactation, death occurring within 12 months of birth.

To establish whether an independent existence had occurred, we were advised to take the child to one of the country's leading expert Forensic Pathologists who worked from a city in the north. (I will not identify the Pathologist or the city although he is now deceased.) I spoke to him by telephone and he said that, although he could not come to us, if we took the body to him, he would do the Post Mortem immediately. He also said that his facilities were much better at his mortuary for this type of examination.

We therefore had to obtain the permission of HM Coroner to take the body out of his area. This was granted and I arranged for a Traffic Patrol car to take us on the journey with the poor child carefully packaged in a small casket in the boot. I have often wondered what would have happened if we had been stopped for any reason in another Force area or if we had had an accident en route but these considerations were part of the reason for using a marked patrol car. The other reason for using a driver was that the Detective Sergeant and I had been up all night and were already tired.

On arrival, we were greeted by a friendly, affable character who put me in mind of a Shakespearian actor or some of the best Barristers with his lecturing manner and classroom style. I discovered that he did indeed run his post mortems like a classroom lecture and even had a viewing gallery for students.

His reputation was clearly well justified and his methods were nothing short of brilliant, even if a little gruesome. He told us that, if the baby had drawn breath, the lungs would retain some air and would float in water. He removed them and put them in a tub of water. They floated.

The Pathologist said, unequivocally, that the child had drawn breath and we were looking at some form of homicide. The one thing I really disliked about his methods was that, having completed the full examination, he used a scalpel to shred some of the internal organs! The reason he gave was that the defence were entitled to have a second Post Mortem carried out to dispute the first findings and he was not prepared to have some lesser pathologist argue with his.

I declined his offer to join him for lunch after that experience and we returned to Kettering General Hospital with the body, which by then had been put back together by his technician. There, I consulted with the CPS and fully agreed with them that no charges should follow because it was clear that, even though there was technically a homicide, it was unlikely that a Court would find her guilty on the fine judgement of whether a breath had been taken or not. In any event, this girl needed care and help, not punishment. I felt, and am still sure, that even if convicted, she would not have been given anything other than a probation order.

Sandwiched in amongst all of the mayhem, I decided to take a holiday, something I always tried not to miss, and we decided to take the children to Cornwall for a fortnight. A few weeks before we were due to go, I had occasion to visit the home of one of the well-known solicitors who dealt with the most difficult defences and who had a reputation of being anti-police. I had to serve some papers on him and had agreed that I would drop them in on my way home as he lived in a large house on the outskirts of Kettering. "Oh come on in and meet my wife" he greeted me, with unexpected friendliness and enthusiasm. The general conversation turned to holidays and I told him that we were going to Cornwall and the date we intended to leave. He told me that he had a farmhouse at Salcombe, which is not too far from the route we intended to take. He said that they would be there on that date but then said, "Why don't you leave home a day earlier and come and stay the night with us. We have a guest flat that you and the three children can use. It will break up the long journey and we can have a nice meal in the evening."

I politely declined but he would not hear of it and insisted that we stay with them so, at considerable difficulty, I took an extra day off and we set off for the journey, one Friday morning, with the three children and our luggage packed into the estate car we had at the time. I was not truly looking forward to the overnight stay because I prefer to do such a journey in one go if I can, and I was not sure whether he had some ulterior motive for wanting me to have dinner with him.

Salcombe is a beautiful little Devon town and we began to enjoy the scenery as we searched for his farm. It was very remote but not hard to find and we pulled into his drive at about 5pm. He was up a ladder cutting his hedge, wearing a deerstalker hat and wellies, whilst his wife stood below holding the ladder. As we got out of the car and began to stretch our legs he saw us and exclaimed, "Bob, how nice to see you. What on earth are you doing down here?"

"You did insist that we come and stay the night with you, had you forgotten?" I replied.

"Of course I hadn't forgotten, we'll have to get the bedding down for the guest flat." But he had really forgotten the whole arrangement and I felt so embarrassed that I just wanted to leave.

We were exhausted from the drive and he said he would make some tea. It took him almost an hour to make a pot of tea and we drank it in the driveway as he continued with his tree cutting. Then he finally went to fetch some bedding for the guest flat – or more accurately – the room over the pigsty with no running water or electricity.

He then said, "So what are you planning to do for dinner?" and I was too embarrassed to remind him that he had invited us specifically to join him for dinner so I replied, "I don't really know, is there a restaurant in Salcombe?"

"No, but there is a good fish and chip shop on the quayside," he replied. He did not offer to join us and we spent an uncomfortable evening sitting on Salcombe quayside with our makeshift supper. When we returned to his farm, he just handed us the key to the pigsty and went to bed.

It was the oddest experience because he was not, as I may have given the impression, unwelcoming. He was very friendly, as was his wife, but they seemed to have totally forgotten the offer they had jointly made. It was one of the most uncomfortable nights we have ever spent. It was cold and dark, with no lights, toilet facilities or even water to drink but we somehow got through it and, in the morning, I went over to the house, hoping to just wish them goodbye and get on our way.

I broached this with him when I found him in his study working on legal papers but again, he would not hear of it. "I'm just going to make some toast and tea," he said and proceeded to make a huge plateful of toast (he forgot the tea) and then left it standing on the table without offering any to us or taking any himself. His wife was nowhere to be seen and after a while Jackie came in with the children and we were still not offered any of the now cold toast or a drink.

Finally, I could stand it no longer and I said, " — — —, we shall have to get going now or we will catch the traffic." As I said that, his wife appeared and said, " You can't go yet, I'm just about to get breakfast." This at 10.30am and we still had a long journey ahead of us. Nevertheless, we could not get out of it and had to wait while she cooked, what transpired to be a very nice breakfast.

We finally escaped at 12 noon and met a huge traffic jam all the way to Cornwall, the journey taking us another six hours. We had effectively wasted a whole day on the strangest visit I have ever been involved in.

On the social front, we were very friendly with the car dealer who had helped us when I first moved to Kettering and we changed our cars quite often when he had a bargain available. We even made a small profit on the sale of some of them and the overtime I worked had led us to a position when we could afford for Jackie to have a car as well. One of her cars will always stay in my memory. It only cost us £50 and was worth no more than that. It was a Ford Escort, hand painted in red with a huge stripe down the sides (like in Starsky and Hutch). If that was not spectacular enough it did not have a conventional horn but a switch that, when depressed, played the 'Marsellais'.

One day, Jackie had taken our oldest son, Martin, to the Doctor's surgery, which was in the next town and decided to go on to Northampton afterwards. Martin could not resist the Marsellais and when they were well out of town, he pressed the switch. Unfortunately, it broke off as the tune began to play and they had to drive all the way to Northampton playing the Marsellais before someone managed to switch it off for them.

Chapter 19

The pressure of work on me was quite intense at this time although I absolutely revelled in it. I found that it was necessary for me to go back and work in the evening on at least three, sometimes four evenings per week. I had detectives working a late shift (6pm to 2am) every night and they would be rostered to work one week of evenings every fourth week.

I would sit in the office and catch up with the paperwork until about 10pm on the nights I was there and it became my habit to call them then and join them for a drink at one of the local public houses. This habit was supposed to be to meet informants and see who was meeting with whom. I have no doubt it achieved the latter but I never met any informants in a public house. It would be the last place an informant would wish to be seen with a detective and in a small town like Corby, they would be spotted very quickly.

Although not entirely for pleasure, most of this drinking was done for the benefit of the detectives not the job. At closing time, it was also the habit of most shifts to go for a Chinese meal or fish and chips and I would join them for that too. Unfortunately for me, they only did it on their 'nights' week but I was doing it every week. The effect of this on the constitution of a man of my build was most unfortunate. A couple of pints of beer and a meal on top of my normal intake, three or four times each week soon had the inevitable effect and my weight climbed to 19stones and 7 pounds. There was another Detective Inspector at Northampton who had the same problem and we used to be referred to as the book ends, which, although I treated it as a joke, I found a bit hurtful.

I also drove a Ford Capri, a very low-slung, sporty car, and I began to notice that my knees hurt when I tried to get out of it, particularly in the garage where space was limited. I decided that enough was enough. I went on a diet. I stopped drinking completely and while still going out with the night shift, I would not have a meal and in the roughest pubs insisted on a slimline tonic.

This was the most successful diet I had ever undertaken and in four months, my weight had dropped to 15stones and 7pounds. I have never drunk beer since then and I did manage to keep my weight under 16 stones for at least ten years. My colleague at Northampton did not do so and he continued to put on weight until he weighed almost thirty stones (and still does).

They do say that you can never find a policeman when you need one but another brush with violent death in my time as a Detective Inspector was to disprove that saying. It also proved a saying that police officers have, that if you do something you shouldn't, it will be then that you come across a job that will either make you a hero or finish you.

Les Carnie was a young officer who was the kind you always would want with you if there was trouble. Intellectually, he is not necessarily the brightest but I have always had the greatest respect for him for his enthusiasm and certainly for his ability to handle himself in a fight. Indeed, long after this incident, when he became a dog handler, he was regarded as being more dangerous to criminals than his dog.

At the time of the incident, he was a local beat officer and on the Saturday afternoon in question he decided to go off his beat to go to his aunt's house for a cup of tea and see the day's football results. An hour or so before this, a man who lived close to the aunt's house had been drinking during the Saturday lunchtime. He had then returned to his house and sat watching the TV. He had two teenage daughters and they were out playing in the local square.

An old drunk, who was well known as a harmless old man, would go to the local pub at lunchtimes, get drunk and then buy a bottle of whisky that he would take back to his flat. The combination that came together that day was when the two teenage girls began to tease the old drunk, and tried to take his whisky from him. He tried to stop them and swung his hand in an attempt to knock them away. Whether he actually hit either of them is doubtful but it was clearly enough to scare them and they ran home to tell their father that the old drunk had 'interfered' with them.

In his drunken state, the father misunderstood and thought he had sexually interfered with them and promptly went in search of the man. He found him wandering in the Square and without seeking explanations he launched into the old man, knocking him to the ground and then began to kick him about the body. Two young boys saw this happening and having also seen a uniformed policeman going into a house (his aunt's) they ran to the house and called the policeman to come quickly.

Although he was well off his beat and could get into trouble, Les Carnie did not hesitate and there could not have been a better officer to attend. He ran to the Square and very quickly overpowered the father who was still kicking the old man on the ground. Les Carnie needed no assistance to make his arrest but called for transport to take the father, who he arrested for GBH, to the Station. An ambulance was called and took the old drunk to Kettering General Hospital.

I had gone off duty for the day and was at home when I received a call to the effect that the old man was badly injured and was undergoing surgery at the hospital. I returned to the Station and decided to join one of the Detective Sergeants in an interview to get an early version of events from the father.

We took him to an office for the interview, as he was perfectly calm and composed by now. There were still no tape-recorded interviews and we were using the contemporaneous note method of interview. Suddenly, the phone in the office rang and I answered it as the Sergeant was just writing down an answer. The father had just admitted quite freely what he had done and was now regretting it because he had been made aware that his daughters had not been sexually interfered with and indeed, probably deserved what had happened to them.

The call was from another Detective Sergeant at the hospital, who told me that the old drunk had just died whilst undergoing an operation. I was then faced with the problem of what to do in the light of the news I was receiving while the suspect sat opposite me. I had to retain my composure and just casually thank the Sergeant for the call before going on with the interview as if nothing had happened.

There was little to dispute in the facts of this case. He could hardly say it was not him when he had been pulled off the (now) deceased by a police officer and the crime had been committed in full daylight and seen by the two young boys who called the officer. The only questions to be resolved were the motivation for the attack and the final cause of death.

Could his misunderstood message about interference with his daughters be sufficient reason for him, in a somewhat inebriated state, to believe he was entitled to take revenge on this person, some twenty years his senior? Clearly not in law, or in moral justice. Had the victim not died, the charge would have been GBH with Intent and that would have been extremely clear cut, after all, he could hardly say that he did not intend to inflict GBH. However, now the victim was dead, the issue would be whether there was a possibility of a defence to Murder with a plea of Manslaughter? This was much more likely because there are several ways in which the defence can seek to establish this defence, such as by claiming that the balance of his mind was temporarily disturbed. Indeed, such a plea was subsequently offered but rejected by the CPS.

The final cause of death was to prove more difficult for me. I was very well aware that the attacker had repeatedly kicked the victim about the body. The doctors had also been told this although it would have been obvious from the bruising. I was told by the Sergeant at the hospital that the victim's blood pressure had been dropping (consistent with internal bleeding) but he had died as they performed a skull operation to relieve pressure on the brain.

I obviously did not have sufficient medical knowledge to question the skilled doctors on their diagnosis but I was concerned about what the forensic pathologist might say. A priority therefore was to get the post mortem examination completed and this was done on the Saturday evening. In fact, the pathologist was quite dismissive of the fact that the operation had been performed on the head and not the body. Death had resulted from massive internal injuries caused by the kicking and he had no trouble in saying that death had resulted directly and completely from the attack and that the head operation, although possibly unnecessary, had had no impact on the patient.

This did not totally alleviate my concerns because I anticipated that the defence would have a second post mortem carried out with their own interests in mind. However, this was for later resolution and my immediate problem was that I had a prisoner in custody, who believed he was going to be charged with GBH but was de facto, now in custody for Murder.

The Detective Chief Superintendent, with whom I had by then established a close working relationship, had arrived and we decided that I should now inform the man that he was now in custody for Murder. As it was so late in the evening, I would re-interview him the next day. It is not difficult to imagine how he must have felt when I delivered the fateful words.

The next day, I re-interviewed him and charged him with the offence. When the trial began, there was no challenge to my evidence and the second post mortem, which had been carried out by a distinguished pathologist from another area, had concurred totally with the findings of our own pathologist so, was not used in the trial.

He was duly found 'Guilty' by the jury and sentenced to Life Imprisonment, which, in his case meant ten years in prison followed by a lifetime on parole, any breach of which would lead to a return to prison to complete the original sentence. Some years later, I heard that he did in fact breach the parole but, this time, his victim declined to press charges and he escaped spending the rest of his life in prison 'by the skin of his teeth'.

And so, my time as a Detective Inspector in charge of my own Department was coming to an end. As I looked back on it I reflected that it had been a time of great stress, enormous amounts of work but immense pleasure too. I had certainly grown in maturity and stature as a Police Officer and manager.

There were many, many more incidents during that time that space prevents me from recounting. Some were funny, some traumatic and some that simply took hard work and effort to resolve. We had seen a massive strike at The Steel Works, followed by a demonstration and march by the National Front and finally, the closure of part of the Works with the loss of thousands of jobs. It was fascinating to note that the pattern of crime changed as the social structure of the town changed. When they were on strike, there was no money and therefore drinking stopped and with that the violence level dropped. Then came redundancy and payouts, which led to more drinking and much more violence, as well as an influx of con-men taking the money from a group of men who had not been used to having large sums available.

Chapter 20

I had been at Corby for almost four years and I knew, deep down, that it was time for a change. I saw an advertisement in Force Orders for any Inspector who wished to apply for the Junior Command Course at Bramshill Police College and, having nurtured the desire to attend the college since I joined the Force and having been rejected as a Constable for the Special Course (accelerated promotion), I decided to apply.

No officer from Northamptonshire had previously attended this course and, knowing that competition would be quite fierce, I did not hold out too much hope. I underwent an interview with the Deputy Chief Constable and was very pleased and surprised to discover that I was the only successful candidate from our Force.

There was one final twist to my time at Corby. My last day was New Year's Day 1981 and, although it was a Bank Holiday, I had to work to clear up the last few outstanding jobs. These took me all day and I was finally ready to leave for the last time about 5pm.

On one of our visits to Cornwall, Jackie had bought me a specially made coffee mug, with 'The D I' on it. This always stood on a shelf behind my desk next to the legal reference books and despite the fact that I swear I did not touch the shelf that day, just as I stood up from my desk and turned to the shelf, the books fell over and knocked the mug to the floor, smashing it into many pieces. I could not help but think that this was spooky and prophesied that I would not be a 'DI' again.

Before I could reflect too much on that strange happening, I took the last of my possessions out to my car and, in the yard, I encountered two of my Detective Constables who were just on their way to a report of a domestic incident that had resulted in a stabbing. I decided to wait until they got to the scene before leaving and it was as well that I did.

They reported that a woman had stabbed her husband with a kitchen knife following an argument whilst she was peeling potatoes and he was dead. Thus I spent my last evening attending a murder scene, going to a post mortem and liaising with the officers who would be carrying on the enquiry as I was due to travel to the college the next day. I finished work at 1.30am. The woman was subsequently convicted of manslaughter and received a non-custodial sentence because of intense provocation and years of violence on the part of her husband.

My life then changed dramatically as I settled into the routine of six months of travelling weekly to Hampshire and enjoying an academic lifestyle.

The National Police College, Bramshill, is a large medieval house set in acres of rolling countryside with beautiful lakes, stocked with fish. And hundreds of geese (how I came to hate those geese). If it isn't honking and waking you at the crack of dawn, it is the goose pooh that seems to be everywhere. It is all green and goes into a sort of slime when it rains.

There is also a herd of white deer in the grounds and rumour had it that the Commandant of the College used to cull them occasionally, though I doubt it. It is a curious title, The Commandant, reminiscent of a prison camp yet the titleholder was necessarily a highly respected intellectual who carried the 'rank' of Her Majesty's Inspector of Constabulary (HMI).

The staff members were a mixture of academics and experienced police officers and the concept of the establishment was that this was the centre of excellence for policing for the whole country. The potential was for it to be just that. It had the best police library in the world (and still has) and it should have attracted the best brains from academe and the police service. Unfortunately, too many staff members were failures in their field and the police officers were mainly those seeking a sinecure for the end of their service.

The Special Course, which was then of 12 months duration (based on a concept borrowed from the military), was intended to prepare outstanding young officers for starring roles in the service. An officer could attend the course as a Sergeant and then, subject to passing the Inspectors examination at the first attempt, would immediately be promoted to that rank and would have an assured future, probably to the rank of Assistant Chief Constable.

The Junior Command Course, which was the one I attended, was intended for Inspectors with potential and it was expected that they would be promoted to Chief Inspector as soon as a vacancy arose after the course, although I truly did not know that when I applied.

There were also the Intermediate Command Course (then six months but later reduced to three) for Superintendents and the Senior Command Course (also six months) for those carefully selected individuals at Chief Superintendent rank who were likely to go on to Chief Officer. There were very few short courses although a 'carousel' of one and two-week courses on various themes was being introduced.

The main problems were that the long courses were all very similar in content with a bias towards management theory and six or twelve months is far too long to keep bright young officers away from their careers.

I found the change in rhythm after my years of hard grinding work, very refreshing and unlike many of my colleagues, I decided that I would certainly not become cynical about the prospect of an academic sabbatical. As a result, I thoroughly enjoyed myself even though there was no doubt that the course was a month's work crammed into six months, and Wednesday afternoons were free for games anyway. Fridays were early finish days, as students had long journeys to make and there were also many free periods for study and research (not always fruitfully used).

I gained some major benefits from the course. I made some very dear friends who I have remained in contact with; I gained an early insight into the Phillips Commission on Policing, which was to stand me in very good stead later when the Commission's Recommendations were transposed into law in the Police and Criminal Evidence Bill (PACE) and most importantly, I went there with a very limited view of police issues and I came away with a greatly expanded view of the world.

During the course, it was known that the Deputy Commandant, Mr Maurice Buck, who was a Deputy Chief Constable from the West Midlands, was applying for posts as a Chief Constable. Maurice Buck is one of the most dynamic and powerful leaders I have ever had the privilege of meeting. He was a former Metropolitan Police Detective, who had risen through the ranks of the CID to Detective Chief Superintendent and possessed all of the cunning and political acumen commensurate with such a background. He had also been the Project Manager for the introduction of the Police National Computer (PNC), which was one of the more successful Government IT projects.

His style was an anathema to the academics at the College because he worked very long hours and drove anyone working for him just as hard. They did not understand that, a) he was their boss and b) they really did have to do what he said, when he said it, and we students were often privy to the major rows that would take place when he felt they had not acted upon his wishes properly. He was a perfect foil for the more gentlemanly, but just as determined, Commandant.

About half way through the course, Maurice Buck achieved his ambition. He was selected as the next Chief Constable – for Northamptonshire! Suddenly things started to happen to me. The first was that he sent his Staff Officer to see me to find out about Northamptonshire

Police as I was the only officer from that Force on campus.

The Staff Officer and I had an unfortunate crossing of swords in the canteen one day when he asked me to tell him about Northamptonshire. I instantly realised he meant about personalities but I started to tell him about crime rates and the length of Motorway in the county.

He told me that he knew all that but "what about that difficult Chief Super at Northampton?" To which I replied that I had never worked in that town and had never met the officer in question.

"Well you must know the Admin Chief Superintendent," he persisted. My reply was not what he expected. "Look Sir, you have the wrong man here," I said. "If you want to know about my Senior Officers, you will have to ask them; not me". At this, he quickly left the table and did not speak to me for some time, although we did become well acquainted later and I do have considerable respect for him. Clearly Maurice Buck had sent him and I believe my loyalty to colleagues may have won me some credit with my new Chief Constable.

Maurice Buck sent for me personally and I went with some trepidation but he did not mention my encounter with his Staff Officer and just wanted to tell me that he already had a project for me on my return to the Force so I could get started on it immediately in my spare time. I was to research the whole Prosecution procedure used by the Force and make recommendations to overhaul the system. I would be returning to the Force at the end of June and my report was to be submitted by 31 October. That was the only direction he gave me and he then expected me to progress it and have it completed by his deadline.

Towards the end of my course, I heard that he had arrived in our rather backward little Force like a whirlwind and that a number of Chief Superintendents were 'on their way out' including those he had indirectly asked me about. It seems he had arrived on his first day before 8am and found that Headquarters did not really wake up until about 10am so he could not find a Senior Officer to brief him. This had apparently led to a confrontation with the Admin Chief Superintendent who retired soon afterwards. I was quite pleased because he was the bully who had told me, on promotion to Sergeant, that I had no choice of accommodation.

I was even more pleased when I received a message to attend Headquarters one Monday morning instead of returning to College on the Sunday night. I was a little worried but thought it must be related to my project. On arrival, I found myself waiting outside the Chief's office with a Superintendent and a Chief Inspector. It still did not dawn on me, until I was called in to see the great man, that I was being promoted to Chief Inspector in the chain leading down from the Admin Chief Superintendent's retirement. He told me that it was College Policy to see attendees on the Junior Command Course promoted to Chief Inspector and he could hardly breach that policy in his first few months as a Chief Constable even though I was really quite junior in service. Upon my return from the College, I was to be posted to Kettering as the Sub Divisional Commander.

I could not wait to get back to the Force and, being still at the College, I was able to ignore the jealousy within the Force that my appointment had caused. On my return, I was soon thrust into the new role and still had to complete my project, which I duly did and handed it to his Staff Officer, a good friend of mine, on 31 October 1981.

I heard nothing from Maurice Buck and as Christmas approached, I was at a function one evening when he walked up to me and began to tear a strip off me on the dance floor. "I can't think what came over me promoting you. I gave you a project to do in April and here it is December and I haven't seen it yet. When I say I want something by a certain date, I mean by that date yadda yadda yadda."

"Just a minute Sir," I said quite angrily," If I am given a project to do, or anything else for that matter, by a certain date, I do it and I submitted the project on time by placing it in your Staff Officer's hands on 31 October."

"Oh, that's alright then. I knew I could rely on you". Was all he said as he walked away. I later spoke to the Staff Officer and it transpired that he had thought the report was to go direct to the Chief Superintendent who was running a much larger project to reorganise the whole Force.

I know that Maurice Buck did read the report but he still did not comment on what were, in fact, some very major reforms that I had proposed. The next time he spoke to me about it was casually to ask when I planned to introduce the changes. He had accepted them all without question and I came to realise that this was part of his leadership style. He would ask people to do things and then he would trust them to do it; but Lord help them if they did not.

He was in the process of going round all of the Stations to talk to ALL staff and I had to arrange a meeting of all my officers and support staff at Kettering except those actually dealing with incidents at that time. It would be an understatement to say that he was aggressive at the meetings.

He spent half of the meeting telling the Force where we were going and inviting them to 'come on board'. Then he spent some time inviting them, if they did not want to be part of his progressive new Force, to leave and find another job. There is always at least one officer at every Police Station who is brave or foolish enough to take on a senior officer and the one who did it at Kettering was the same officer who had been 'attacked' by the man who threw himself to the ground to get him into trouble.

This officer was himself aggressive, quick-witted and able to stand his ground but he was no match for Maurice Buck who simply tore him into small pieces publicly without even 'breaking sweat'. It seems this happened several times during his tour but gradually officers came to realise that they had a Chief in the image of Mrs Thatcher, who was the Prime Minister and a role model for Maurice Buck.

At the same time as all this was happening, two Detective Chief Inspectors managed to land themselves in deep trouble with Maurice Buck. One was alleged to have tortured prisoners by holding them over a banister and threatening to drop them if they did not confess, and by giving another hardened criminal, (by an odd coincidence, the same man who had broken into my home when I was ten), a cold bath to make him confess his latest crimes.

The other Detective Chief Inspector had not dealt with a rape allegation as Maurice Buck expected it to be treated. Police treatment of rape victims had changed dramatically since I had last been involved with one as a result of some notorious cases including a 'fly on the wall' TV documentary in which a Detective Constable in Thames Valley had put the victim under ridiculous pressure, probably playing to the cameras and thinking he was in a TV drama. Our Detective Chief Inspector had allegedly, allowed similar treatment and had failed to take positive action.

The first Detective Chief Inspector was disciplined and reduced to Constable, subsequently retiring on a sick pension and the second simply took early retirement. As a result of these two vacancies, the Force had a distinct shortage of experienced CID Officers to fill the important ranks. Thus, my time as a Uniformed Chief Inspector and Sub Divisional Commander was to last only eight months.

During that time, however, I was involved in a very serious crime enquiry, but this time in a totally different capacity. As a Uniformed Chief Inspector, I did not expect to be deeply involved in such enquiries so I was quite surprised when I received a call to attend Wellingborough Police Station.

Three gypsies had been found shot to death in their caravans, in Ditchford Lane near Irthlingborough and I was called upon to conduct the ground search. How the Police carry out these searches is now very well known from TV shows and news clips but then, our Force had not carried out such a search on this scale, and I had certainly not managed one but I was soon to become the Force expert.

The weather was very cold indeed and I was allocated fifty officers with the brief to carry out a fingertip search for 100 yards on either side of the road where the caravans were parked, searching for bullets. The methodology was to have one officer peg out a section of the field, one sergeant to keep the officers in line and then the remaining 48 would go forward on their hands and knees. If anyone found anything the whole line would stop until it had been marked and bagged as an exhibit. This was obviously a cold, soul destroying job, particularly as Ditchford lane is well over a mile long and we had to cover both sides.

The circumstances of the murders came to light when a passer by had noticed the door of one of two caravans, which were always parked in a lay by in Ditchford Lane, standing open and had gone to investigate. Inside he had found one elderly man and his dog, both shot dead with a .38 handgun. The witness had run to the other caravan for help, but there found the occupier and his wife also shot dead with the same gun. There were numerous bullet holes in the caravans and it was clear that the assailant(s) had reloaded the gun more than once.

Even with the voluntary aid of a local metal detectors club and expanding the search to 150 yards each side of the road and covering the whole length of Ditchford Lane we found nothing of any interest whatsoever. The search is well remembered by those taking part for two reasons. One was that it was so cold that I had had to have hot soup delivered at regular intervals but, after several frustrating days, I took it upon myself to spice up the soup with a bottle of whisky one afternoon , a previously unheard of treat from a Senior Officer and although, actually allowed within the Discipline Code, a very unusual thing for the Uniformed Force to do.

The other memorable matter was the question of six hedge slashers that I had arranged to purchase for the job. At the end I was asked by Admin to account for them and I had no idea where they had gone. My suspicions were firmly with the Uniformed Support Group who were always used for this type of work and would have a use for them. However, they steadfastly denied having seen them and it took me many weeks of painstaking detective work to finally get the Group to return them. If they had only known, I was about to give up the search when they finally handed them over.

Regrettably, the person(s) responsible for the three murders have never been traced despite a massive enquiry that continued for many months and was resurrected, whenever any clues emerged, for many years after.

Chapter 21

In February 1982, without any choice in the matter and as a direct result of the alleged misdemeanours of the two Detective Chief Inspectors, I was transferred to Headquarters as Detective Chief Inspector in charge of Support. This included Staff Officer to the Detective Chief Superintendent, Dog Section, Fraud Squad, Scenes of Crime, Stolen Vehicle Squad, Special Branch, Criminal Records, Intelligence, Fingerprint Dept, CID Admin, Crime Prevention and, in addition, I had to act as the Press Officer for the Force.

This was an unbelievable range of tasks and far too much for one person to cope with, particularly as I also had to see through the implementation of my project as part of the Force Plan and this involved writing a manual to be published and issued to every officer in the Force. The Press role took up quite a part of every day and, as I had not previously had any experience of such a role, I was sent on two courses to learn how to deal with the News Media.

One of these course was run by Kent Constabulary and the Officer in charge of the course was David Hatcher, their resident expert on The Media, who later, on my recommendation, became the presenter of BBC's Crimewatch UK programme and held the role for 15 years. He had a talent for dealing with TV personalities and was able to get some big name news journalists to help out with the course (Kate Adie was one). He also arranged for the whole course to attend the BBC studios to see the News broadcast and the offices of *The Sun* to see how a newspaper is produced. This was a new and fascinating experience for me and it began an affinity with the News Media that stayed with me throughout my career.

The role as 'Detective Chief Inspector in charge of everything' was a period of unrelenting hard work and long hours with no respite or even funny interludes. The Detective Chief Superintendent made a virtue of the lack of effort he personally had to put into the job and this was exemplified at the Christmas of that year when, coincidentally, we both acquired new briefcases. The one his wife bought for him was wafer thin and mine was a 'Pilot's Case'. When I pointed this out to him, he just laughed and told me that it was my job to do all of the paperwork and his to make decisions.

I was, therefore, somewhat pleased when a decision was made to split my job into two with me continuing as the Staff Officer and a new Chief Inspector to take on all of the other roles. This was part of the overall reorganisation of the Force and took place on 1st April 1983. On that date, every member of the Force up to and including Chief Inspectors had been allowed to apply for whatever post they wanted within the reasonable limits of their experience. With almost no exceptions, Constables and Sergeants were given their first or second choice of job and most Inspectors also got what they wanted.

I had an interview with the Chief Constable, as did all other Chief Inspectors, but mine was limited to 30 seconds. He felt he knew all about me and that I would want to continue in the role of Staff Officer. You knew better than to argue such a point with Maurice Buck so that was the job I took.

I was not happy with it and felt that I wanted to be back on outside duties. The eight months at Kettering had not been long enough to make much progress, although I felt I had improved the morale there a little. I did let the Chief know that I did not see myself in the new limited role for too long but he barely acknowledged my comments.

A few months into the new arrangements, Maurice Buck became the Secretary of the ACPO Crime Committee, an extra responsibility borne by Chief Constables with Crime experience but also a very prestigious position, leading, as it did by tradition, to the Chairmanship of the Committee in due course. There was great deal of work attached to the position and Maurice Buck decided to appoint a second Staff Officer with a secretary of his own to deal with the correspondence for him.

I was walking along the Chief Officers corridor one morning when the Deputy Chief Constable called me in to his office. "You're going to be offered a job in about twenty minutes. Take it and don't tell anyone I told you" he said, and would add nothing to that mysterious statement. I guessed what was coming and went to find a telephone so I could at least have a quick discussion with Jackie. As usual, she gave me her full support and told me that I should take it if I wanted it, knowing that it would involve long hours and hard work, as would any job working directly for Maurice Buck.

Sure enough, he already had someone out looking for me and a few minutes later I was in his office. "I've got a new job for you if you want it," he said. "It's a good job and its one I want you to take but you can go and think about it and talk to your wife if you want to," although his face said that I would be crazy not to take it. After he had told me what the job

entailed he said, "Well, do you want some time to think about it?"
"No Sir, thank you very much, I would love to take the job," I said and so began a whole new pattern to my life and my career.

My first task was to appoint a secretary and I set about arranging adverts and interviews. I wanted someone with initiative, intelligence, good shorthand and typing skills and a personality that would not be intimidated by dealing with very senior officers from all over the country. I selected a short list and arranged tests for the applicants. The choice quickly came down to two ladies. The final choice was made on the more accurate and speedy typing test although I was concerned that the losing applicant was more mature and had better educational qualifications. Having made the selection and told the unsuccessful candidates, my selected choice turned the job down.

I decided to offer it to the second choice and she told me that she did not want the post as second choice: a perfectly reasonable decision but one that I would not accept. She must have wondered what she was getting into because I asked her if I could meet her for coffee when she finished work in her current post. I must confess that I turned the pressure on full blast, with my most persistent persuasion and charm, and I convinced her to work for me.

I was really pleased because it transpired that her typing only let her down on the test because she was nervous and her MA from a Scottish University together with several languages and a standard of grammar that was at least a match for my own, plus her experience as a teacher would have made up for any deficiency had there been any. But there were no deficiencies and we soon built up an excellent working relationship. Meanwhile, I had to take over the reins from the previous Secretary's Staff Officer. The Chief Constable of Thames Valley, (later to become Commissioner of the Metropolitan Police), was the incumbent and was about to assume the Chairmanship of the Committee.

I was despatched to Oxford for two weeks to work with his Staff Officer and get to grips with the job. I soon discovered that it was a most enjoyable role accompanied by harder work than even I had experienced. I was made most welcome in Thames Valley by the Chief and one of his Assistant Chief Constables and I was even given an afternoon out in their helicopter, acting as observer, on a search for a missing elderly man. That in itself was a most interesting experience, particularly as I soon discovered that helicopters on a search pattern do not fly straight and level. They go in lines and when they make the turn at the end of the line it involves a swing from perpendicular to horizontal and back that can quickly unsettle the stomach but I managed to hold onto my lunch and was grateful for the experience.

The Assistant Chief Constable had made me so welcome because he had had the responsibility, under his Chief, for liaison with the Home Office on the implementation of the recommendations of the Phillips Commission on Police and Criminal Evidence. He was pleased to see it passing on because it had got off to a most inauspicious beginning under the Chairmanship of an Assistant Chief Constable from another Force who had retired after making some terrible mistakes and concessions during the progress of the Commission.

I saw immediately that this part of my role was going to be very important and difficult as the recommendations passed into law. I also had to acquire a huge knowledge base of all of the current issues facing the Police Service as a whole and I had to build up a bank of contacts in all Forces at Staff Officer level.

The ACPO has two distinct roles. It acts as a sort of Trade Union for Chief Officers of Assistant Chief level and above and it also acts as a policy making body for the police service. It achieves the latter responsibility by dividing into a series of Committees, such as the Crime Committee, and delegating the responsibility for policy to the Committees, coming together periodically as a General Council to formally approve decisions made by the Committees.

The power they wield is enormous. Far more than that given to the Police Federation that represents all Officers up to Chief Inspector or the Superintendents Association and this is to be expected as the Committees were composed entirely of Chief Constables at that time (Assistant Chiefs are now involved much more).

The Crime Committee was the most prestigious of all of the Committees, dealing with anything requiring a policy decision on matters of a criminal nature. This was far reaching, touching as it did on matters of International crime, Terrorism, Scientific developments and Evidence. On this Committee sat the most powerful of the Chief Constables including the Chiefs of Greater Manchester, Merseyside, West Yorkshire and Avon & Somerset as well as my own Chief and the Chairman (then the Chief of Thames Valley) and several others of only slightly less stature.

The Chairman was the most incredible man. He had a very avuncular style and a level of suave sophistication that set him above the rest although I was later to see the harder side of his character when he mercilessly chastised two of the more unruly Chiefs on the Committee.

The Author with the Producer at the first broadcast of 'Crimewatch UK'. Readers may recognise ex Superintendent David Hatcher who was introduced to the show by Bob Thorogood and presented it for some fifteen years.

The way in which decisions were made on a daily basis was that I would receive correspondence from bodies requiring a decision or opinion, such as the Home Office, Prison Service, Inspectorate of Constabulary or one of the Forces faced with something they had not experienced before. I would then research the issue and draft a reply for my Chief if a policy was already in existence. If there was no existing policy, I would write to all of the members of the Committee and, on receiving their replies, form a consensus decision.

This could be quite tricky, as the opinions given would quite often be at variance. There was a tacit acceptance that one Chief's own view might have to be ignored in favour of the majority and it was very rare that I could not establish a logical response from the replies. In fact, Chief Constables are so busy that they would mostly delegate the preparation of a reply to Staff Officers and therefore would not be terribly offended if their view did not prevail. I have often wondered how far down the ladder the real decisions were being made. Certainly Maurice Buck did not view any of the replies and would usually accept my responses. Thus I was effectively making some quite weighty policy for the Service.

I soon found that the hardest task was to convince Maurice that my grammar was accurate. We would debate the first paragraph of a letter and, if I was not confident that I had used the correct words and punctuation, he would examine every word thereafter and change virtually every line to my enormous chagrin. If however, I could argue with him and win the first paragraph, I could be fairly sure of winning the whole letter. Thus my secretary was a wonderful boon because Maurice, like me, had no formal educational qualifications and I would often cite her MA in support of my cause.

A Sub Committee was formed to deal with the Royal Commission recommendations and to liaise with the Home Office who were just beginning to formulate a new Act of Parliament to encompass all of the recommendations. This was to be known as The Police and Criminal Evidence Bill (PACE) and it would govern all police activity in relation to arrest, detention, stop and search, warrants, custody arrangements and complaints.

The Sub Committee met and appointed me and a Detective Sergeant from Scotland Yard's Policy Department to be the everyday contacts with the Home Office. Effectively, this meant that the Sergeant and I would do all of the donkeywork and my Chief would be involved on a daily basis, only going back to the Sub Committee on really major issues.

Liaison with the Home Office was an unusual experience. Picture the Home Office at Queen Anne's Gate and you conjure up an image of the corridors of power a la 'Yes Minister'. Nothing could be further from the truth. The offices tend to be small and dusty and my main contact shared his with numerous paper aeroplanes and mobiles supplied by his children. He was a little eccentric but with a mind as sharp as anyone I have met. He was located on the fifth floor in a maze of identical offices and was most easily found by tracing the aeroplanes.

I had to meet him at least once a week and quite often twice. This would involve catching the early train from Northampton, taking the underground to St James Park where I would walk to Scotland Yard and meet my colleague before walking back through the station to emerge at the Home Office. I developed quite a local knowledge of the cafes and shops in that area and had an amusing encounter one day when I was suffering badly from a sore throat. A hard day of negotiation made it worse and I went into a small Jewish Chemist's shop opposite New Scotland Yard. I asked him if he had something good for a sore throat. "Certainly Sir," he replied and handed me a razor blade (he was kind enough to replace it with some suitable medication). He then told me the price was £1.50, including the paper bag. I, naturally, was lured into asking him how much without the bag. To which he replied. "£1.50".

The Bill went through numerous versions as various contributions were made and considered and then it began its passage through the stages of Parliament. The first was the Committee stage where a panel of MPs drawn from both sides of the House in the same proportion as the ruling party's majority in the House sit to consider the draft and propose amendments.

They sit within the Houses of Parliament and my colleague and I, together with the Home Office representatives had to attend each meeting to advise MPs as and when required. Needless to say, we soon built up a close relationship with some of the MPs, particularly on the Conservative side. Some famous names were involved in this group including Robert Kilroy-Silk (TV's Kilroy), Leon Brittain, Douglas Hurd, Gerald Bermingham, Gerald Kaufman and many more.

A pattern emerged of Conservative MPs coming to the meetings poorly prepared but confident in the huge majority they enjoyed in those days. The Labour side, in contrast came prepared with detailed briefs prepared for them overnight by various left wing or liberal groups.

Mr Bermingham, a lawyer, would begin the assault on the Government position whilst Mr Kilroy-Silk, a barrister, would prepare the next stage of the attack. They would then defer to Mr Kaufman (the Shadow Home Secretary) who would invariably deliver a well-reasoned argument for rejecting whatever proposal had been put forward in the Bill. This would promptly be rejected on a vote because of the Conservative majority.

The drafting stage would then continue and the Bill went through at least eight versions during its passage through the Committee Stage. Each time a new version was issued, I had to read all 130 plus clauses in detail to see what Machiavellian schemes our friends at the Home Office had slipped in to cripple the police even more (our view at the time and probably totally unjustified).

This was a massive task and was guaranteed to occupy me for a whole weekend each time a new version arrived. We were also preparing a set of Codes of Practice to accompany the Bill and these were more detailed even than the Bill. These too had to be written, amended and debated by the Committee of the House and I found that I was now spending 80% of my time travelling to London and working on the Bill. Maurice Buck was very supportive and when any tricky negotiations were to be held, he would always make the time to accompany me and he had a good grasp of the issues involved.

It was a treat for me when he did go with me because we would go in the chauffeur driven staff car and park in the Home Office car park. We would even occasionally lunch in the Senior Officers' Mess at Scotland Yard, although I would always have to pay and recover my outlay later because Maurice Buck did not carry money.

When I had first taken on this job, I had been told that Maurice always took a mountain of work in the car with him and I had been very worried because I cannot read more than ten words in a car without feeling sick. On our first trip together, we got into the car and he told me to sit in the back with him. I promptly told him I hoped he had not made a mistake in appointing me because I was likely to embarrass myself if he tried to force me to read in the car. "What bloody use are you to me if you can't read in a car? Who ever heard of a Staff Officer who can't work in a car?" he said. Then he opened his newspaper and read it thoroughly in between listening to news broadcasts on the radio. The briefcase was untouched.

On the return journey, we listened to a play on Radio Four until he fell asleep and keeled over with his head on my shoulder. Again the briefcase was untouched. This became the standard itinerary on our trips together and I became very used to having my Chief asleep on my shoulder. I never found out if he had deferred to my disability, or whether the truth was that he never worked in the car anyway, but I suspect the latter.

The other point of interest on these journeys was the level of discussion between him and his driver, a constable of many years experience. Particularly in London where Maurice had worked for many years, they would fight like cats and dogs about the best route to wherever we were going. It was the driver's job to know the route and he usually did but Maurice would always 'know' a better way and would berate the poor driver until we were hopelessly lost.

Theirs was a strange relationship. Maurice Buck always liked to make an impression with his silver hair, silver grey overcoat, flopping pocket handkerchief and large cigar so, not surprisingly, he always wanted to be driven to the steps of wherever he was going to make a grand entrance. He was most put out, therefore, when we arrived at the House of Commons, when the driver stopped some 200 yards short and told us that he was dropping us there because it would be easier for him to park. I was amazed that the driver kept his job but that was the nature of their relationship.

Maurice was always quick to spot trouble on the horizon and he had evasive tactics ready should anything go amiss on his car journeys. One day, when I was not going with him, he left Headquarters well before 8am to go to London. He had been gone for about half an hour when I received a phone call from the president of ACPO, The Chief Constable of Lincolnshire. He asked me where my Chief was and when I told him, he clearly did not believe me. He said I was very loyal as my Chief was obviously having a lie in and would not accept my repeated reassurances that Maurice Buck always started work before 8am and really was on his way to London. "When he does eventually get in, tell him to call me," he said.

He added that it was urgent before putting the phone down on me. I thought that I had better try to contact the Chief and, as this was long before mobile phones became de rigueur, I decided I would have to try the forlorn hope that he would have switched on the car radio. I contacted the Control Room Inspector and asked him to try to pass the message to the Chief to ring the President as soon as possible.

As this was all I could do until he reached his destination, I promptly put it to the back of my mind. What I did not realise was that the Control Room Inspector was a man of initiative. Had I known that, I would certainly have dissuaded him from the action he took.

Having failed to raise the Chief on the radio, he contacted all of the Forces between Northampton and London i.e. Thames Valley, Bedfordshire, Hertfordshire and the Met, and asked them to ask their patrols to keep an eye for our Staff Car and if they saw it, to stop it and pass the message on. I would not have condoned this because I knew that, secretly, Maurice Buck did not discourage his driver from exceeding the speed limit if he was in a hurry.

Sure enough, the driver saw the blue lights in his mirror as they passed through Hertfordshire and, over his shoulder, said to Maurice, " Sorry Sir, I think we're being stopped for speeding." As quick as a flash, Maurice replied, " Eh, eh, Oh what did you say, I was fast asleep," making it quite clear that the responsibility would lie with the driver. It transpired that the passing of an important operational message from the President of ACPO was the only thing on the minds of the Traffic Officers but neither the Control Room Inspector nor I would be allowed to forget it quickly.

Maurice Buck, as can be seen, was not always the easiest person to work for and I have a vivid memory when his ambivalent view of the breach of some rules was to annoy me immensely.

By then, the second Staff Officer had changed and Peter Barclay, a very close friend of mine to this day, had taken on the 'domestic' Staff role. A very intelligent and articulate man, this officer was located two offices away from me and, like me, always had to make an early start.

One morning, when Maurice Buck arrived at Headquarters in the Staff car, a member of the Civilian Support Staff was caught by him, going out of the Headquarters car park via the 'No Exit' entrance. Maurice promptly ripped into this poor man, who was actually just unlucky to be caught doing something most of us did when not being observed. That could and should have been the end of the matter but Maurice was incensed and came into my office. "Tell me," he said, "When you leave the car park, which way out do you go?"

"By the exit, of course," I replied.

Maurice said, "Now, I have always told you that you must tell me the truth if I ask you something. I've got to be able to rely on that."

Wishing I did not have to and moderately confident that I could get away with it if I tried, I decided I had better tell the truth. "Well, sometimes, if it is late and there is no-one else around, I do occasionally go out the wrong way." I foolishly replied.

"Why do you do that?" said Maurice gently.

Thinking on my feet, I replied, "Well, I had not previously thought about it but the exit is nearer the way in to Headquarters and it would be more logical to have the exit where the entrance is to avoid vehicles crossing over but I suppose it was also a bit of laziness on my part."

"So what have you done about having it changed," he continued patiently as the hole I was digging got bigger and bigger."

"I've done nothing about it because I didn't even think about it until you just raised it," I defended myself. He instantly tore my head off, ripped me into shreds and left me lying, bleeding on the carpet. For more than fifteen minutes he continued his tirade against me. "You want me to make you a Superintendent. How could I put you in charge of 150 men when you see a sign that says 'No Exit' and you just ignore it? Do you think you can just break the rules because you work for me?" and so he continued.

I thought it best not to mention that I did not have to admit anything and he would not have known about my transgression, nor did I feel it was the moment to mention his speeding escapades so eventually he got tired of me and went looking for new prey.

He found Peter Barclay in his office and as he began the patient build up questions as he had with me, I hovered in the background, making negative motions to my colleague when he was asked if he ever broke the 'No Exit' rule. Unfortunately, Peter did not see my signals and confidently explained that, yes, he did break the rule sometimes.

The tirade took the same pattern as mine had with one exception. In the course of this ranting, Maurice Buck told Peter that, of course, if he had an accident going through the wrong exit, he would not be covered by his insurance. At this, my colleague with more courage than I could have mustered, reminded Maurice that he was a Law Graduate and yes, he would be covered by insurance in such circumstances. This was not the answer that Maurice was looking for and he managed to extend the telling off well beyond the fifteen minutes I had endured – and believe me, it takes some doing to find enough expletives and different ways of explaining a fault to make it last that long.

Eventually, Maurice tired and we were both able to return to our work and lick our wounds but it did not end there. For three days, every encounter either of us had with Maurice would leave us tongue lashed and reminded that neither of us was fit to hold the rank we held, never mind promotion. The member of the Support Staff who was the only one who had actually been caught out had, of course, been long forgotten in all this.

We both reached a point where our patience was exhausted and the injustice was becoming intolerable when, late one evening, Maurice called us both into his office. "How's it going lads?" he asked and, not trusting this affable new mood, neither of us answered. "Look, I hope you're not sulking, if you couldn't take a joke, you shouldn't have joined" he laughed. And we were forgiven. But even now, when I have been retired for several years and there have been three Chief Constables since Maurice Buck, I cannot bring myself to leave that car park by the 'No Exit', which still has not been changed. Nor indeed, can Peter Barclay, who also retired as a Chief Superintendent.

However, if support was needed, Maurice Buck could be relied upon totally. Whenever I had a difficult meeting at the Home Office, he would be there and I have to say that we made a formidable team in our negotiations, even if some other Chief Constables did not realise how hard we were going in to bat for them.

The Bill had passed from the House of Commons Committee to the House of Lords Committee, which actually consists of the whole House and I was now sitting in that illustrious setting twice each week.

One day, when I did not have to attend, I received a telephone call. My secretary put the female caller through with the whispered warning, "It's Baroness …"

"Hello Ma'am, how can I help you?" I said. "Oh Hello, Chief Inspector, I want you to do me a small favour" she said. "I want you to tell me all you know about unfairly obtained evidence."

This was not as daunting a prospect as one might imagine because the Bill was just going through the clauses dealing with those issues and I had fully researched the stated cases. I began to explain the law to her. "Oh do stop, do stop. What I would really like you to do is jump in your car, pop down to London immediately and just chat it all through with my friend Lord Scarman".

Lord Scarman was one of the most senior Law Lords and was famous for his enquiry into the riots of 1981. His reputation was enormous and any police officer could be forgiven for being slightly intimidated but I was not about to let that show. "Of course Ma'am, I can be there in two hours" I said. Then I thought about the implications and went to tell Maurice Buck.

I had barely related the content of the conversation when he said, "I had better come with you". And the driver was rounded up to take us straight to London. I briefed Maurice on the way and soon after we were being welcomed by the very tall, impressive Lord Scarman, who took us into his office and poured us a coffee.

For the next hour and a half, we had a most robust debate, with me referring to an Australian case involving a murderer who had made a confession during the time he was transported from one province to another. This had been held to be an interview not under caution and therefore improperly obtained evidence. On appeal it had been accepted that the evidence was improperly obtained but that in the interests of justice, it was admitted.

Lord Scarman was proposing an amendment to the Bill that would automatically exclude any evidence obtained improperly and he had already laid his amendment in the House Library to be debated the following day. We were, therefore, most surprised when, at the end of one and a half hours, Lord Scarman thanked us profusely for our time and said that, if we wouldn't mind, could we just pop in to see The Attorney General and tell him that Lord Scarman had been convinced by the two police officers and, if an alternative amendment was proposed, Lord Scarman would accept the alternative, provided it incorporated the views of the police officers.

I was so glad to have had Maurice Buck there for his support and his preparedness to deal with anyone of whatever stature. It would be no exaggeration to say that we both walked out of the House three feet off the ground with elation. We tried to 'pop in to see The Attorney General' without much success but we did manage to send a message via the Home Office and received his thanks before we set off for home.

The next day, I was even more glad that Maurice had been there. I went to sit through the debate and had managed to get a seat for Jackie to join me. The two alternative amendments were put to the House and I was totally amazed when Lord Scarman used every argument we had put to him the previous day in support of his own amendment. I could not believe my ears.

There was a very substantial debate with a major supporter for The Attorney General (and us) in the shape of the formidable Lord Denning, who, despite his advancing years was as sharp as ever and told one of his captivating stories to illustrate why evidence might be tainted but still should be heard by a Jury. He warned of the American position and counselled against allowing our law to create some of the nonsense that exists in their law. I thought his intimate style in relating conversations he had held with the top American Judges, about the anomalies they had faced, might just win the day. Certainly the Attorney General, because he had been briefed that he would not need to do so, was in no position to combat the power of Lord Scarman.

Lord Scarman won the vote easily and his amendment was inserted into the Bill. As he left the Chamber, I managed to position myself where he could not fail to see me as he left and I was disappointed that such an eminent person as Lord Scarman could not look me in the face. He certainly saw me and cast his eyes to the floor. I dread to think what Maurice Buck would have thought if he had not been there in person for the session with Lord Scarman the day before.

Some months later, there was to be a sequel and although I cannot confirm the truth of this, I was told that a certain 'Iron Lady', ensured the amendment was overturned in favour of the Attorney General's version when the Bill returned to the Commons. It is that version that now appears in the Act.

Chapter 22

Another very notable memory arose from the drafting of the Codes Of Practice. My Sergeant colleague from the Met. and I had spent a very difficult and trying day at the Home Office arguing the merits of the case to exclude a solicitor from a police interview in exceptional circumstances.

The Home Office had been subjected to intense pressure from the Law Society (who are of course disproportionately represented in Parliament) to include a provision in the Codes that made it impossible for a Solicitor to be excluded from an interview, even if the police believed him to be dishonest and in league with the suspects. Presumably, this was on the basis that *all* solicitors are honest. Obviously, not all are honest, although, equally obviously, the vast majority are and their integrity is beyond challenge. Many police officers would strongly argue that there are dishonest lawyers who are prepared to break the law for their clients.

After an all-day session, we were all tired and irritable at 8.30pm when we broke up. As we did so, the leader of the Home Office team said to us, "I've had enough of this particular point. If you can come back here at 8.30am tomorrow with a sensible draft, I will accept it."

As we walked back through the Underground station, my colleague said, "There's no way we can do that now, it's much too late and we've got to get home, rest and get back for 8.30. That will be hard enough without us trying to come up with a form of words." I told him that I had an hour on the train to Northampton and an hour back the next morning so I would write out something and check it in the morning if he could get a typist into Scotland Yard early enough to present a neat typed version at 8.30am. That was exactly what happened. My first draft on the way home set out the principles and it was refined the next morning and typed up in time for us to walk into the Home Office dead on 8.30am and present a new version, which was accepted and appeared verbatim in the Codes when finally approved by Parliament.

It provided for an Inspector to have the authority to exclude a Solicitor if he reasonably believed that the solicitor was disrupting the interview or acting dishonestly. The suspect would then have to be allowed to select a different solicitor and a Superintendent would then have to consider the facts of the exclusion and consider reporting the matter to the Law Society.

I think it is a matter of regret that court decisions after the Act became Law contrived to change the will of Parliament and the provision did not survive into the second version of the Codes when they were amended some years later. I always refer to the provision as my 'fag packet code' because it felt like it was, figuratively speaking, drafted 'on the back of a fag packet'.

Finally, we reached the end of the drafting and all that was left for us to do was to have one final reading and to agree the version that would be approved by Parliament to become Law. To achieve this final reading, a pair of houses at Ryton-on-Dunsmore Police Training Centre (where I had undertaken my initial training many years before) was rented for three days and the full team of Home Office draftsmen met my colleague and me to go through each clause of the Bill and each sentence of the Codes of Practice. This was an exhausting task and took up the whole of the three days, working late into the night.

At last it was done and the Bill became the Police and Criminal Evidence Act 1984, coming into force on 1st January 1986. But there was much work to be done before it came into force.

Maurice Buck told every Chief Constable that if they wanted to know anything about the Bill, they should contact me at any time and, as every Force set up their own version of an implementation group, my telephone was red hot. Not all callers were friendly, far from it. Many of the older breed of detectives thought that it spelled the death knell for policing. They had been used to the looser 'Judges Rules' controlling police behaviour and could not get round to the idea of planned interviews, the presence of solicitors and the dreaded Custody Officer (a Sergeant at every 'Designated' Police Station) who had a direct line to the Superintendent if he was in disagreement with a more senior officer about custody issues).

We never claimed that PACE was a panacea for policing. In fact it was less than perfect from the point of view of any police officer with its emphasis on the safeguards for the suspect, but we were satisfied that we had achieved the very best possible outcome with the provisions, in the light of the recommendations of the Royal Commission, which were far more stringent than those that finally appeared in the Act. In fact, earlier Chief Officers had made our task very difficult by telling the Home Office what they thought they wanted to hear, and not what really existed.

Examples were the concept that every Police Station already had 'Station Sergeants' who fulfilled the role of Custody Officers. When we tried to explain to Home Office officials that there would be a need for hundreds more Sergeants throughout the country, we were simply not believed, because the Met already had Station Sergeants, though few, if any, other Forces had them.

Chief Officers had been asked how control was exercised over the rights of detained persons and who filled in the records of custody. They had not known and had said that it was the Station Sergeant when, in fact, no-one really checked on prisoners rights other than Courts when any doubts were raised, and the records, allegedly completed at the time, were truthfully, often completed in the quiet hours of the night after the prisoner was released.

What the Act did was to force the police to act more ethically, and they (or some of them) did not like it. Many members of the public might say that they think prisoners have too many rights, but my experience is that such a view only holds until it is a close relative who is detained, and then that member of the public wants to ensure that every possible right is upheld.

I had been told by the Staff Officer to the President of ACPO that the President had asked Maurice Buck how he intended to reward me for my efforts and that Maurice had replied that he had not yet decided whether to put me forward for some honour or whether to promote me two ranks. I had dismissed this as rumour mongering but it was impossible not to live in some kind of hope that I would be acknowledged in some way. I felt that my Met colleague deserved something because he had been involved in the Bill far longer than I, and could not be promoted because he could not, for some odd reason, pass the Inspector's examination. He was subsequently awarded the British Empire Medal in the next New Years Honours List and I was a little disappointed that I was simply waiting to see if I could sit the next year's promotion board to Superintendent. In fact, I was successful at that board and I suppose I should be grateful, as I did not think I had performed very well at the interview.

Chapter 23

In June 1984, I was appointed Superintendent Personnel and Training. This was, of course, a Headquarters post and I was selected for it because it kept me available to advise other Forces on the impending legislation (to be undertaken as a sideline whilst I learned my new job and new rank).

I had made it known that I wanted an outside operational post and for this rash claim, I was allowed to take charge of the policing of Silverstone village for the weekend of the British Motor Cycle Grand Prix. This was less than two months into my new role and I had little preparation for such an onerous task.

The Motor Cycle Grand Prix was an annual nightmare for Northamptonshire Police. Thousands and thousands of motor cycle enthusiasts, many of whom were of the 'Rocker' or 'Hells Angels' fraternities, would descend on this tiny village on the A34, which is a main holiday route to the south, just at the time when families were heading that way for summer holidays.

Favourite pastimes for the rowdier elements were making 'doughnuts' (braking the front wheel of the bike and revving up to make the bike spin through 360 degrees, burning the shape of a doughnut onto the road surface – (and wearing the tyre out very quickly), pulling a 'wheelie' with a naked girl on the back or standing outside the village's only pub on the main road and stopping holidaymakers cars. Thereafter, if the car had a sunroof, beer would be poured over the occupants and if they objected, the car would be lifted bodily, with the motorist inside, and turned to face the other way.

All this is good innocent fun for a Hells Angel but not much fun if you are a law abiding resident or motorist. The job of the police was to try to control this over the whole of race weekend, at Silverstone village, Towcester village, and the racetrack, where there was also a campsite.

The campsite is in Thames Valley so the whole affair was always a joint operation and I knew that previous years had seen some frightening scenes, one of which involved a Thames Valley Superintendent having his car burnt out. It was with some trepidation that I took command of the Police Support Units (PSUs). These are groups of police officers consisting, then, of one Inspector, two Sergeants and eighteen Constables – since changed in numbers and composition. I had four PSUs although there was a total of 17 PSUs deployed in the whole operation.

I was assisted by the local Chief Inspector whom I knew to be a robust and very experienced leader with an excellent local knowledge and previous outings with the race weekend. We agreed that we would have a fallback plan if we could not keep the drunken motorcyclists off the main road. We would divert all traffic through tiny villages and lanes until we could get the revellers all back to the campsite and I deployed one PSU at 7pm on the Friday to ensure the safe passage of the holidaymakers.

All went well – for about 30 minutes – and then the crowd became too big for the PSU to hold back and I had to deploy the remaining three PSUs. Then a bus driver panicked and his bus was in a slight collision with one of the officers. No injuries were caused but I decided to divert all traffic. This was fine until the rowdy elements realised that there was no traffic coming and therefore no sport to be had. They then began to get angry and difficult and began throwing beer glasses and cans through the windows of the pub. We had not been able to persuade the innkeeper to close voluntarily because this weekend normally provided his best income all year but I was advised by the Chief Inspector that the time had come to close the pub, a decision I had been thinking was perhaps due.

I took a group of officers with me into the crowded bar and told the innkeeper that he was to close immediately and he did so. This turned the wrath of the whole crowd onto me and as we retreated from the bar, missiles began to fly. Amazingly quickly, we had gone from a rowdy but happy crowd to a baying mob of at least 5000, all out for my blood. A gap opened between the lines of police and the crowd but, at the front, I became the main target without even a helmet to protect me (Superintendents wear flat caps). A Sergeant, who is well known for his martial arts skills and strength, suggested that he and I could go behind the line of rioters and might still calm them down. I am not a coward but I am not stupid either and I decided that it was time to deploy officers in riot gear for the first time ever in Northamptonshire.

My request was agreed in seconds by the Assistant Chief Constable but it is easier to decide than to deploy and we had to wait at least 30 minutes under fire from bricks, cans and notably a set of darts, one of which hit me but luckily failed to penetrate my uniform, before the units were kitted up and ready to march. Finally the units were ready, behind the lines of unprotected officers and I told them to advance in two lines across the whole road. The first line was to push the crowd up the hill towards the racetrack, where they would be steered to the campsite by a group from Thames Valley. My second line would be ten yards behind and if any of the crowd sat down in the road, the first line would march over them and the second line would make arrests. The tactic worked and we pushed 5000 people where they did not want to go for about one and a half miles.

At the campsite they then began to throw petrol bombs and that is very scary though there is less risk than it looks provided you go forward quickly enough to avoid catching fire. I will confess to a moment, about four hours into this situation and in a quiet moment, when I just wanted it all to go away and I knew what it must feel like to be in a battle. But it doesn't go away and on this night it lasted until 2am, by which time we were all exhausted and had no more than about 15 prisoners to show for it. Luckily. the next night and race day all went with few problems but I came away with the dubious honours of having had darts thrown at me, being petrol bombed and being the first Superintendent to deploy a riot squad for real in the County. I still have one of the darts to this day.

Perhaps the Chief did not feel able to let me loose on Silverstone village the next year because I was deployed to Towcester for what was supposed to be the quieter of the two villages. Just my luck to find that the motorcyclists had decided to make that the main venue for their pre-race frolics. Towcester is the junction of the A43 and A5 main routes and on the Friday night before race weekend I found several thousand half drunk revellers, many of whom had just come to watch the fun as motorcyclists pulled 'wheelies' on the A5 with naked ladies on the pillion or drew 'doughnuts' on the road with their tyres. It sounds a little amusing from a distance of many years but on the night it was potentially a disaster. If a motorcycle had gone out of control in that crowd there would have been many deaths.

I set the objective that we would breathalyse as many of the participants as we could but this needed a little cunning on our part because we could have caused a riot if we had done that in the crowd. The trick I adopted was to wait for the moment when a motorcyclist had just completed his 'doughnut' and was accepting the plaudits of the crowd and then I would step in and take his ignition keys, whisper in his ear that he could push his bike up a side street to get his keys back and then I walked smartly away before anyone else knew what was happening. When the biker came for his keys he would be breathalysed and reported or arrested for dangerous driving.

My only problem with this tactic was that I could not expect anyone else to take on the dangerous job of taking the keys so I had to do that myself. I was particularly grateful to a sergeant from Warwickshire (helping us on mutual aid arrangements) who took it on himself to watch my back and arrested one man, as he was about to hit me on the head with a bottle. Dangerous it undoubtedly was, but it worked because the attraction of being the centre of attention soon paled when they discovered that friends were disappearing soon after pulling such stunts and the night's festivities were over in quite a short time.

The Chief Constable must have thought I liked that 'action' type of role (as I actually did) because on December 20th 1985, he transferred me to Operations Dept, in charge of Firearms, Dogs, Underwater Search, Air Support, Support Groups and Planning.

I have always enjoyed a challenge but when I commenced the job on 20th December and the Chief told me that I had five days to place on his desk, the Force Major Incident Planning book, which my predecessor (who had been promoted) had been working on for three years, I did baulk at that particular test. The discerning reader will have noted that five days after the 20th December is a significant date and as the book had barely been started I thought it a little unfair to expect me to place it on his desk on Christmas day.

I cannot be sure if that was the cause of me falling out of favour with the Chief but I certainly felt somewhat ostracised from then on. It may also have been connected with the fact that virtually my whole Firearms Team were suspended from carrying firearms because of an incident that had occurred before my arrival.

I was also faced with the problems of their low morale because of the investigation into the incident. It related to some violence at a football match and they were accused of reacting with too much force. Firearms were not involved in the incident in any way but they were suspended because of the fear that, if they did have to shoot someone at a time when they were under investigation, the Force would be heavily criticised. The logic could not be faulted but the morale issue was very serious.

This issue was to blight the whole of my time with the Operations Department. I was battling with the combined problems of low morale, a Chief Superintendent who, though a good and true friend was probably more out of his depth with this department than any of us, a new Chief Inspector who thought he was 'Action Man', always dressing up in the coveralls favoured by Firearms Teams or Police Support Units on an operation and not wanting to spend any time on his office duties and, perhaps worst of all, an Assistant Chief Constable who disliked me and went out of his way to make my life uncomfortable.

I found myself trying to cope with most of the policy issues of the department, which also seemed to land on my desk and this was a very uncomfortable part of my career.

It was something of a surprise to me that I was asked to lead another major ground search but I was still the only Senior Officer with experience of managing that type of search.

This time, the search was in connection with the disappearance of a little girl at Corby. The little girl had left home on a winter morning to walk to school alone. It was not a long walk but surprising, that a child of that age should have been left to walk it alone. It was not until she failed to arrive home at 4pm that her parents knew she was missing. Obviously the school had thought she was off for the day.

Police Officers get a feeling about some of these cases and we certainly did not think she had gone off of her own will. We treated it as a case of Abduction and feared Murder from the start.

My role was to organise the search of every piece of open ground within the town. Corby had been designed as a New Town with lots of these open spaces and I realised from the outset that it was going to be a thankless task.

I was allocated fifty Officers and we set about our daunting task in the dark, knowing that we could not afford to wait for morning in case she was alive and out in the cold. The darkness was not complete because there had been a sprinkling of snow and we were able to cover some of the parkland quite well.

Unfortunately, by 2am, we were exhausted and I had to call a halt until morning. Well-meaning members of the public who, having heard about the incident, were determined to help, had hampered us. Some of these were quite aggressive when I called my men in and I had to explain to them that it would not help if exhausted searchers missed some vital clue.

A search of this kind must be detailed if it is worth doing but in this case, there was too much open ground for a 'hands and knees' search but it had to be done shoulder to shoulder.

I persuaded the volunteers to return at 9am and we all managed a few hours rest (except me who had to spend most of the night planning the next day's search). The Saturday passed in a blur as we continued to cover an ever-expanding area with no positive results. Concentrated CID enquiries were no more successful and our fears were growing deeper with every passing hour.

During that day, more and more members of the public were joining in of their own volition, sometimes covering areas we had already covered in more detail than they could hope to achieve and other times walking areas we had yet to reach and risking damaging any evidence there might be. Finally, towards the end of the day, I went on local radio to appeal to the public not to search haphazardly but if they felt they must help us, to meet at the Town Boating Lake at 10am the next day, where they would be given instructions.

With still no sightings of the little girl and no leads for the CID to follow, I sent my team home for the night and planned out the next day's searches, by now expanding beyond the limits of the town. I went to the Boating Lake to organise any volunteers and soon found that I had some urgent reorganising to do. A crowd of at least 1000 volunteers greeted me. The only hope I had of organising such an army was to ask them to split up into groups of twenty and to allocate an officer to each group. This officer had a radio and could therefore be directed from my Control Post. The officers then had the unenviable job of keeping their groups in order but it worked extremely well and by lunch time, we had covered all of the main areas, including the fields all around the outskirts of the town.

It was not a well-recognised fact at that time but a helicopter can cover open areas like that far more effectively than can an army of ground based searchers. We had borrowed a helicopter from Thames Valley Police and I went in it to satisfy myself that we had covered all areas. In the hour that I was in it, we covered again every inch that had been covered on foot. At a height of fifty feet we could see clearly anything on the ground and if there were places we could not see into we could direct ground searchers to check them out. We had effectively covered all of the possible places in the open air twice and still there was no trace of the child.

I thanked the volunteers and explained to them that my fifty officers would now be deployed in a different way to cover garages and sheds where volunteers could not be used. I must confess that I was overwhelmed by the willingness of the volunteers and the nature of community within Corby.

On the Monday and Tuesday, my team continued with our very demanding searches and we were all becoming emotionally drained, particularly those Officers with children of their own. During the afternoon of the Tuesday, I was told to recall all of my men to the hall being used as an incident room to be addressed by the Assistant Chief Constable. We all tiredly trooped into the room, grabbing a coffee as we went, and there we found that all of the team of well over 100 officers including the CID and Enquiry Teams were gathered.

The Assistant Chief Constable stood to address us and in solemn tones told us that the body of a small girl had been found, wrapped in a carpet, in the roof of a house in the town. That was probably the most difficult and emotional moment of my career and I looked around to see that I was in good company because, like me, every officer present was crying.

We then learned that a Uniformed Constable, assigned to the Enquiry Teams, had found himself with an hour free and decided to try to execute a couple of arrest warrants for non payment of fines he had previously been given. He went to one house and although there was no answer, he was sure there was someone in. He persisted and finally, somehow managed to get in the house where he found his quarry who had just cut his wrists in an attempted suicide.

The officer thought that was a bit drastic in response to an arrest warrant and began to ask questions. It was not long before the man admitted that he had been at his own house (he was arrested at a girlfriend's house) on the Friday before and he had grabbed the little girl on her way to school, dragged her into his house, assaulted her and murdered her before putting her body into the loft.

There was enormous anger in the town when the news was released and the officers who had spent so many hours searching were suddenly cast into the role of protecting the prisoner from an angry mob who gathered outside the Police Station when he appeared at Court. He subsequently pleaded 'Guilty' to Murder and was sent to prison for life.

One of the reasons the ACC disliked me (I believe) arose because he had been one of two internal candidates for the post and the other internal candidate was a far more personable man whose professionalism was beyond doubt. When the appointment was made, the Chief Constable had called me in to his office (as one of his staff officers) and asked me what I thought the Force in general would think to the appointment.

True to the instructions he had always given me, I answered honestly that I thought the Force would be truly disappointed that the job had not gone to the other internal candidate. I have reason to believe that the Chief Constable promptly told the new ACC what I had said and I was very disappointed that he had left me so exposed. Soon after that he announced his retirement and a new Chief Constable was appointed. I was very pleased that it was a man I respected who had, at some time before been our ACC, been the successful candidate.

Bad things, like good ones all come to an end and after about eighteen months, the Deputy Chief Constable sent for me and asked me if I would be prepared to go to Corby as the Sub Divisional Commander on a temporary basis.

The Author on his first day as the Sub Divisional Commander at Corby 1987

The Sub Division had gone through a very unsettled time for many months following the transfer of the previous permanent incumbent. There had been two temporary Commanders who had combined to bring the morale of the Sub Division to its knees.

In the weeks before my arrival an incident had occurred involving the use of firearms and the last temporary Commander had, in the opinion of most of the local officers, put police officers lives at risk rather than approach the ACC for permission to deploy firearms. I must confess that, based upon the experience I had gained in Operations Department and the accounts related to me, I tended to agree with them.

I resolved in my mind that I was not going to be another temporary Commander; I was going to take the role on permanently. Just before my start date, I was invited by the temporary Commander to attend his management meeting. During the meeting, an issue arose that I felt required a decision and my predecessor began to prevaricate, probably because he knew he would not be there to see the matter through. Even though I was only there as an invited observer, I stepped in (rather theatrically I thought) and said, "No, we shall not leave that decision until another day, this is what we shall do...." And I gave an unequivocal decision. There was a shocked silence but no argument and I knew I had set the pace for the future, which was exactly what I intended to do.

On the Sunday before I was due to start work, Jackie and I went to the office to put my own 'stamp' on it and clear out old rubbish. On the stairs I encountered a young female officer who, not knowing who I was, greeted me with a friendly, "Hello". Still realizing that the station needed to be pulled up by its bootstraps, I stopped her and said, "Hello, it's nice to meet you but the next time you meet me, I expect to be addressed as 'Sir'". That may sound harsh but I knew that the morale had sunk so low that officers were whispering in corners and had stopped addressing senior officers in a respectful way and I was determined to change things around.

I immediately called a meeting of the Management Team and was staggered to find that only six members attended (the team consisted of about fifteen). They had apparently become used to attending only if it was convenient. Ten minutes after the scheduled start time, when it was apparent that no one else was coming, I announced that the meeting was adjourned for three days and I had memos sent to every member of the team, telling them that, henceforth, Management meetings would be a duty commitment and their presence was required no matter whether they were on rest day, night duty and the only exception would be annual leave. The memo also advised them of the rearranged meeting and the fact that failure to attend would result in disciplinary procedures.

It was no surprise that we achieved 100% attendance for the first time in years. I told them that there was only one issue on the agenda and that was how business would be conducted in future. I said that I would allow as much open debate as was necessary on any issue but at the end of the debate I would take final decisions and responsibility. I told them that I was prepared for anyone to express any views they held but at the end of debate, we would all abide by whatever decision was made, as it was a team decision.

Finally I dropped a bombshell. I said that I expected everyone to stand if I walked into a room and they were to ensure that it happened. Also if I met officers on the street, the senior officer present would salute. In fact this was no more than the Force discipline required, but they had grown so used to ignoring the protocol that they were shocked and expressed doubts about whether they could make it happen.

I made it very clear that it would happen and I explained that in my view, it was necessary because, if I was to lead the station from the front, I had to know that if I gave an order on the street to jump, the only question would relate to how high and not if. This style is far from my natural demeanour and I certainly felt that I was acting a part as I said it but I truly felt that it was totally necessary if we were to turn the Sub Division into a successful crime fighting force. I also resolved that I would go out on patrol at least once or twice per month at night and make sure I knew what the problems were at first hand.

I stuck to these principles throughout my time at Corby and they stood me in good stead. In fact there was no difficulty in getting officers to stand when I walked into briefings and they soon got to like the idea of me going out on patrol with them when they found that I meant it when I told them to behave exactly as they would if I was not there – including tea breaks etc. In fact I was critical if they did not know where to get a 'cuppa' at 2am because I felt they should know who was at work at that time and they could gain more intelligence than they could by just patrolling aimlessly.

I even agreed to them going into the back of McDonalds for a bag of chips in the late evening because the drunks soon realised that the police got there very quickly if there was trouble. I was also lucky in that I got involved in a number of fights and violent arrests which endeared me to the staff.

One of the first contacts I made on my return to the town was with the Police Surgeon. He was a GP (my own doctor) and a friend since he had come to the town at the beginning of the 1970's. We had shared some difficult court cases when I was a young detective and again when I was the Detective Inspector and I trusted him implicitly. I was also aware that he could give the appearance of being drunk when he was overtired, and he frequently was overtired because of his devotion to police work and his willingness to be called out at any time of the night even though he may have worked all day. Because of this, he was completely teetotal and would only ever drink 'Irnbru' (a soft drink similar to 'coca cola').

I felt that he was very important to me in running the Sub Division because he was so well known and respected by all of the staff, who he would often help in many unofficial ways. As a result of my desire to have him work closely with me, I had a long talk with him during the first week I was there and we parted with a clear expression of how we could improve morale etc.

I was therefore staggered when I arrived at work to find a letter from him on my desk. In it he tendered his resignation for personal reasons. I immediately hit the roof and rang him in his surgery.
"What the hell do you think you're playing at?" I said when I was put through to him. "Do you mean you don't know?" he replied, "Well you better come to the surgery and I'll tell you all about it."

Still fuming, I drove to his surgery at the end of the morning practice. When I sat down he explained that he had received a visit the previous night from two Superintendents from the same Division but not the same Sub Division. They had come with a message from the ACC and the message was that they knew he was an alcoholic and that his behaviour was such that the only thing he could do was to resign if he wanted to avoid being dismissed. He had told them that he did not drink at all and they accused him of misusing drugs because, they told him, they had evidence that he was often unfit for work and one of them had the temerity to quote an instance when he had been on a sea trip on the doctor's boat when he had begun behaving oddly.

The doctor had declined to defend himself and had reluctantly agreed to resign, though even before morning he was beginning to regret having caved in so easily and was considering what legal action he could take. I am not a man who is given to displays of anger easily but I made an exception on this occasion! How dare two of my colleagues come onto my patch and start taking actions that affected the way I ran the Sub Division? What on earth could have possessed them to think they could walk all over my command in this way and why had they been so presumptuous without even getting the facts checked first with me. I believe they thought they knew him better than I did but they clearly did not.

And then I started to think about the ACC who had supposedly sent them. Frankly I did not believe it to begin with but then I started to wonder if he had some Machiavellian scheme to get rid of the doctor and undermine me at the same time. Surely not? But how odd that it should happen in my first week at the Sub Division.

I asked the doctor if he really did wish to leave the job in which he had been so happy for so long. Of course he did not. I therefore handed him the letter of resignation and invited him to tear it up in my presence. He was quite touched because he had thought I was in on the plot to get rid of him – I could not imagine why he would think that and I reproached him for thinking it.

How then to unravel the plot? I had some powerful enemies to deal with and did not feel that I had many allies who could support me but I did feel confident that our Divisional Chief Superintendent was friendly towards me and would not have condoned the actions taken. I rang him as soon as possible and revealed the whole story to him, asking him what advice he could offer. He soon convinced me that he knew nothing about it and he was absolutely outraged that two of his Superintendents should have taken this action without telling him first, particularly as the orders had come from the ACC without going through him.

The Chief Superintendent promptly rang the Chief Constable who was also apparently unaware of what had been done. The risk to the Force of legal action was one that obviously did concern the Chief directly and I understand that he was not slow to let those responsible know his views. The specific incident was thereby ended without losing my Police Surgeon but I did receive a warning from the Chief Superintendent that he and I now certainly did have at least one very powerful enemy and I should watch my back.

The only time the ACC ever referred to the incident to me was some months later when he appeared with his friendliest head on at my office on his way home one Friday afternoon and during the conversation, he casually said that I should not have persuaded the Police Surgeon to withdraw his resignation, to which I replied that he should have spoken to me before taking action on my Sub Division and the whole thing could have been avoided. Indeed I pointed out that if it was necessary for anyone to be removed from my Sub Division I was perfectly capable of doing it without interference from my colleagues (neither of whom ever mentioned the incident to me).

Chapter 24

I was also busy renewing contacts from my earlier time in Corby and I soon established a very good working relationship with the Local Council and the Magistrates. So good did this relationship become that my confirmation as the Sub Divisional Commander on a permanent basis became a foregone conclusion.

But a problem came from the local Victim Support Scheme. This scheme was in its infancy and the Corby scheme was a pilot for the County. Funding had been obtained from charitable sources for a full time coordinator and that post was already operational when I arrived. The scheme had a number of volunteers who would visit victims of crime and help them with counselling and practical advice.

It had been attempted before but a previous Chief Constable had insisted that volunteers could only be given crime details after the victim had given his specific written consent. This had effectively killed the scheme because police officers did not have such consent as their highest priority and traumatised victims were not usually thinking about such support immediately after a crime. This second attempt at the scheme was working better because the incumbent Chief Constable allowed volunteers to have the data they needed and was happy to rely on victims to decline help if they did not want it.

Unfortunately, alarm bells started ringing for me when I discovered that the coordinator had not submitted the previous year's financial accounts and the current year's were almost due. I had, by then, been joined by a new Deputy Sub Divisional Commander in the shape of Chief Inspector Laurie Owen about whom I knew little other than he was a long serving Regional Crime Squad officer who had just returned to uniform duties. I did know that he had a reputation as a likeable, avuncular character but not the most thrusting or ambitious person to have supporting me. In fact we made a perfect blend with Laurie always supporting me and taking on many of the personnel tasks that he enjoyed.

Victim Support was one of his responsibilities and he undertook the initial work to try to get the accounts produced and the scheme running efficiently. The scheme had its offices away from the station and Laurie went to inspect it. He reported back that it was in chaos and it was unlikely that they would be able to account for the expenditure as records were only kept haphazardly. I had previously dealt with many minor frauds (often at Working Men's Clubs) and the symptoms at the scheme were classic signs of such a fraud. One person left in charge of the money and the accounts, poor record keeping and little supervision. It soon becomes easy for such a person to take a little money fully intending to repay it but then either forgetting or not being able to repay the debt, then falsifying records to cover it or simply not keeping a record.

I decided to interview the coordinator myself and soon found that his answers to my questions were very evasive so I set up a small team to conduct a short investigation. The report confirmed my worst fears. Money was indeed missing. Sums allegedly paid to volunteers were not receipted and they usually could not remember whether they had claimed their expenses or not (most often not).

Unfortunately, as again is often the case, the person responsible will not admit having committed a crime and indeed often, I believe, they do not accept that what they have done was criminal. I did manage to get enough of an admission from the coordinator for me to be able to caution him though I doubt if I could have achieved a conviction if it had gone to court so I had to settle for his resignation and a re-start of the scheme.

The Local Council then came to the rescue. My best contact, Councillor Jim Sands whom I had known for many years through my time as a detective, managed to come up with Council accommodation and a free telephone line, together with stationery and a donation of cash to get a new scheme going. I went to see a retired headmaster whom I also knew from my earlier time in the town and I persuaded him to chair the new scheme. He was not keen initially but once I had convinced him that it was for the good of the town he soon settled in to become a stalwart and keen driver of the scheme with Laurie's help and support.

The morale of the Sub Division soon started to climb and the statistical results started to improve rapidly as the staff became better motivated. It was not a very large Sub Division in terms of staff (about 120 officers and 50 support staff) and I took great pride in knowing all of my officers by their first names. Of course this was made easier by my previous service at Corby so I had a head start with the older officers and Support Staff. I even tried to get to know the names of their wives and how many children they had, and so on.

Although the number of staff was not huge, the area covered was quite extensive and incorporated many villages as well as the small town of

Oundle (54 parishes in total). So we had a wide variety of problems to deal with, ranging from inner city issues that the largely Glaswegian population of Corby had brought with them, through to speeding in villages, the expectation that rural style policing could be provided to villages whilst city style problems were being handled by town officers who were often short handed. There was also the Royalty Protection we had to provide for the Duchess of Gloucester at Barnwell Manor.

This consisted of permanently armed officers on 24-hour duty. These officers were drawn from the Sub Divisional staff but could not be used for other duties. One was on armed foot patrol whilst another had to sit in a bombproof hut called a 'Bothey' whilst a third officer was on car patrol within a mile or so of the manor. It is not hard to imagine the difficulties this drain on resources caused us because none of the officers could be withdrawn for any reason and if they were short, the numbers had to be made up even though the town of Corby, with its 50,000 inhabitants, might be covered by three officers on the street.

Also the officers at the manor had to be trained in physical fitness and weaponry but then found themselves with virtually nothing to do as visitors to the Manor were fairly rare. They had to have hobbies or they would have gone quietly mad with such a soul-destroying duty. The fitness regime meant that it could not be a duty for the elderly or infirm yet the job was so undemanding that young fit officers would not volunteer. I was well aware of the sort of things they were doing, such as growing vegetables in a small part of the grounds (with the permission of the Duchess). One officer did leatherwork and another studied, and gained an academic qualification in history. Others used the time to rest so they were able to carry out some illicit part time work that they could not make me aware of. I am sure they did not realise I knew about the grave digging, funerals, game keeping and even at one time nocturnal decorating of doctors' and dentists' surgeries. Eventually, I had to insist that the patrol car included Oundle in its ambit but of course, there was always the possibility that a job in Oundle would leave the Manor without back up.

In Corby, my relationship with the Council was very close and we achieved some outstanding results by working together. I had a strong aversion to the travellers who would descend on the town quite regularly. I know they have to live somewhere and if they are moved on from one location they only become someone else's problem but they caused such disruption with rubbish when they left and stealing while they were there, that I received regular complaints from the Councillors who wanted to know what I was going to do about it.

Jim Sands was the loudest complainer and seemed to anticipate that I would make excuses for inaction but do nothing. The biggest problem for the police with the travellers was that if they refused to move on, it became necessary to arrest them and then the caravans became the responsibility of the police while the hordes of children became an impossible task for Social Services. It could be guaranteed that several of the travellers would have urgent hospital appointments so could not be moved (they said).

Jim Sands was therefore surprised when I threw the ball back in his court by saying, "Yes, we will be glad to move them on – with the condition that the council supplies the tow trucks and accepts the responsibility for the caravans if we make arrests."

Good friends we were but it was not always a happy go lucky relationship. Jim Sands was left with no alternative but to agree the conditions, and in fairness to him, he did so willingly. As a result we soon found a formula to rid ourselves of these unwelcome visitors. As soon as we discovered a new camp, the council officers would visit with a police officer and give them 24 hours to go with a warning that if they failed to leave, the tow trucks would be there within the hour. Soon we developed a technique of turning up with a couple of clearly marked council lorries and our guests would immediately depart.

So practised was our technique that, when a new group pulled off the A428 one day and began to set up camp in the woods behind the council offices, I immediately sent an Inspector with a group of officers to tell them not to even unhitch their lorries. Jim Sands had been advised of their arrival and telephoned me from the council offices. My reply was to the effect that if he looked out of the window he would see that we had already taken action. He was fairly impressed when he did just that and saw them all pulling away.

This relationship I had with the council caused some senior officers to look with concern because they were worried that I might be becoming too close because of all of the council functions I was invited to with my wife. Indeed we were invited to a great many functions and I attended whenever I could because I wanted the whole town to know that the police and the council were closely co-operating. My relationship with the Chief Executive, John Salmond developed into a close friendship and he and I used to meet regularly. Indeed we continued to do so long after I had left the town and until John sadly died.

The danger was, of course, that a situation would arise when my relationship prevented me from taking action against a councillor or someone favoured by them. This was a danger I knew only too well and I was never naive enough to do anything that would have prevented me from doing my duty. I did not consider that the fact that I received a formal invitation to attend shows, Civic Balls, the Annual Highland Gathering and similar events would affect me even slightly if I discovered that anyone, including John Salmond, Jim Sands or the Labour leader of the Council, had done anything to warrant their arrest.

The trouble was that this group, always acting in the interests of the town, would often act in arbitrary fashion and did undoubtedly receive favours in the sense of sponsored trips to encourage trade with the town (incidentally, remarkably successful trips) and there was an opposition group who desperately wanted to unseat the Council. They took every opportunity to criticise publicly the very group I was working so closely with.

Long after I had left the town there were serious allegations of corruption made and the Council did eventually fall. John Salmond was suspended and a major police enquiry was undertaken. No charges resulted despite a massive amount of police time and effort and I truly believe that the enquiry hastened the death of my friend who was a very honest and ethical man as well as being a gifted and thoughtful lawyer.

Although it is out of sequence with my story, I must relate here the fact that, after I had retired from the Force, I heard that John, whom I knew to be suffering from cancer, was very ill and had refused to see any of his old friends. I telephoned his wife Doreen to ask after him and to express my regret that he did not want to see anyone. Doreen told me that his refusal to see anyone did not extend to me and he would be very pleased to have a visit. Jackie and I went to see him a few days later and found him to be terribly ill, drifting in and out of consciousness and weighing less than half his normal weight. We had quite a long conversation, during which he brought up the investigation and asked if I had heard anything about its progress, as it had been ongoing for several years and he wondered if it would soon be concluded.

I did have a little knowledge of the enquiry although I had not been involved in it either as a police officer or as a witness. I did not really know how close it was to a conclusion but I did realize that John would not be there to see the conclusion. So I said to him that from my experience I felt sure that he would soon receive a letter to the effect that no legal proceedings were to be taken against him. He showed immediate and enormous relief to hear that and I left him in a much better condition than I had found him in.

I then sent a message to the Chief Constable explaining that John could not be expected to live for more than a week or so and when Doreen phoned me five days later to say that John had died, she said that she was sure he had felt able to let go having heard from me that he was not to be prosecuted. She also told me that a letter had come from the Chief Constable a few hours AFTER he died, saying that there was to be no action against him. I do wish the post had been a little quicker and that he could have seen the confirmation in writing but I thought it was very kind of the Chief to send it.

Chapter 25

Although I was always very careful to ensure that I never personally accepted anything that could be seen as corrupt it would have been impossible to refuse the hospitality of the Labour Group on the council if I was to achieve all that I wanted for the town. I therefore went to great lengths to ensure that I never had too much to drink at a function even when the councillors perhaps did imbibe a little too much.

Of far greater concern to me was the 'Wonderworld' project. This was a major private undertaking to create a theme park to rival Disneyland on the outskirts of Corby. It had been in being for some years as a concept and £5m of finance was in place. 1000 acres of land had been purchased for the peppercorn sum of £1m and elaborate plans had been drawn for the building of hotels, golf courses, railway station, car parks and even a Police Station. All of this as infrastructure for the main theme park which would have sections for commerce, history and the future with rides and amazing attractions.

A few members of staff were in place and exhibitions were held in the town for all interested parties, including the Police, Fire and Rescue service and the Council. The only thing missing was the money to build the park. Without doubt, the cost would have run to hundreds of millions of pounds and I could not see Corby competing with Paris, Los Angeles, Florida or other such exotic locations. Indeed I believed that we might be witnessing a major fraud even though I could not see how it was to be perpetrated or who the beneficiaries would be. Certainly the land was worth many times the price paid for it as it was in a prime commercial location but the vendors (indirectly British Steel and their associated companies) had an option to re purchase the land for the sale price if the project failed to materialise.

I resolved that one of my CID officers would maintain an interest and a file on the project to at least give the Fraud Squad a head start if it did all end in tears. In the end no fraud was disclosed but the project came to an end some fifteen years after it had started with losses of the £5m it had spent, when the potential financiers worldwide finally decided not to provide the funding.

In addition to the relationship with the Council, I also renewed and developed my contact with Lord Brookes, the Chair of the Magistrates, who was also a member of the Police Authority and Chair of our local Police and Community Consultative Committee. We spent many hours trying, with only very limited success, to get the community interested in policing matters. We did 'Road show' committee meetings in various parts of the town with enormous amounts of publicity but apathy reigned in the town. It was easy in the villages where we once had an attendance of over 300 but in Corby itself, the worst attendance was 2 people who I discovered to my chagrin transpired to be the parents of the local beat constable.

I suppose I could have concluded that the people were happy with the standard of policing they received but I fear it was more to do with the competing attractions of 'Bingo' or the pub. Indeed I even considered holding the meetings before a Bingo session but rejected the idea as inappropriate (and I doubt if Lord Brookes knew what Bingo was).

The demands of policing took a huge amount of my time but I recognised that, if I wanted to go beyond the rank of Superintendent, I would need some academic qualification. I knew I could not afford the time to study for a degree but decided instead to go for the slightly less demanding Diploma in Management Studies (DMS) on a part-time basis. Even this, which is really a postgraduate qualification, was destined to take me two and a half years including the final 6 months for a 10,000-word thesis. On reflection, I have no idea how I managed the 20 hours of study per week required in term time. I frequently arrived home at 8pm with two or three hours of study ahead of me. Every weekend off involved at least one day of study and there was a weeklong session at a distant college and a period of study in a commercial environment. Nevertheless, I managed to achieve a pass with distinction and was tempted to consider continuing my studies to convert the Diploma into a Masters Degree in Business Administration (MBA) but I eventually rejected this idea as impossible in the time I had available.

Fortunately, there were not too many serious cases during my time at Corby (a little over four years) but one firearms incident was potentially very serious and I was proud to resolve it without bloodshed. It began with an armed robbery at a petrol service station when a man in a balaclava helmet and carrying a sawn off shotgun walked in and demanded the takings. Fortunately, the attendant handed over the money and was uninjured. Within a few days, a well-known drug dealer was held up at the point of a sawn off shotgun and robbed of his money and drugs.

I was off duty for the weekend and my Deputy co-ordinated the enquiry to trace the offender. Several times during the weekend, he and the ACC had been involved in abortive attempts to trace and arrest the offender, based upon information from an informant. Even after his identity was established, the offender seemed to lead a charmed life and was not captured.

I was called out at about 6am on the Monday morning because the informant had come forward again to say that the man was hiding in a house in Chelveston Drive with a woman and her young child. The informant added that the offender was desperate for more money and intended to rob a post office on the Monday morning.

I drew up a plan to arrest him without creating a siege situation at the house, which would have put the woman and child at risk as well as, possibly, leading to a long drawn out negotiation. My plan was to hire two rental vans and park them at either end of the street, each containing five members of the armed Uniform Support Group and one dog and handler. There were no other vehicles parked between the house and the two vans so we knew the offender had to walk past one of the vans. An observation point or 'nest' was found at a house in the street so that Intelligence Officers could keep me informed of activity at the scene.

The most serious danger was, of course, that someone else would appear on the scene just as he walked out but we had no alternative but to hope that would not happen and make a value judgement if it did. The fall back would be to let him walk past and follow until he reached a point when a safe arrest could be made.

The ground rules I laid down were that no action could be taken without my authority unless the radios failed at the critical point, in which case, a sergeant in the nest could authorise an arrest. I instructed that, should someone else appear, or if the woman left the house with the offender, they would have to follow and advise me of the best opportunity to take him out but under no circumstances was he to be allowed to get to the Post Office.

The waiting is the worst. Adrenalin is pumping but as time goes on, the whole team begins to feel deflated and tired. Luckily for us, we only had to wait until about 10am. Then came the call from the nest, "Subject is leaving the house alone and carrying a holdall. Heading towards van B".

"Is there anyone else on the plot?" I asked.

"No one in sight, it looks good for a 'go'" came the reply.

Things happened very quickly after that. "Van B go, go, go," I instructed (it is repeated three times to ensure that there can be no mistake or word missed because of radio problems). It is a nightmare for the controller at the station because, until we have CCTV at scenes, you have to rely on the commentary from the nest to know what is happening. It was only later that I learned exactly what happened next.

The dog and handler emerged first from the back of the van and I could hear the dog barking frantically via the radio. This failed to phase the offender and even when five armed officers, dressed in their black coveralls and baseball caps, four of them brandishing Heckler and Koch MP5 automatic guns and the fifth a repeating shotgun, emerged shouting, "armed police, drop the bag" he still failed to drop it and just stood looking at the officers.

It was only when he heard the racking sound of the Police Officer's shotgun pumping a shell into the chamber and the final warning to drop the bag that he reacted. It was his good fortune that he did drop the bag when he did because he was literally the time it takes to squeeze a trigger away from being blown in half. He followed the standard instructions given by the officers to place his hands on his head, move away from the bag then sink to his knees and finally onto his stomach. He had undoubtedly got the message by this time.

He was handcuffed using plastic cuffs, searched and placed in a waiting police car before the firearms officers looked in the bag. In it they found a balaclava helmet and a loaded, sawn off shotgun together with extra cartridges. The officers made the weapon safe and returned to the Police Station, where, by that time, I had seen the prisoner detained and placed in a cell.

I never cease to be amazed at how small and insignificant many serious criminals are. This man was no exception. A slim man of less than medium height, he went meekly to his cell to await an eventual sentence of seven years in prison. But I have no doubt that, in the moment before he saw that the shotgun officer really was prepared to kill him, he was considering whether he had time to get his own gun out and use it.

I am so sure of this because, many years later, after his release from prison he went on to murder an elderly man in Corby and then calmly behead him and take the head away with him – but that is another story.

Firearms were involved in quite a few incidents in Corby and I came to respect the professionalism of the Uniform Support Group. Their work can be so dangerous and the judgements they are required to make, so difficult.

On another occasion, whilst I was the Duty Superintendent for the weekend, I decided that I could afford to attend a retirement party for a respected colleague at the other side of Northampton (a distance of about 30 miles). Sure enough, just before 10pm, I received a call to the effect that a man had been seen chasing another man in Greenhill Rise, Corby. The chaser was carrying a handgun. The man being chased had run into a public house, leapt over the bar and run out to the back rooms. His pursuer also jumped over the bar and as he did so the gun had gone off whilst it was aimed at the ceiling. All this in front of a crowded pub – none of the drinkers admitted to seeing anything.

The two men had disappeared into the night via a rear door but not before the landlord recognised the one with the gun as a man with previous convictions for violence and even a siege, when he had been cornered in a house he was burgling.

Obviously, I was needed urgently at Corby so I arranged for a Traffic Patrol car to meet me at Force Headquarters and get me to Corby as soon as possible. When we got to the notorious Barford Bridge, about half way between Kettering and Corby, we were confronted by a car and trailer that had overturned on the dangerous bend at that point in the road. Imagine my horror when I realised that it was the Uniform Support Group and their weapons trailer! Luckily, there were no injuries and it was to their credit that they continued on to Corby to carry out the operation to arrest the offender.

This was particularly difficult because we knew that he was unlikely to come quietly and when we discovered where he was, we decided to make a sudden and devastating entry to the house as the safest of the poor choices open to us. This was not a recommended option but we had, by then, established conclusively that the weapon was a blank firing 8mm pistol. The discharged cartridge was found on the floor of the pub and, of course, there was no hole in the ceiling. Despite this, who would wish to confront the owner of the weapon in 'Dixon of Dock Green' style and ask him to come quietly?

In the event, he appeared at the top of the stairs brandishing a baseball bat, but a furry missile, of the German Shepherd variety, persuaded him to surrender. I am not a lover of police dogs. In fact, they scare the devil out of me. I keep remembering 120 pounds per square inch of bite power and 30mph on the flat, a combination of which is likely to make any thinking person think! But I would not be without them and their handlers. The handlers, in the case of the ones stationed at Corby at that time, were far more dangerous than the dogs and I pitied any villain foolish enough to take on such a combination.

In another firearms incident, the weapon was again known 'for certain' to be a replica and the offender had gone into his house, not knowing that the police were on to him. Two of the dog handlers went to the door, knocked and when he innocently answered it, promptly dragged him out and restrained him to the floor. A bit foolhardy but very effective and very courageous.

One more firearms incident during this period caused me concern. One evening, two charming young ladies had been out drinking, met two young men and took them back to their house in Gainsborough Road, Corby. During the evening, as things got a little intimate, the live in boyfriend of one of the girls came home and was less than pleased. He promptly went upstairs and came down with a shotgun with which he threatened the two courting men. They decided to make their excuses and leave (to coin a Sunday Paper reporters words) and they made off at a high rate of knots back to their van, which was parked nearby.

One of the two tripped and fell as he ran and as he fell he heard the pellets flying just over his head. The blast hit the van and blew out the front window. A second blast did more damage to the van but the young heroes managed to run down the road and did not stop until they reached the Police Station.

I was called out and took charge of the operation. It was clear to me that I needed the armed support of the Uniform Support Group and, as was standard practice, the Constable Firearms Adviser, an ex Para of enormous experience and totally without fear, was already at the Station. There was no question that this was one situation when there could be no short cuts even if a long siege resulted. As a formality, I rang the duty Chief Officer (not the regular ACC but he shall remain nameless to protect the guilty) to ask for authority to issue firearms.

He first asked me if I was sure it was a shotgun that had been used, to which I retorted almost flippantly,"Judging by the holes in the van, I would say so Sir." Then, to my amazement, he instructed me to get the Firearms adviser to crawl up to the van to try to recover some pellets or otherwise confirm that it actually was a shotgun and not an air rifle.

Then he asked me if I had called out a Chief Superintendent and, being told that I had not, he asked me why I had come straight to him. I patiently explained that I did not need a Chief Superintendent but I did need his authority to issue firearms. He told me to get the results of the search by the Firearms adviser and then ring the Chief Superintendent.

I was deeply concerned on a number of levels. Even though I had established an unarmed cordon around the house, I could not be sure that the offender could not escape and dispose of the weapon or cause injury to someone else or himself. I was appalled at having to ask the Adviser to put himself at risk by going into the scene. I was disgusted that the officer did not trust my judgement and wanted a Chief Superintendent involved, and finally, I was concerned that the Chief Superintendent, a friend of mine, would be in trouble somehow because one of his Superintendents had failed to call him. I immediately phoned him to warn him but too late, the Chief Officer was already on the phone to him.

The Adviser expressed his own view of the requirement to search for pellets at 3am but nevertheless went and came back to report that it was undoubtedly a shotgun even though he could not find any pellets. He had not expected to.

The Chief Superintendent rang me and rubber-stamped my plan, apologising for having to do so and saying that he would attend but I need not wait for him.

With the usual professionalism, the Uniform Support Group surrounded the house and one officer (coincidentally the same one of shotgun racking fame) approached the house and told the occupants to come to the front door where they would be met by armed police officers.

They complied precisely with the instructions, which were the standard for such a situation. There were two women and, in fact, two men in the house. The women came first, one at a time, hands on head to the road, sinking to her knees, lying forward onto her stomach and then being handcuffed behind her back with plastic cuffs. She was taken away to a waiting police car and the operation was repeated three more times until all four were in custody. The odd thing was that by this time it was 6.30am and one or two people emerged from houses within the inner, armed cordon and calmly made their way off to work as if nothing was happening even though there were officers covering the target house with their MP5's.

The house was then entered in the prescribed manner, with officers covering each other as they carefully went from room to room ensuring there were no other threats or persons inside. When they were sure, a separate unarmed search team entered and searched the house from top to bottom including under the floorboards. No weapon or ammunition was found. Of course, the offender may have disposed of it before police even arrived at the scene but we can never be sure that it was not removed while the Duty Chief Officer was prevaricating.

The two women and one man were released without charge but the offender admitted having fired at the van though he denied attempting to shoot the fleeing lovers. He was sentenced to eighteen months in prison and although I do not know if he has since committed further offences, information was later received to the effect that he was an active supporter of Sectarian violence in Northern Ireland and that the gun was intended for shipment 'across the water'.

The Chief Officer concerned never mentioned the matter again to me and I have never discovered whether he really did lack confidence in my judgement or whether he was just plain scared of making the wrong decision.

Chapter 26

My time at Corby passed in a blur of activity and I enjoyed almost every moment of it, with one notable exception. I still suffered the enmity of one or two colleagues arising from the incident with the Police Surgeon. It was most unfortunate that one of the two Superintendents involved was promoted on a temporary basis to Chief Superintendent of our Division, which consisted of the towns of Corby, Kettering and Wellingborough, together with the surrounding villages and countryside. He was based at Rushden Police Station so that he could not be seen to interfere with the quasi-autonomy of the Sub Divisions.

My Sub Division was selected for an inspection even though the next one due was this Superintendent's own Sub Division. The explanation given was that, as the Temporary Chief Superintendent, he could not inspect his own Sub Division. Inspections have never been conducted very successfully in Northamptonshire despite numerous attempts to get the formula correct. They either seem to become a bureaucratic exercise that finds little to criticize or they are seen to be a simple fault finding exercise.

I resolved that I would ignore the enmity that had gone before and I instructed my Deputy and all of the staff to ensure that they did not attempt to hide anything from the inspection team, which consisted of the Temporary Chief Superintendent, Detective Superintendent, Divisional Detective Chief Inspector and the Chief Superintendent's Staff Officer (an Inspector). It was my intention that we would seek, in a spirit of openness and constructive progress, to learn whatever we could and improve on our performance – how naïve was that?

I maintained this approach even though members of my staff told me several times that they had found the Chief Superintendent sneaking around their offices before they arrived and then asking questions to which he obviously already knew the answer. The Temporary Chief Superintendent never did get around to interviewing my Deputy formally, or me for that matter, although we had a few informal chats, during which I did advise him that some staff members were concerned about his approach. I did this in a friendly manner and with the intention of assisting him.

When the inspection was complete, I waited to see his report but nothing emerged. Several times, I rang him to ask how it was progressing but he would simply say that it was being prepared and he would get it to me as soon as possible. He also suggested that it was not of great importance so I had no need to worry about the delay.

About six weeks after the inspection had been completed, at 5pm on a Friday evening when I was due to be off for the weekend, a motorcyclist arrived with two copies of the inspection report. This was an unusual occurrence because, contrary to the TV image, police motorcyclists are rarely used for delivery services.

Laurie Owen called me to tell me that it had arrived and I said that it could wait until Monday as I had had a very long week and wanted a free weekend. I carried on working in my office for a while and then Laurie called me again to say that he thought I should read the report and that I would not like it. I took it home to read at the weekend and soon discovered that Laurie was right. I did not like it at all. It was extremely critical of my personal management style and Laurie's communication skills. It found criticism of almost every aspect of the work we undertook and the only grudging praise was for the forbearance of the staff who had to work under such a poor regime.

I was incandescent with rage. Apart from the personal criticism that I felt was totally unjustified and the picky fault-finding with administrative procedures that I knew from covering his Sub Division at weekends, were worse on his area than on mine, I had been given no chance to defend myself or the Sub Division.

I was also sure that copies of the report would have been sent to Headquarters for the information of the Chief, and the ACC who was not well disposed towards me. If I let this go, my career was certainly over as far as further advancement was concerned and I had to work out a strategy to respond to what I considered was a libellous and offensive attack on my integrity.

During that weekend, I sought advice from Jim Sands, whom I knew to be a master of politics from his work with the Trade Unions. His advice was simple. "Go on the attack with all guns blazing. You have nothing to lose and if you do it well, you might even win." Very sound advice and I worked out a plan.

On the Monday morning, I called Laurie in and told him my plan but I gave him the opportunity either to disassociate himself from it, offer alternatives, or back me totally, knowing that we could both be seriously harmed if it did not work. He backed me without reservation.

I then rang the Temporary Chief Superintendent's secretary and booked an appointment with him for the next morning. The Chief Constable's Secretary was the lady who had been my own secretary when I was a staff officer, before being promoted to the Chief Constable's office, and I telephoned her for a large favour. I asked her to book Laurie and me in to see the Chief late the following morning but not to enter it in the diary or tell him about it. She just had to make sure he was available and free at that time.

As instructed, Laurie arrived at work the next morning, not in uniform but in his best suit, as I had also. We armed ourselves with copies of the report marked up with every point upon which we felt it was incorrect and more importantly libellous. I had previously learned as a Staff Officer, how important it can be to arrive for meetings, not early or late but dead on time. Some of Her Majesty's Inspectors of Constabulary had been known to wait at the end of the drive so they could arrive on time.

Therefore we walked into the Temporary Chief Superintendents office, precisely at the agreed time. He was waiting there with his full inspection team to support him, all arrayed on one side of the conference table, with two seats on the opposite side for Laurie and me. His first comment was, "You're both dressed smartly today aren't you?" this said with a smile as if in a friendly greeting.

I coldly replied, "Yes we are dressed smartly because we are going to see the Chief Constable directly we leave here, if you do not withdraw your disgraceful report, and it is our intention to make a formal complaint about the manner in which you conducted the inspection, and your libellous comments in it."

With this, the Detective Superintendent, Detective Chief Inspector and Staff Officer all rose as one and left the room. The Temporary Chief Superintendent then asked if I would mind if Laurie also waited outside and I signalled him to go. He asked me if I was sure and I confirmed that he should, feeling tremendously grateful for his support. As soon as we were alone, the Temporary Chief Superintendent tried to regain the advantage by warning me that if I did go to see the Chief Constable, I would certainly lose and it would cost me dearly.

"You may be right," I said, "But I will definitely lose if I don't and there is no way you are going to get away with this".

He tried to bluster and continue with the aggressive approach but I knew by then that I had him on the run. It was not long before he started to take a conciliatory approach by saying that he could not understand why I was so upset because it was only a discussion document upon which we could base a more formal discussion about management styles.

I accused him of telling lies and said that I knew the ACC would have already seen the document. He was adamant that it was not so and that the only copies that had left his office were the two sent to Laurie and me. I could not prove that was not so but I again told him I did not believe him.

He then said that to prove he was telling the truth, if I was prepared to go through the report with him and tell him what I wanted altering and how I wanted it worded, he would have it fully amended in accordance with that.

Clearly I could do no other than give him the opportunity to withdraw the offensive parts because his defence to an allegation from me would be as he had said, that it was only a provocative discussion document so I asked if I could use his telephone and, to show him that my threats were not a bluff, in his presence I rang the Chief Constable's Secretary and asked her to cancel the appointment I had with the Chief that morning, adding that I might need to re instate it later if necessary.

The rest of the team were then allowed to rejoin us and we spent an hour and a half going through every point we wanted changing. At the end of this, he agreed to make all of the changes I asked for and said that he hoped we would still be able to work together. Some chance! I told him that I would never ever trust him again or forgive him for his actions. About three weeks later, we received a copy of a much-amended report but I sent it back again for further changes, which were also made and then I heard no more about it for months.

I had more or less forgotten the report (if not the way it was done) when I received a call from the Chief. He said, "That report was nothing like as bad as you expected was it?" I replied innocently, "It was about what I expected from the inspection but what made you think I was expecting a bad one?"
"I just had an inkling that you were not very happy with the inspection," he replied but would not elaborate on how he had heard such an inkling. I later learned that the Temporary Chief Superintendent was given a real 'ear bashing' for the lateness of the report, but I still have a suspicion that the ACC had at least been told that my inspection report would be bad and had told the Chief. How else could he have had any idea about the original contents of the report?

Suffice it to say that the Temporary Chief Superintendent returned to his Sub Division as a Superintendent and eventually retired at that rank. I take no satisfaction from that fact, but I despised the stupid petty politics that abounded during that era in the Police Force and still have no real idea why that ACC and his junior colleagues wanted so desperately to make my life a misery. It is not my nature to be vindictive and I know that I give the impression of being an easygoing person but I have always had a very determined streak and can be difficult if pushed. I just wish it were not necessary to demonstrate the harder side of my character before some people are convinced.

After a very enjoyable working relationship with Laurie, he was eventually transferred to the Complaints Department as a Senior Investigator, where he stayed until his retirement, although we still keep in touch to this day.

Chapter 27

One huge attraction of the Police Force for me has always been the unexpected that can happen during a perfectly normal working day, and one such event, that was later to have a considerable impact on my life, occurred one day in October 1988. My family and I had been on our first foreign holiday to Spain a couple of years before and I had felt very embarrassed that I could not speak a word of the language. So I had bought a small book and cassette to learn the rudiments. I studied it very thoroughly and when I progressed to first level evening classes, I had found that I was able to keep up easily with the other students. I had mentioned this new interest to a few senior colleagues and thought no more of it.

I sat at my desk at Corby when suddenly the telephone rang. It was a Chief Superintendent from Headquarters who asked me how my Spanish was going. I said it was OK and asked why the interest as I knew that he was a busy man and unlikely to call purely out of interest. He then asked if my passport was up to date and I realised that he was thinking of sending me on a trip. On discovering that my passport was indeed up to date, he told me to go home and pack for about seven days and a car would collect me from home to take me to Headquarters for a briefing and immediate journey abroad. He could tell me nothing more on the phone and I drove home wondering where I was going and why.

Jackie had gone shopping for the day and I had no means of contacting her so I simply packed and a Traffic car took me to Headquarters. There I was given an envelope containing £1000 in pesetas and told that there was no time for a briefing, I was to be accompanied by a young Detective who could not speak Spanish but he would brief me as we caught the British Airways flight to Barcelona that was due to leave from Gatwick in one hour and forty minutes time.

As we travelled down the M1 and M25 at speeds well over 100mph in a Patrol car with blue lights and siren going, the young detective told me a fantastic story. I was a little distracted because the sirens were supposed to go 'bee-bah bee-bah' but ours was broken and it just went 'bee bee bee' (isn't it odd what sticks in the mind?)

The story that unfolded was that a Kuwaiti businessman, who dealt in diamonds, had been kidnapped at gunpoint in a village just outside Northampton and a ransom note, demanding that £1,000,000 be paid into a specified bank account at a bank in Girona in Northern Spain, had been left. The note warned that he would be shot if it were not paid.

Enquiries had been commenced and a total news blackout had been agreed with the national press. This had taken place a few days before and the officers had established that the kidnappers were from Belgium but had access to a villa near to Girona. It was not known if the victim was still alive or where he was. The Spanish Police (Policia Nacional as opposed to Guardia Civil) had agreed to make whatever enquiries were needed but insisted that a Spanish speaking police officer be sent to liaise with them (and I was the only one in the Force – with my one year of evening classes under my belt).

As we flew (Club Class – was the only available seat) I explained to my colleague that, from my knowledge of the Spanish, it was most unlikely that we would be met at the airport so we would probably have to take a taxi. We did not even get as far as the passport control before two Inspectors identified us, pulled us out of the queue and whisked us straight through to their car and took us to meet the Police Chief for the whole of the Barcelona region.

He told us that we would stay in a hotel in Barcelona that night and be taken to Girona the next morning. I politely suggested that we would prefer to be in Girona that night in case anything happened and he simply turned to the two Inspectors and told them to take us straight to Girona. It was only later that I learned they had already been on duty for 12 hours and they now had a 130 mile round trip in front of them.

Before leaving, and while some arrangements were being put in hand, the more senior of the two suggested that I might like to ring home. All calls were paid for by the national telephone company Telefonica so I rang Jackie to ask if she could guess where I was. As she was explaining to me that she had received a call from the Detective Chief Superintendent and therefore knew I was out of the country, I noticed that the Inspector was showing my colleague his guns. He had a large, loaded Colt 45 automatic in his hand and like the eyes of 'The Laughing Cavalier' its muzzle seemed to be following me around the room. This was his 'desk gun', kept in case of attack by ETA (this was Basque country and the terrorist group was quite active). He also had a .38 revolver that he kept in a handbag and a .22 ankle gun that went everywhere with him.

Our two new friends made no complaint about the lengthy journey I had got them into and they happily had a drink with us at the hotel they had arranged in Girona before setting out on the return trip to Barcelona. Also, before leaving, they told us that they would collect us from the hotel at 10am and I was staggered when they arrived exactly on time and looking quite fresh.

They took us to see the Chief of Girona who asked what we wanted done. My Spanish was now being tested to the full and when I explained that we wanted them to check at the bank to see if the account had indeed been opened, if there was any money in it and what were the terms of its opening, he simply nodded and indicated that that had been done. "No Senor, eso es lo que queremos a hacer" *No Sir, that is what we want to do.* He just nodded, "Que mas?" *What else?* I asked if they would also search the villa where we believed the kidnappers had an interest. He said that this had also been done and I was amazed to find that, as soon as they heard how urgently I viewed it, they had gone to a Judge for a warrant for the bank, turned out the manager, checked the account, obtained a statement from him and then searched the villa.

The villa was empty but they had arrested the caretaker just because he was ex Guardia Civil and they did not like the Guardia Civil anyway. It transpired that the account had been opened some months before by the individuals we suspected. There was no money in it but the terms of opening it were that they should expect £1,000,000 in sterling in the near future. The offenders had been at the villa some months before but had not been seen recently.

So, where were we to go from there? Everything we needed to be done in Spain had been done already and in a most satisfactory manner. I rang Headquarters and was told that there were developments taking place in England, Kuwait and Belgium and all we could do was to wait in Spain in case rapid action was required. It seems that the family of 'El Desaparecido' *the man who has disappeared* were able to pay the ransom but the Sultan had been consulted and refused to allow them to pay, no matter what the outcome. One does not lightly disobey the Head of State in Kuwait and it was most unlikely that the ransom would be paid but we had to ensure that, if it was, we were on hand.

Therefore, we were at a loose end and being entertained by our very good friends at the Policia Nacional. It was more like a holiday with Spanish lessons thrown in as well as lots of good food and the occasional small glass of gin and tonic, though it was a little disconcerting when we were being driven in a Police car by a drunken Inspector who was carrying two guns.

After almost a week of waiting in the Girona, Lloret and Tossa del

Mar areas, we received information from England that the victim had been recovered in London, having been tortured with an electric cattle prod, chained to a bed and threatened with being shot. We later learned that the gang had finally realised that they were not going to get the money and decided to kill their victim. They had the weapon but lacked the cold courage actually to shoot him.

One member of the gang, therefore went to Belgium to recruit a 'hit man' and somehow, the Belgian Police (where we already had a team) discovered the details of the plot and the location in London where the victim was being held. Our Metropolitan colleagues sent in an armed team who soon recovered the damaged, but breathing victim and arrested the gang except the one still in Belgium, who was soon picked up there.

Apparently, there was still some slight danger that the money would be paid and we were instructed to remain in Spain for a further three days. We did transfer to Barcelona to make life easier for our hosts and had a very eventful night on the town there. This night began at 10am and ended at 5am the next day and it included a memorable ride across the city's main thoroughfare, 'El Diagonal', which, as its name suggests, runs diagonally across the city. This is a four-lane highway in either direction with no central barrier. It was also very busy when our host (only one Inspector by now) wanted to take us to a club on the waterfront.

He simply put on his siren and 'Kojak' lamp and drove at 60 mph. When traffic became heavy in our direction, he simply switched into the fast lane coming towards us, with cars swerving in all directions, then across four lanes and onto the footpath to get through a difficult spot before returning to the opposing fast lane again. I have related this story a number of times and I promise that it happened exactly as I have described. At the end, my colleague said he saw nothing as he had his head on the seat but he knew every time we had done something particularly outrageous because he could hear me saying, "Oh no, don't do it Jose –. Oh s—-, he's done it!"

By the time the night was over, Jose was driving with at least twenty gins and tonic inside him, and two guns about his person. I had a real fear that he would shoot someone if they said the wrong thing. We had also visited several seedy clubs and one very high-class flamenco club but I never saw money change hands. At every venue, I offered to pay but Jose would not hear of it insisting that we were his guests and he would settle the bill, though I never actually saw him do so.

The final day, we were invited to lunch at the home of one Paco, who owned a club called Paco's Porno Club. At his beautiful home in

Casteldefels, we enjoyed a very good paella and I was invited to bring my wife for a fortnight's holiday at his guest flat. I might have accepted had his wife not shown me some family photos featuring their adult children taking part in the porno shows!

It was time to leave and I was amazed when Jose, the hardened and tough detective began to cry as we left him at the airport. I am staggered that I have never had a reply to my letters or cards or even the phone calls I made to thank him for his hospitality and I have no idea why. I was totally hooked on Spain, the language, the culture and the general style and generosity of the people.

As a footnote to this adventure, the Kuwaiti victim went on National TV and said that he owed his life to the professionalism of Northamptonshire Police. He also offered to throw a champagne party for the team but our Chief sensibly declined because of the pending case. I never have understood the vagaries of our justice system but none of the gang received more than six years in prison and even this was reduced on appeal.

Chapter 28

I continued at Corby for about a total of four years, having two more deputies during that time but it is a fact that there are only so many times a Superintendent can keep coming up with new ideas to take a Sub Division forward, and I believe that four or five years is about the correct length of time to stay in one role, even if very successful. I am aware that there is a view that there must be stability in the command of a Basic Command Unit (BCU), which is the latest term for a unit of command.

I was, therefore, not terribly surprised when I was asked to take on a major project at Headquarters to review the whole prosecution procedure for the Force. This project had been offered to a Chief Inspector who had considerable experience in prosecutions but he had had the courage and honesty to say that he felt it was beyond him to complete such a major undertaking.

A young and ambitious sergeant had been assigned to assist with the project and although I did not know until later, the Sergeant (who held degrees in English and Military History) had been briefed to keep the Chief Inspector on his toes by challenging his views and when the project was given to me, no one thought to tell him that he did not have to challenge me quite so rigorously.

I was therefore quite surprised when, on the first day, we could not agree what the title of the project was to be. We argued fiercely for most of the day and I reached a point when my patience was becoming exhausted and I began to think that the Sergeant would have to go. In the end, I said, "This is what we shall call the project......"

"How can you just make a decision like that?" he replied. To which I replied to the effect that it was because I had a crown on my shoulder and if he didn't like it, his options were open.

I went home fuming about the arrogant little upstart and only later found out that he had gone home saying the same thing about me. It was an inauspicious start to what became a very close friendship and the formation of a very complementary little team. This arrogant little upstart is now a Deputy Assistant Commissioner in the Metropolitan Police Service and I am sure he will soon be a Chief Constable on merit.

We certainly had some interesting times during the project, including a trip to Edinburgh where we saw a tremendously advanced computerised reporting programme that, in 1991 was more advanced than most Police Forces have today.

Perhaps the funniest moment was when visiting a Chief Superintendent in another local Force. That worthy addressed all of his conversation to me and towards the conclusion, turned to me and said, "I know we have been talking about high level issues but do you think your Sergeant will have been able to understand?" I could not believe he had said it in front of the said Sergeant, who was obviously very annoyed, so I gave him a look to warn him to keep his own counsel and I responded to the Chief Superintendent, "Well, I know some of the things we have spoken about are a bit difficult but I think that with his Honours degree in English and a second degree in Military History, he'll probably catch on quite soon, don't you?" We left the Chief Superintendent red faced and we laughed about his incredible rudeness and arrogance all the way home.

During that year, I had applied to attend the Senior Command Course at Bramshill Police College (since re named as the Strategic Leadership Development Programme). This is the course that senior officers must attend if they wish to be considered for posts at, and above, the rank of ACC. At that time it was a six-month course and to qualify, one had to pass a three-day interview based upon the Civil Service entrance exam. Only a very small number are successful and I failed the interview but was formally told that I was only just short of skills in one area and should try again the next year if I could develop certain personal skills.

I managed to arrange a course to resolve these problems and returned the next year when I was successful and was selected to attend the 1992 Senior Command Course. In between the two attempts, I had also applied to attend the European Police Studies Course in Madrid and had a tremendously interesting six weeks at the National Police College, learning about Spanish Law and the Constitution each morning with Spanish language lessons every afternoon from a Catedratico *Professor* from Madrid University.

There were students from England, France, Germany and The Republic of Ireland on the course and we were required to speak only Spanish for the whole six weeks. This proved to be very arduous but at the end, I found that I could easily converse in Spanish and even think in that language.

At the weekends we were taken on visits of interest to such amazing locations as El Prado Museum, Salamanca, Segovia, Toledo, El Palacio

Real, La Valle de los Caidos and San Lorenzo de el Escorial. My love of Spain was increased even more and I found Madrid to be the most beautiful city I have ever visited. El Parque Retiro on a Sunday morning is absolutely wonderful with its lake and many footpaths where there are stalls with many kinds of entertainment and novelties as well as Tarot readings. At night, La Plaza Mayor and El Puerto del Sol attract huge crowds of happy revellers with none of the atmosphere of threat that exists in so many cities elsewhere. A visit to Los Mesones de Tapas, where the challenge is to visit all forty houses and have a drink and tapas in each is not to be missed. I also made some very good friends in the Police Forces of Spain and Germany, with whom I am still in contact 13 years later.

Attendance on the Senior Command Course does not guarantee promotion to ACC and students begin to go on the circuit of interviews for ACC posts. This was more difficult for me because I was still a Superintendent and at that time, although in theory it could be done, it was not really possible to go directly from that rank to ACC without serving as a Chief Superintendent (that has since changed) so I was applying for posts as a Chief Superintendent and finding it difficult to get a job because some Forces felt that I would just be there for a short time before seeking further promotion and, though I did not realise it then, I was already being considered to be too old at 48.

Although other Superintendents on the course had the same rank problem, I was far older than most of them and after a series of failed interviews, I confess that I became discouraged and my self-confidence reached a very low ebb. This became self-defeating and I then began to have some very poor job interviews concluding with one awful performance before a Metropolitan Police board, when the combination of a very hot day, a hostile reception and my poor self-esteem combined to reduce me to (comparatively speaking) a gibbering wreck.

On my return to my Force, I decided to give up on job interviews for a while and settle into my new role, which, I was surprised to find, was to be as a Detective Superintendent, having been out of operational detective work for over ten years. I walked into a baptism of fire! On my first day – yes, the very first day, I was greeted by a very serious case of blackmail. The supermarket chain Budgens had received a letter to the effect that their goods would be contaminated on the shelves if they failed to pay a ransom of £100,000 to the blackmailer. Instructions on payment were to be sent later.

Examination of the letter revealed that it was printed on a word processor on a common but fairly expensive 'Conqueror' paper. The letter had a local postmark and the nature of the threat made it obvious that the sender had an intimate knowledge of the Company's Distribution Centre at Rushden, in Northamptonshire.

When the follow-up letter was received, the instructions were that the money, in used notes was to be placed in a particular type of 'Pilot' case and carried by a courier from the Company up the escalator of the Northampton Grosvenor Centre, where the courier would be intercepted by 'a member of the Organisation'. He should hand over the case and continue walking. No guarantees about the safety of Budgen products were given.

The larger chains of stores have contingency plans for such a situation and they have a team of senior managers identified to make corporate decisions on these increasingly common offences. At that time Budgens had no such plans and I was impressed by the co-operation shown by Tesco's who lent them their assistance.

This type of case is extremely difficult to resolve and special expertise resides with the Regional Crime Squads (now the National Crime Squad). I was really grateful for their assistance and the resources they could bring to bear. One hundred and twenty officers including Intelligence cells, Surveillance teams, Communications experts and a full command team attended the first briefing. I retained overall command of the operation but the truth is that the expertise available far exceeded my own experience and I am sure they could have managed quite well without the local input.

Nevertheless, no attempt was made by them to take control and any actions were always put to me for approval. We purchased a Pilot case of the type demanded and soon found that only one retailer in the Northampton area sold this type of case and they also sold the brand of paper used and word processors that produced similar type faces.

Given time we would have identified the offender from this line of enquiry but in the meantime, we agreed with the Managing Director of Budgens and his security staff, that we would provide the courier, but the case would contain no money and instead a letter to the blackmailer inviting him to ring a telephone number because there was problem with getting the money.

A direct line was set up with a Rushden code but it terminated in fact in an office at my Headquarters where a trained negotiator was waiting. The handover went like clockwork. A Regional Crime Squad Inspector was selected as the courier and a less 'Policeman like' Police officer I have never seen .He was approached by a man at the top of the escalator and he handed over the case. From that moment on, the offender was never out of sight of the surveillance teams.

He took a bus to the outskirts of town, collected a Mountain Bike from a Tesco's car park and made his way across fields to another location where he had a car waiting. From there he drove around country lanes for several hours, obviously making sure he was not being followed. How wrong he was.

Eventually he went to a house in the Towcester area and we waited for him to open the case. Soon after, the phone rang and our negotiator introduced himself as a representative of the firm. Whilst they were talking, the surveillance team established whereabouts in the house the phone was situated and as soon as I gave the OK to enter, they were able to overpower the offender and his wife before any attempt could be made to destroy evidence or even put the phone down.

The word processor was recovered and examination of its ribbon disclosed all the contents of the letters. The offender was a disaffected employee who had been fired and the reason for specifying the type of case to be used was as simple as the fact that he had seen them in the store and wanted one. Two years in prison was probably about right for his first offence, particularly as it was a fairly amateurish attempt at blackmail and he was something of a 'Walter Mitty' character.

The problem was further complicated by a copycat threat made to the same company by someone using the dramatic name 'The Terminator' and threatening to inject foodstuffs with AIDS infected blood. Initially we believed that this threat might have come from the same offender, as the threats began before we made the arrest and were copied to a major National newspaper that immediately published the details including the name of the company involved. After the arrest the threats continued and our offender was then on bail but we found that he could not have committed this second offence because he was under surveillance when some of these second series of letters were posted, although at least one was postmarked Northampton.

This second threat caught the media attention even more than the first because of the name used. My Brother in Law, who lived in New York, was amazed one day when he heard my voice on a radio interview, having been picked up by one of the American networks. Unfortunately, even though these threats suddenly came to an end, the cost to the company was enormous because the premature publicity led to a huge drop in sales and could have bankrupted a less secure company.

We had barely cleared the paperwork for this case when another most difficult case arose and was destined to remain undetected to this day. At

10.30am on Friday 22nd January 1993, I was en route to Wellingborough for a meeting when I received a message to contact Headquarters at once. I was then informed that I should attend a pet shop in Wellingborough Road, Northampton, where a murder had occurred.

I made my way there as soon as possible and on arrival found that uniformed officers had cordoned off the front of the shop but, as I have found in the past, they were sheltering inside the cordon because of the heavy rain that was falling. I instantly made myself unpopular by sending them out in the rain while the 'brains department' (CID) were inside.

A Detective Inspector and a Detective Sergeant were already there examining the scene. The shop was owned by Mr and Mrs Dumayne who were on a month's holiday at their villa in Portugal and the shop had been left in the charge of the part-time manager, Albert Bunting. Albert Bunting was 76 years of age and had worked at Police Headquarters until he reached retirement age. Indeed, I knew him by sight.

Two young lads, aged 18 and 16 assisted him at the shop and the arrangement was that the 18 year old would open the shop each morning and Albert would arrive about 11.30am and take charge for the rest of the day, cashing up after closing time and putting the takings into a night safe bag. Albert made a habit of staying at the shop until late in the evening, looking after the small animals they sold, watering the plants and generally looking after the shop. Quite often, he would be there until 10pm.

The shop was a most unwelcoming environment. It was cold, with only a couple of small electric heaters. It was very cluttered because many items on sale were kept outside during the day and placed inside the shop at night. Just inside the door was the counter and beyond that, several aisles all heavily laden with sale items. To the left, about halfway down the shop, was a door that led to the cellar and at the rear of the shop was a toilet and another door giving access to the rear yard.

The cellar was used for storing boxes, cardboard and a whole collection of items for sale. Upstairs, in what had previously been the bedrooms of a house, were a kitchen, an office and further storage space. It was Albert's habit to sit in the tiny kitchen with a heater and have his coffee during the evening.

In addition to the cash that was placed nightly into the night safe, there was a small amount of banknotes that were left, hidden under some old envelopes on the stairs leading from the shop to the upper floor. There was also a small quantity of change, left in the till drawer, which was placed in the toilet (the theory being that any burglar would find the change and think there was no more cash on the premises).

A cursory examination of the premises revealed that the window of the upstairs kitchen was open, a chair had been placed in front of it and there was a boot mark and a small splash of blood on the seat of the chair as if someone, with blood on their shoes, had left the premises via the window. It could be inferred that they had climbed down a drainpipe and gone out through a rear entrance. There was also a boot mark on the outside windowsill, adding to the appearance that someone had gone out that way.

On his arrival that morning, just before 9am, the 18-year-old assistant had been surprised to see Albert's car parked at the front of the shop. He had then found that the front door of the shop was only secured on a 'Yale' lock instead of the mortice as well. On entering, he found an electric heater switched on and standing in front of the cellar door. He then noticed that the shop's cordless telephone was broken and lay on the floor. He opened the cellar door and saw the light was on down there. By this light, he could see the body of Albert Bunting lying at the bottom of the steps. He went down the steps and found a horrific sight. Albert had been battered to death with an iron bar and with such violence that blood had spattered up the wall, across the ceiling and down the opposite side. He was almost unrecognisable because of over 20 separate blows to the head.

The youth ran back up the stairs and used a second phone to call the sixteen-year-old son of the Dumaynes. The son told him to phone the police and then made his way to the shop and was there before I arrived. Also in the shop, by that time, was the sixteen-year-old assistant.

I then arranged for the Fire Brigade to attend to cover and then remove the upstairs window where the chair had been placed, in order to prevent the inclement weather from destroying any evidence.

The first few hours of a murder enquiry are always chaotic but they are also the most vital hours because it is a well-known fact that murders, not detected within the first 48 hours, are often extremely hard to resolve. There are literally dozens of things for the Senior Investigating Officer (SIO) to do and make decisions upon. Many of these cannot be delegated because they are so vital. The first priority is to decide if the enquiry is large enough to use the Home Office Large Major Enquiry System (HOLMES) which is the computer system introduced following the enquiry into the 'Yorkshire Ripper' investigation when the person convicted of a series of murders of women, was found to be on the card system used at that time, on no less than six separate occasions.

HOLMES is a wonderful asset because it can search all records created in the enquiry for any reference to a word, number, description or name.

However, to be able to search those records, they must all first be typed into the system so it is very intensive in human resources, requiring typists, indexers, statement readers, allocators and computer experts. The decision to use it involves a very high financial cost from the outset but it is now almost an automatic decision except in the smallest of homicide enquiries. It was not a difficult decision to set up a HOLMES team in this case.

Secondly, resources are required on a large scale, not just for HOLMES but also for enquiry teams, Scenes of Crime Officers (SOCO's) Ground Search teams and House-to-House teams. In addition, it is usual to call a Forensic Pathologist to the scene and sometimes Forensic Scientists.

Meanwhile, the press will have found out about the enquiry and will be clamouring for information so the Force Press Officer must be briefed, as will senior officers. Premises are needed for the investigation (although Northamptonshire Police have a series of fully equipped Incident Rooms located with the permanent base of the HOLMES team).

The SIO is also under pressure to give a briefing to his staff who are all desperate to get the enquiry under way. There can easily be up to 100 people waiting for their briefing and this is at a time when the SIO has barely had time to discover what he is dealing with. Depending on the time of day, it can even be better to leave the call out of resources until the next morning, despite the earlier comment about early detections.

In this case, I set the briefing time for 1pm and was forced to put it back to 1.30pm to enable people to get to Northampton. The Uniformed Support Group were anxious to start ground searches for the weapon and any blood staining but I could not allow them to start until I had at least a vague idea what they would be looking for.

I asked for a team of Forensic Scientists from the Huntingdon Laboratory to attend as well as the local Forensic Pathologist from Leicester Hospital and they were soon on site and working. Our own SOCO's always work with these experts and can provide expertise in photography and even some techniques that require as much expertise as that of the scientists. In this case, because of the extraordinarily cluttered nature of the scene, the scientists were on site for five days, during which time the shop obviously had to remain closed.

I attended the Post Mortem examination that evening and was amazed by the ferocity of the attack on a defenceless elderly man. Indeed there was only one defence wound on his forearm, the other 23 blows having landed on his head and face, fracturing his skull and making him almost unrecognisable as a human being.

Clues were in remarkably short supply. Obviously there were hundreds of fingerprints in the shop but, after many weeks, only six remained unidentified and these were all in the public area, mostly on the external door. The boot marks on the upstairs chair and windowsill came from a sole made in Portugal for several types of fashion boot including 'Timberland', which were commonly used by young men at that time.

No trace could be found of the murder weapon but the Post Mortem revealed that it was probably a tyre lever with a forked end and the shop owner was able to tell us, on his return, that such a tyre lever was missing from the shop. The cash float normally hidden on the stairs was missing.

Our next problem was that we had a large number of suspects. Two brothers who were self-confessed burglars were seen in the area that night and it transpired that they were living in a street at the side of the shop. They did not have a very strong alibi but there was no other evidence against them.

Another, well-known, violent criminal from the same area, was on the run from prison and he had gone to hospital that night with a wound on his arm. This was verified but when arrested, he admitted breaking into a car and cutting himself as he did so.

A man had been seen in the area, wearing a yellow road workers jacket at 10.30pm on the night of the murder and enquiries were in hand to trace him. A further sighting was of a man in a yellow tracksuit who had been seen to throw something into a builders skip and was thought to have blood on his clothing.

We then received information about another local burglar who had broken into many of the shops in that stretch of Wellingborough Road and was known to be strongly addicted to drugs. He was arrested for other matters and interviewed but denied any knowledge of the murder.

It was then that we decided to publicise the case on BBC's 'Crimewatch' programme and they agreed to do a reconstruction and make it the top case of the month. I have the utmost regard for the researchers and staff of the programme. I had helped to set the programme up at its inception as the Staff Officer to ACPO Crime Committee and I had previously met the presenters so I was not as unfamiliar with the way it worked as some of my colleagues. It is nevertheless a very stressful programme to participate in with the time constraints on each item, the requirement to help out with all of the phone calls relating to all of the items and, if you are the SIO, the thought of talking to 16,000,000 people.

Our presentation went well and calls began to flood in, including one from a lady who worked in a Social Security office in Liverpool who claimed to know the identity of the man in the yellow road workers jacket. Our detectives patiently explained that the man she had seen on the TV was, in fact, a police officer playing the part of the suspect. "I'm not stupid," she replied, "I know that was a police officer but I can tell you who the man in the yellow jacket in Northampton was." She later explained that, the day after the murder, she had been at work in Liverpool when a man wearing such a jacket had come in to apply for emergency assistance and told her that he had just arrived from Northampton, where he had spent the evening wandering the streets before getting a lift to Liverpool.

She gave us his name and when he was traced and interviewed, he confirmed that, yes, he was indeed the man and had been hanging about in the relevant area at 10.30pm although he knew nothing about the murder and was not even aware of a pet shop there. The odds against the lady identifying the correct man must be astronomical. Unfortunately, the man in the tracksuit could not be traced despite our appeal on the programme and a search of the skip had failed to identify what he was thought to have thrown into it.

There was another call from a young woman that was far more significant. I cannot reveal the details of this call but suffice it to say that she claimed to know the identity of the murderer.

This man was quickly arrested but there was no firm evidence upon which to charge him despite lengthy interviews and even extended detention authorised by the Magistrates so he was released on bail.

During the course of the enquiry, another witness came forward, who said that he was driving past the shop at about 9pm on the night of the murder, when he saw Albert, whom he knew slightly from visits to the shop, standing just inside the shop doorway with a young man whom he described in detail but from the back, which was all he said he could see. In the interests of justice, I am unable to relate some other facts surrounding this case but the description given by this witness did match another main suspect.

I submitted case papers against both of my main suspects, separately, to the CPS, and predictably, they declined to prosecute either, partly based upon the fact that neither man knew the other, but after disclosure of the prosecution case, either would use the obvious defence that the other did it.

Yet another witness came forward to report that they had been in Wellingborough Road at about 8.30pm when a young man had run, very fast, down the road from the direction of the shop, towards the town centre and the witness had noticed this youth particularly – because he was stark naked. Could this have been the murderer, having dumped his bloodstained clothing or was it someone a little odd or was the witness mistaken? It was a long time after that he came forward.

So, who killed Albert Bunting and why? Was it really a casual burglar who had entered the shop without realising that Albert was there? There was no sign of a forced entry and the marks on the upstairs window were almost certainly made by someone leaving the shop. Or was it someone he knew and admitted to the shop after hours as seemed to be indicated by the evidence of the witness who drove past during the evening?

Despite a massive enquiry involving dozens of detectives and uniformed staff and costing a fortune in police time, the case remains undetected and, as in all serious cases, still open. It remains a source of great interest to me even at this length of time although I believe that the offender is most likely to have been one of the suspects interviewed.

Chapter 29

Although I did not realise it then, this was to be the last serious crime I would investigate personally. As I finalised the reports on the two suspects I was promoted to Temporary Detective Chief Superintendent and I soon discovered that this role, despite the glamorous title, is in fact largely an administrative post and is more concerned with policy than direct investigation.

The role does involve supervising the Senior Investigating Officers (SIO) but generally, these are very experienced, capable detectives who need no supervision or guidance. The only control truly experienced by the DCS is control of the budget and this is a source of much argument with the SIOs whose only concern is with detecting the crime and not saving money. They are nevertheless, responsible people and do not believe in wasting money but they do not believe in saving money to the point of hindering the investigation.

I remained in this post for the next four years, being promoted to the permanent rank of DCS in the course of that time. As I have said the role was mainly concerned with policy and although I was consulted about many difficult and serious crimes in that time, including a headless corpse at Corby, a contract shooting at Rushden, a very complex murder enquiry of a woman at Corby and the murder of a prostitute whose naked body was found on a railway line near Northampton, these were all matters dealt with by the SIOs and therefore do not form part of my story.

The only two that I was more closely involved in were a case of transporting guns for the Protestant paramilitaries in Northern Ireland which resulted in armed officers from Northamptonshire, working with the Regional Crime Squad and Special Branch following the suspects from Corby, through various other Force areas and finally carrying out an armed stop on the suspects in the Lake District. This was an excellent operation with full co-operation from all of the Forces involved and led to the recovery of guns and ammunition and the arrest of a dangerous little gang who received prison sentences.

The other was an attempt to extort money from the grocery giant, Tesco, by threats of food contamination. Although this was dealt with by an SIO various factors meant that I would take a much closer interest than I would have for most serious crimes.

Not least of the matters that affected my role was the death of the first appointed SIO, who had been suffering from cancer for some time but had continued working until the last possible moment. The death of a colleague is always hard to take but this was particularly hard because he had been so brave and stoical in bearing the pain and continuing with a difficult enquiry at the same time.

The circumstances of the case began when a loaf of bread was injected with dye and left on the shelves of the Tesco Superstore at Kettering. A note left for the manager demanded a huge payment to avoid future contamination with something more deadly than dye.

As I had found on a previous enquiry, the hardest part of this type of crime for the criminal is working out how to get their hands on the money and get away with it. This criminal had worked out a particularly clever and complicated method of getting his money.

His instructions were that Tesco must advertise an experiment with a 'loyalty card' (something that had not been invented at that time) to be issued only at the Dudley (West Midlands) store. The card was to be made available on one Saturday only and it was to resemble a credit card. The odd thing was that he demanded that it should, in fact, be a credit card that could be used to obtain cash from ATMs with the correct PIN code.

Tesco's were then to publish in 'The Times' a secret coded message to include the PIN code so that the only person who would have both a card and the number would be the blackmailer. He could then use cash machines at will, provided Tesco kept enough money in the account.

This scheme was particularly ingenious because parts of it had been previously used by a blackmailer who was an ex policeman but the public in this country had not heard of loyalty cards and Tesco said they had no plans to introduce them (though, in fact they had been planning such a scheme for some time).

Initially, Tesco said that the proposal was impossible but after we consulted with a major credit card company, who have their Head Office locally, it was concluded that it was possible to produce such a card and we would have an opportunity to catch the blackmailer. The plan that was finally agreed was that the Dudley store would advertise a day when the experimental cards would be made available for anyone who wanted them. We arranged for CCTV to cover all of the people who took a card and each was to be followed to their car by experienced surveillance teams. Then when the tapes were reviewed, any suspicious characters could be identified. The coded PIN number was published in The Times and Tescos made available a fund to allow the criminals to use the card and hopefully be caught red handed.

On the day, the plan seemed to work like clockwork with every person who took a card being followed to their cars and the number being recorded. A team of officers carefully reviewed the tapes at the end of the day and one person was identified as a likely suspect. This person purported to be a woman but the officers felt that it was a man dressed in women's clothing. This person was followed to a Ford Mondeo car and the number recorded. It was traced to a company rep living in the West Midlands and his house was placed under surveillance. Unfortunately, no one even remotely resembling the woman went anywhere near the house and we took the decision to obtain a search warrant.

A very shocked but totally innocent company rep suffered a few hours of considerable trauma being interviewed by the Regional Crime Squad but he was able to prove his whereabouts on the day of the incident and both he and the car were nowhere near Dudley at any time that day. Nevertheless, the card and PIN began to be used extensively in the West Midlands area. We had placed a limit on the amount of daily transactions but the criminal managed to obtain several thousands of pounds without being caught. At that time, very few ATM machines were equipped with cameras to record users so we had to wait until a pattern of use was established and then police cameras were established in a selected number of ATMs. At least two of these caught images of the person obtaining the money and it was clear that it was a man but the police did not know his identity.

Eventually, we decided to stop the card and risk the wrath of the blackmailer. It was not long in coming! He wrote to Tesco's Head Office but, unaccountably, agreed to give them one more chance on the basis that the machine might have seized the card in error. He demanded that the whole exercise be repeated at Dudley store and this was duly carried out with a new PIN number published in The Times.

This time however, we had the advantage of having seen an image of the face of the blackmailer so when, at about 3pm, he walked into the store and took a card, Regional Crime Squad officers were able to follow him out of the store, out of the car park on foot and down the road to a car (not a Mondeo) that was waiting for him with one passenger. The passenger was soon identified as the woman who had taken a card the first time and a decision was made to follow them until they attempted to use the card.

This proved to be quite a long pursuit because they took a motorway towards Birmingham and then across country before turning south towards London. It was there, on the outskirts of London that the man went to an ATM and was in the act of inserting the card in the machine when he felt the heavy hand of the law on his shoulder.

There was little point in denying the offence, especially when a search of his home revealed that his computer still held the letters of blackmail he had sent. These were quite well hidden in the files but we were fortunate enough to have on hand in Northamptonshire, one of the country's leading experts of forensic computing and he quickly imaged the hard disk and located the incriminating letters.

Also found in the house was a set of number plates which were identical to those on the Mondeo we had identified on the first card issue. On interview, our suspect explained that he had guessed that we would try to follow people who took cards so he had written down the number of a passing Mondeo, had a set of plates made and then hired an identical car, which his wife used to go to the Dudley store.

All round, it was an ingenious plan, though he never did tell us where he got he idea of loyalty cards from or whether he knew that Tesco's planned to introduce them. Throughout the interviews and subsequent trial, both the man and his wife (who could now be clearly identified as the 'man dressed as a woman') insisted that she had only acted under duress from her husband and I was amazed when the jury returned a verdict of 'Not Guilty' on her. The man pleaded 'Guilty' and was sentenced to eight years in prison and Tesco went ahead with their very successful loyalty card scheme. Another effect was that many more ATMs were equipped with cameras thereafter.

I personally, could take very little of the credit for this highly professional operation and I was left with a very high regard for the ability of the Regional Crime Squad and my own staff, particularly the Superintendent who so tragically died during the operation and the Temporary Superintendent who took his place.

It becomes obvious that the higher up the rank structure of the Police Force one climbs, the less one is able to take a personal part in investigations and operational work. That is probably why many good detective officers do not seek promotion beyond Superintendent because that is effectively the highest rank at which involvement is personal and detailed.

Chapter 30

From my earliest days in the Force, after having found what the job was about, I had nurtured the ambition to achieve the rank of Assistant Chief Constable. Realistically, I knew I could get no higher than that given my age when joining and my educational background. Quite suddenly, however, I was thrust onto the stage of this higher rank when I was invited to become the Acting Assistant Chief Constable (ACC) for several months.

I was a little surprised to find that the job actually was as an assistant to the Chief Constable and therefore the rank carried little authority of its own, even though it was the third highest position in the Force. This is not to say that there was no responsibility because the job involved all of the operational command of the Force.

The Chief Superintendents all answer to the ACC but they have such a degree of independence and indeed, experience that they need little control or guidance. The Chief Constable, on the other hand requires to know all about anything that catches his (or her) eye and expects the ACC to know the answers.

I was part of a chain of acting appointments that included the Acting Chief Constable and Acting Deputy Chief Constable, both of whom were ambitious to make the posting permanent. This did tend to make my job slightly harder than it might have been but I did thoroughly enjoy about 5 months in this challenging role and, although I did not exactly see eye to eye with the lady who was the Acting Chief Constable, I knew that I had carried the responsibility well enough and was quite hopeful that I might be successful in my application for the permanent post.

I was supported by the HMI and the new Chief Constable (the lady was unsuccessful in her application) said that he could happily work with me as his Assistant. On the day of the interviews I found that the competition appeared to be between myself and a young candidate from a neighbouring Force. Two other candidates appeared for interview but it was fairly obvious that neither was properly prepared or suitable for the level of responsibility that they would have in a small Force.

I knew that I had a good interview and made a sound presentation on a subject we were given the night before. At the end of my interview, the Chair of the Police Authority thanked me and said she was sure they would 'see me later'. The implication of that statement was considerable because the format of such interviews is that the successful candidate is recalled to be offered the job whilst the Chief Constable informs the unsuccessful candidates at the end of the day. Therefore to 'see me later' seemed a hint that I was likely to be successful.

Unfortunately for me, I was not successful, losing out to the young candidate from the neighbouring Force. It was small consolation to be told later that I came a close second but on the day he had 'walked on water'.

Many officers become bitter at such a setback but those that do only cause suffering to themselves and I was determined not to do that so I immediately threw myself into my work. Had I been successful, I would have had to undertake to serve for at least four years and I had always promised Jackie that I would retire after thirty years. Four years would have taken me to thirty-two years so I took consolation from the fact that I would, after all, be able to retire as I had promised, at thirty years.

My thoughts then turned to the fact that I had never actually served in Northampton even though it was my hometown and I had told the Deputy Chief Constable on joining all those years before that I wanted to serve there. I had, of course worked on various enquiries in the town but never as my posting. Coincidence then took a hand because I was talking to Peter Barclay, by then a Chief Superintendent and the Area Commander at Northampton and he was very keen to return to CID. We both spoke to the Chief Constable and were given permission to swap jobs!

It is most unusual for a Detective Chief Superintendent voluntarily to give up a CID post to return to uniform duties, but that is precisely what I did and soon found that I had taken on a far bigger and more responsible job. Taking into account support staff and the Special Constabulary, Northampton had a staff of over 500 people and a budget approaching £13,000,000 per year.

My introduction to the command of Northampton started with a bang – quite literally. I was due to start work at 9am on a Monday morning but at 3am some ne'er-do-well decided to firebomb Weston Favell Police Station. Hence I received my first call out 6 hours before I even started at the place.

The town of Northampton has a population of just fewer than 200,000 people served by two main police stations. The Area Headquarters is at Campbell Square, in the centre and Weston Favell on the outskirts. It is interesting to note how management fashions seem to go round in circles in the Police Service. At one time Northampton was a single Force with its own Chief Constable, then the fashion became for fewer Forces and the Borough was absorbed into the County Force as a Division. Subsequently, the town was split into two, hence the reason for the two Police Stations.

However, the fashion changed again and the town became one Area and this restructuring had reduced the management staffing from one Chief Superintendent, two Superintendents, four Chief Inspectors and about 20 Inspectors, supported by two Resource Managers and all of the back up staff, to one Chief Superintendent and fourteen Inspectors with one Resource Manager. In fact this senior staffing level was totally inadequate and I found that I was working enormously long days and then being recalled to duty whenever something required a Superintendent's authority, or there was a firearms incident – these occurred roughly every two weeks and always seemed to be at night.

A Superintendent's authority was required if a prisoner was to be detained for more than 24 hours, if an intimate search was required or intimate samples were to be taken (for example, pubic hairs in rape cases or penile swabs, and so on). For some of these authorities the prisoner had to be allowed to make personal representations to the Superintendent in person so it was necessary to actually return to the station. Luckily for me, the Inspector (Operations), Andy Dickson was one of the most competent senior officers I have ever encountered, and he was perfectly capable of dealing with any incident that arose, including firearms incidents, although he was not then permitted to deal with them without my direct supervision.

I was soon able to arrange to have him promoted to Chief Inspector and to attend the relevant course that enabled him to deal with firearms incidents unsupervised. In this way, the two of us could just manage the supervisory responsibilities we faced. In fact, since my retirement, the management structure has been altered again to provide a second Superintendent.

Andy and I had been in post for only a very short time when we were faced with a major disaster of huge proportions. Over many years, Northampton had been susceptible to flooding in the areas of St James and Far Cotton. However, there had been no really serious floods for two decades and so no one was particularly alarmed during Maundy Thursday, 1998 even though heavy rain had fallen continuously for several days.

No flood warnings had been issued for our area although some minor roads were under water in the south of the county on the Daventry Police Area. The new ACC called me during the afternoon and asked if we had any reported problems and, after checking the control room, I was able to say that we had not. Furthermore, the CCTV system in Northampton was one of the most widespread and sophisticated in the country and we were able to actually see that the River Nene was high but well within its banks.

About 4pm, a narrow boat was making its way upstream through the Midsummer Meadow Park, intending to get to quieter waters on the canal beyond Far Cotton. As it approached the South Bridge in Far Cotton, local residents called to the man and woman crew to warn them that they would not be able to get under the bridge because of the speed and height of the water. The woman was at the front of the boat and her husband was steering at the back and unfortunately, he ignored the shouted advice and tried to get under the bridge. As the front of the boat passed under the bridge, the force of the current became too strong for the engine of the boat and it reached a point, with the front through to the other side of the bridge, when the balance of force was such that the boat would go no further and obviously could not go back.

Gradually, the front of the boat swung towards the bank and the boat hit the side of the bridge, throwing the woman off and into the water, where she was instantly swept away. Responding to the emergency calls, my officers attended the scene and began walking the banks of the river looking for her. Others called the Fire and Rescue Service to try to secure the boat whilst other officers attempted to console the husband.

Andy Dickson went to our 'Silver Control' room (a separate control room used only for major incidents and which is intended to take the pressure off the main control room). When he gave me a situation report, it was obvious that we would need assistance from other Areas to make a proper search of the river, even though we clearly realised that we were searching for a body rather than a live person. It would be unsafe to allow boats on the river and the only thing we could do was to walk the banks. We did however contact Spartan Rescue, a locally based company that specialises in water rescue and they generously volunteered to turn out their boats and use their expertise to begin a water search if they felt it was safe to do so.

I called the ACC for assistance from the other Areas and although they sent as many officers as they could, we soon realised that we were hampered by the fact that some Areas were now suffering from flooding and, because of the Easter holidays, were already short of staff. From the Silver Control, we were keeping a wary eye on the river because it was in imminent danger of bursting its banks in the Midsummer Meadow area and it was there that our staff were searching.

By about 7.30pm, we decided to withdraw our officers because the search was now hopeless and was becoming dangerous as the officers were increasingly cold and wet and night had fallen. The ACC had decided to set up a 'Gold Control' at FHQ to control the whole flooding situation and I went to report the Northampton situation leaving the Chief inspector in command.

My route to FHQ took me past the South Bridge and I decided to have a look at the scene where the accident had occurred. I found that the Fire and Rescue Service had tried to pull the boat through to the bank with a Fire engine but all they had achieved was to pull a piece of railing off the boat. We decided at the scene that the best hope was to use a huge lorry recovery crane to pull the boat to the bank. It was essential that we did this because it seemed that the boat was blocking part of the river and making it run even faster through the bridge.

A local company quickly attended with a massive tow truck and began to pull the boat to the bank. Unfortunately the power of the crane also had the effect of pulling it up the bank, pushing the back of the boat deeper into the water, where it immediately sank. It was however securely fixed to some trees and in no danger.

After the meeting at Gold Control, where I learned the extent of the flooding throughout the county and began to think that we had been lucky to have no flooding at Northampton, I returned to my station and agreed to leave Andy Dickson in command until the incident could be finalised, as I was the duty Chief Superintendent for the whole weekend and would obviously be needed the next morning.

This was a fortunate decision for me because I did at least get a few hours sleep before calling the station at 6am for a situation report. I was therefore surprised to receive that report from Andy, who had been there all night but had not called me, knowing that I would have to take over command of what had escalated during the night into a disaster.

He informed me that he had just about cleared the boat incident at about 11.30pm when reports began to come in of minor flooding of some streets in various parts of the town. He had stayed on to monitor that situation when, shortly before 1am, a torrent of water had come rushing downstream and the St James and Far Cotton areas of the town were inundated. Some streets were under more than five feet of swirling water and the officers on duty were suddenly transformed from traffic control duties to the urgent rescue of householders who were in danger of drowning in their homes.

It is no exaggeration to say that there were many feats of heroism performed that night by my officers. Some had waded, chest deep through the floodwater to get to the homes of elderly residents. Two officers had to be taken to hospital suffering from hypothermia but then changed their uniforms and went straight back to duty to help with the rescue operation.

Those officers who had waded through the deep water had not realised the danger they were in until much later when Spartan Rescue staff advised them that floods often force drain covers off and to step into an open drain in those circumstances would result in certain death.

There is a potential conflict between the role of the police and the other emergency services in the face of a disaster. Strictly, the role of the police (the Constable) is to co ordinate the other services, making access and egress to and from the scene possible and effectively making the people do things they would not without some authority – stopping their cars, for example, or going in directions they did not wish to. A Constable is legally defined as '...a citizen, locally appointed but having authority under the Crown...' But the confusion begins to arise over what he or she has 'authority' for, because the definition includes, along with enforcement of the law, '..the protection of life and property.'

Therefore the Constable has the element of rescuing those in need within his raison d'etre as well as making them do that which they do not wish to do, and the element of protecting quickly comes to the forefront. Sometimes, a senior officer has the difficult task of ordering his men to withdraw from this rescue work because it can mean that the vital task of coordinating and facilitating the other services is failing for lack of available staff.

In the Northampton floods, during that first night, the police had to concentrate on rescue. There was no question of that, or many more people would have lost their lives. The Fire and Rescue Service had no hope of coping with the rescue of the numbers of people at risk that night. It took the combined efforts of the Police, The Fire and Rescue Service, The Ambulance Service, The Northamptonshire County Council, Social Services, Northampton Borough Council and dozens of volunteers including the Women's Royal Voluntary Service, Churches, members of the public and anyone who had a boat to try to get people out of their homes and to Rescue Centres which were set up around the town.

The two areas affected most, St James and Far Cotton, contained many elderly residents in private terraced homes, as well as Council owned properties, and before morning, over 2000 homes and a busy shopping area (St Leonards Road, Far Cotton) were under five feet of dirty polluted water. The number of people displaced exceeded 5000 and in many cases, they were unaccounted for because they had made their own way to the homes of friends or relatives.

The sheer force of the water had to be seen to be believed for, at one stage, a huge petrol tanker was being swept along St Leonards Road, smashing into cars and sweeping them along as it went. In the midst of that chaos, my officers were walking through those streets and forcing their way into homes, getting people out as fast as they could.

The Social Services worked hard to produce a list of all of the vulnerable people they knew of and this was passed to my control room and to the Fire and Rescue Services. The pressure on our two control rooms and the staff in there was unbelievable with the volume of calls being received. When one takes into account the fact that on any weekend evening, the fourteen staff in my control room were hard put to cope with the volume of calls anyway, resulting in some going unanswered; compound this by the fact that this was the Thursday evening at the start of a holiday weekend; then add the fact that we, like everyone else would like to take holidays off, thus resulting in a minimum of staff; then on top of all that, to try to run a 'Silver Control' as well, it is not surprising that mistakes were made.

However, when I called in for a situation report early on the Friday morning, the only death reported was the lady who had been thrown from the narrow boat and we counted ourselves very fortunate.

I arrived at the control room shortly after 6am to take over from Andy Dickson who was, by now, exhausted having been on duty for almost 24 hours but still looked as fresh as when he started. We discussed the situation and agreed that we needed assistance from the Armed Forces – a most unusual step. We were told that they had boats available and would be with us shortly. In fact the first soldier appeared at about 11am and by the time the boats arrived, the water had subsided. It transpired that they had had to come from Peterborough and had been unable to get through because of flooding in the north of our county.

The Military tend to get a good press when they help out in such disasters but I have to say honestly that they were not able to give much assistance with the rescue though I did use them (possibly illegally) to help later with patrols and security when looting began to be reported. All power and gas had been cut off by the relevant authorities to prevent fires and explosions but now it was impossible to reconnect the power until every single home had been inspected for safety and this was to prove a mammoth task.

The water was receding very quickly except in the lowest lying areas by mid morning and the rain had finally stopped. We set up assistance points at strategic locations near to the flooding and directed people to the rescue centres and I quickly decided to have a personal look at how they were coping, after attending the morning briefing at Gold Control at Headquarters.

It was when I returned to my own control room that I discovered we had a second death on our hands. An elderly lady, living alone in one of the worst affected areas, had drowned in her own living room. Later enquiries revealed that she had been on the list of vulnerable people given to us by the Social Services but one of my operators had written the name address down incorrectly in the confusion of the night. The lady herself, who walked with a 'Zimmer Frame' had dialled 999 to say that the water was up to her knees. She had been put through to the Fire and Rescue Service who had tried to reassure her and said they would get to her as soon as possible. She had later called again and said that the water was getting higher but again she had been put through to the Fire and Rescue Service who, by then were themselves overburdened with calls and somehow, her call did not get a response from them.

This was the very worst of the tragedy for us all in the emergency services and we could do nothing to rectify it or ease the pain. It is very easy to apportion blame for such an incident or to seek to avoid responsibility. We could not, and would not, try to do so in this case, and admitted openly that we had made some tragic mistakes. My operator was distraught at having written the name and address wrongly and I can only imagine how the staff at the Fire and Rescue control room felt. We could not even take the time to grieve or even think about those issues at that time so I managed to obtain the services of a very experienced constable from the Daventry Area, who was allocated to take on the task of dealing with the sudden death and making the initial enquiries into the circumstances.

The Electricity Board had sent a team to begin the task of checking each premises before restoring the power and I set up several centres, each run by an Inspector, to identify the houses where we knew the whereabouts of the occupants and could get them back to open up or, in the absence of that information, to have a forced entry made by the police. This was essential because the weather remained very cold and there could be no question of people returning to homes with no power. Surprisingly, the gas authority did not need to gain entry because they were able to place an instrument through the letterboxes to detect any escaping gas and indeed they did not find any. Even more surprising was the fact that the water authority were satisfied that there was no danger to the fresh water supplies but, of course, the water is contained in its pipes and, providing there is no contamination at the source, it is safe. Sewage was naturally a different matter and it was to be many months before some of the homes could be re-inhabited. Indeed, I believe some were still not occupied five years later.

During the course of that Friday, I liaised with the senior manager of the Electricity Board and I told him that he needed to increase the size of his team checking the houses. There were only about five or six in the team and with 2000 homes to check it was obvious that we could not wait before restoring power and getting people back to their houses. Despite the fact that he told me it was almost impossible on a holiday weekend, I was amazed, the next morning, when over fifty electricity staff turned up from all over the Midlands and completed most of their work by Saturday evening.

Our biggest immediate problem was looting, which was being reported in some areas. It amazes me that some people can sink so low as to steal from the homes of those who have suffered so much. But they do, and they did in Northampton in 1998. Regrettably, there were also those who exaggerated the problem for their own political ends. One man claimed to be witnessing looting in the St James area as he spoke on the telephone but a check on the number he was calling from revealed that he was actually about 5 miles from St James – perhaps he had very good eyesight!

Throughout the crisis, Northampton Borough Council was superb. Despite the fact that their main depot, in St James Road, was under water and much of their equipment was damaged beyond repair, they were unstinting in their support with finance and manpower.

The main police operation lasted until the following Tuesday and by then the recriminations had begun. It was to be expected that people who had lost everything and in many cases, were not insured, would seek to place blame for their situation. Two major public meetings were arranged, one in St James on the Tuesday evening and on the Thursday in Far Cotton. I was well aware that the residents of St James were being organised by a committee and there were some difficult characters with political motivation on the committee. I anticipated that there would be some recriminations against the Police and Fire and Rescue Services because of the death of the elderly lady, but I felt sure there would be a major outcry against the Environment Agency for failing to give adequate warning about the impending floods and because they had still been unable to identify the source or cause of the major inundation late on the Thursday evening.

I, therefore, arranged to have a small contingent of officers discreetly available at the hall. The meeting was attended by at least 300 residents and fronted by the Chair of the Police Authority, backed by the Fire Chief, Council representatives, the local MP and myself. I was amazed to become the sole focus of the fury of the residents, not because of the death but because we had failed to warn the residents in time to save their belongings.

They would not listen to my protestations that we had no more warning than them, insisting that we had stood by and done nothing in the face of an obvious threat. Some insisted that we could have toured the streets with loudspeakers in the mistaken belief that police cars are all fitted with such equipment. How they thought the police cars could have toured streets flooded by up to five feet of water by the time we knew we had a problem I do not know.

When someone shouted that we could have used the 'skyshout' public address system on the helicopter, I did not even bother to try to explain that the helicopter was grounded because of the weather; I was so angry that my heroic officers were being blamed so unjustly for the weather and for something over which we had no control.

The Environment Agency had not even attended the meeting and had thereby escaped the initial brunt of the intemperate onslaught, though to this day, I have never heard a satisfactory explanation from them for not giving warnings and for failing to ever identify the source of the sudden 'tide' in the early hours of the first day.

There have been suggestions that it was an overflow from Pitsford reservoir, that some floodgates were not opened when they should have been, that the increase in building to the south of the town had destroyed the natural floodplain and that the build up in the river caused it to change its direction just outside the town, but none has been confirmed. The last two seem the most likely, and there was evidence from a farmer that he saw the river burst and change direction at about 1am, though that was a little late to have been the main cause. Since then, the Environment Agency has spent millions of pounds reinforcing the flood defences and there has, so far been no repeat.

A flood relief fund was set up under the auspices of the Borough Council and I was invited to be a member of the distribution committee. Although the amount of money raised was substantial, it could never be enough to compensate all those who suffered losses and the distribution was a major headache with the need to show scrupulous fairness and ensure no one made fraudulent claims. However, priorities were established and the money was distributed to the best of our ability. Some insurance companies were wonderful, making early interim payments but others were so slow as to make the process very difficult for losers. There was at least one bogus builder going round damaged houses and using the pretext of examining the buildings to steal newly replaced goods – another example of the despicable nature of some citizens.

As for the police, we learned some lessons and will probably not make again the mistakes we did then. Andy Dickson, now a Chief Superintendent, has become an authority on cold-water rescue work and Spartan Rescue still provide training.

The verdict on the elderly lady was Accidental Death and her family accepted that mistakes were inevitable in such circumstances. They therefore made no complaint. The body of the lady from the narrow boat was found five weeks later, several miles downstream and her husband had his boat repaired, though the last time I saw him, at the inquest on his wife, I felt that could have demonstrated more concern for the loss of his younger Thai wife.

That same summer, another water based tragedy occurred in Northampton, when a seven-year-old boy from West Bromwich was reported missing from the caravan he had been staying in at Billing Aquadrome, which is a huge recreation park with about 17 acres of water formed from old quarries and bounded by the River Nene. The family had two caravans at the park and took regular holidays there. They were a very close family and enjoyed the atmosphere of the fishing, amusements, fairground and seemingly safe parkland for the children to play. They had a good circle of friends there and one had given the little lad an old bicycle to play on in the park.

One day, the lad had been with his father who was fishing in one of the lakes near to their caravan, whilst his wife had gone to the laundry, some distance away. The boy decided he wanted to go and see his grandparents whose caravan was at the far side of the lake perhaps a half-mile away and he set off on the bicycle.

In short, he was never seen alive again. The grandparents had, in fact, gone off the site to visit the Weston Favell shopping centre on the outskirts of Northampton. So it was some hours later, when they returned, that the family realised the boy was not with either parents or grandparents.

The police were informed after the family, with the aid of friends, had conducted their own search of the park. The first call came in about 8pm, and officers attended the scene to find the whole family distraught and fearing the worst.

Andy Dickson was called out and soon set up a 'Silver Control', directing officers to commence a proper co-ordinated Police search. The Force has its own specialist search team, the Uniformed Support Group (USG) and they set up a control point at the park.

Some well meaning witnesses claimed to have seen the boy playing with other children in the early evening whilst there were even reports that he had been seen with a man, near to the amusement area. This gave rise to the obvious concerns that he might have been abducted, and doubled the resource problem for us, because we then had to begin investigating a possible crime as well as the massive task of searching hundreds and hundreds of caravans and many dozens of acres of parkland.

Whilst not ignoring the 17 acres of water, this had to take second priority because we had to concentrate our resources on searching for a live boy, whether he had suffered an accident and was lying injured or whether he had been abducted. Through the night the numbers of officers being used expanded until we had no less than 100 on site, and a cursory search of all caravans, occupied or not, was carried out. A checkpoint was established at the gates of the site and officers from the Traffic Department searched all vehicles leaving.

At first sight, one could be forgiven for thinking that the Chief Inspector should have called out his Chief Superintendent but the fact is that we had to have complete trust in each other's judgement and he was perfectly capable of setting up and running an enquiry of this magnitude. He also knew that he could not work all night and all day so he left it until just before 6am before calling me to take over command.

We now had to think about the implications of the search. These included such matters as providing refreshments for this number of officers, detailing and identifying those caravans which had been properly searched, beginning the water search, widening the search area to the countryside beyond the park and making public appeals. Spartan Rescue Ltd again came to our aid, as did the Milton Keynes Search and Rescue team (a voluntary organisation that specialises in countryside searches).

We devised a system of colour-coded stickers for the caravans that had been searched and set up a field canteen to provide meals in a tent on site. We received full co-operation from the owners of the park, who provided staff to assist with the identification of all of the caravans and maps of the site. They also provided rooms for briefings and press conferences.

A really major problem began to develop from the attention of the press. It seems that it was what they describe as a 'quiet' news period and I began to receive calls from all of the major News outlets including ITN, Sky News, CNN and local TV down to the local radio and newspapers.

The effect of all this was that I had to have the Force Press Office on site, but even then, they were not satisfied with a Press Officer and constantly wanted me to respond personally to their questions.

I appointed two Family Liaison Officers to try to protect and help the family members. Family Liaison Officers are specially trained to assist in murder enquiries and are often, as in this case, detectives.

By 11am on the Friday morning, we had set up all of these arrangements and replaced the night shift staff with a fresh 100 officers from all over the Force, but all had been to no avail. There had been no fresh sightings and no new information. The caravan search was well on the way but was producing nothing. Officers had by then walked the banks of all of the lakes and the river without finding anything and Milton Keynes Search and Rescue had expanded their search area well beyond the park.

Spartan Rescue had begun their water search but the size of that task cannot be over emphasized. There are many misconceptions about water searches, largely caused by TV images of underwater search teams going about their business in missing person cases. In fact, visibility under water is so limited that, in my experience, unless there are very well defined parameters, they are unlikely to find a body. Safety procedures for diving make them such an expensive unit that many Forces, including Northamptonshire do not have their own and prefer to pay another, larger Force when they need such a facility. I decided not to use one at that stage.

I had earlier asked the Chief Inspector from Daventry Area to take over my Silver Control so that I could be at the site personally. This was a reversal of the usual roles because it left the Senior Officer making on-site decisions whilst the wider view was being taken by his junior at base, but I did it because the activity needed my authority on site and the press demands could be better met from there. Faced with a similar situation again, I would move Silver Control to the site because it did cause the Chief Inspector a few command problems though it did not affect the overall running of the operation which went well throughout from a policing viewpoint.

A second command problem arose however, because I decided that we should now treat the enquiry as a serious crime enquiry and I appointed a SIO (a Detective Chief Inspector) to take on the crime aspects of the enquiry. My experience is that this often causes confusion if there are both crime and logistical issues to be resolved. A SIO expects to be given full discretion over the enquiries to be undertaken and every item must be entered onto his HOLMES computer system. This does not sit well with the senior uniformed staff who will often have started the enquiry and have more experience in such matters as ground searches etc. In this case I had to tread a fine line between giving the SIO control and ensuring that the lines of enquiry we had already started were satisfactorily completed. In fact, we did achieve this balance but not without some wry faces from both the SIO and the uniformed Chief Inspector.

The press made much of the appointment of the SIO, asking if it was now a murder enquiry and I held a press conference to introduce the SIO and explain that it remained a missing person enquiry but because we could not rule out foul play we wanted to be sure that there was a detective involvement from an early stage. Furthermore the use of the HOLMES system would enhance the administration of the enquiry considerably.

Shifts continued to change and the work continued throughout the night into Saturday morning. I then asked my Chief Inspector to come on duty because I knew that, by evening on that day, I would be exhausted, having had very little sleep since Thursday night. I gave a press conference to coincide with the mid-day news broadcasts but there was little to add. The news crews were still having a 'quiet' time and I found myself doing a live interview on ITN's 'News at One', followed by a similar broadcast on Sky News. This was a daunting prospect, knowing that one has an audience of millions and the slightest slip would be magnified many times over. In fact, the Chief Constable was on holiday abroad but actually saw one of those interviews.

Just at the conclusion of the interviews, my mobile phone rang and Andy Dickson who had now returned to duty, informed me that a body had been found less than 100 yards from where the press were gathered. He was alerting me because the helicopter would be taking pictures to relay to the control post and the activity could cause the press to find out before the parents were aware and we could not let that happen.

I managed to keep their attention away from the activity and went to the control room for a briefing. It transpired that a small boy had been walking by one of the lakes and, looking into the water from his eye level, a much lower point than the officers would have seen, he noticed the outline of a bicycle wheel in the water. He then informed his grandparents who went to see. They made a short attempt to reach the wheel with a fishing rod but could not do so and called the control post.

A young police woman had been first at the scene and she had only just sent the child and grandparents away, when the body of a small boy appeared on the surface of the water. This was about 50 hours after the lad had gone missing and was consistent with the post mortem body gases expanding and causing the body to float. There was no doubt that this was the missing boy but we had great concerns because there was, even on the 'Heli Tele' pictures, obvious signs of bleeding on the face.

The Family Liaison officers had already taken the family to Weston Favell Police Station and I asked a colleague, the Weekend Duty Superintendent, to join them there and tell them the tragic news they had been dreading. As soon as I was told that he had informed the family, I called another Press conference and thought of how I was to break the news to them and the world at large.

I commenced by saying, "It is with great sadness that I have to tell you that, within the last hour and since the last Press Conference, the body of a boy of about 7 years has been found in one of the lakes a short distance from here." As I said these words, a pin could have been heard to drop in the room and I felt a lump in my throat. I am told that most of the population of the park were gathered round TV sets having picked up rumours that an announcement was being made. Many of the holidaymakers burst into tears at the news and many a hardened police officer was seen to wipe a discreet eye.

I then called in the West Midlands Police Underwater Search Team to recover the body and the bicycle and the evidence of what had happened began to emerge. When we finally put the whole picture together, we established that the lad had left his father and gone to see his grandparents but finding them out, he decided to join his mother at the laundry instead of returning to his father.

His path took him round a corner of the lake and it seems that, as he pedalled furiously along, a loose shoelace had caught in the chain of the bicycle, causing him to lose control of the bike. He had then careered off the path, across a six feet wide piece of rough ground before shooting over the handlebars into the water and pulling the bike with him.

The bank at that point was vertical and led straight down into six feet of water. There were no witnesses but forensic examination showed that this was certainly the explanation. The bleeding we had seen was part of the post mortem process.

A week or so later, the Family Liaison Officers and I attended the funeral in West Bromwich as the guests of the family and it seemed that the whole of the council estate where he had lived had turned out because the streets were lined with people. I had never seen so many flowers, including wreaths sent by the West Bromwich Albion football club, of which he had been a fan. No less than six hearses were used solely to transport the flowers.

Chapter 31

Such events as the floods and this tragedy leave their mark on any senior police officer and it was only a few weeks before we were to face another. On a council estate in Northampton another seven-year-old boy was reported missing. The usual procedures were commenced, utilising the lessons learned from the previous incident even though there were substantial differences in that, for example, this boy was known to spend nights away from home and to mix with some bad elements on the estate. He had also been sighted during the evening of the day he was reported missing.

I sent an Inspector to identify a suitable room close to the scene for a forward control post and he reported that there were two suitable Community Centres quite locally. Either would have been acceptable but he chose one over the other, mainly because it was immediately available and open. The other was available but the keyholder would have to be found.

I thank our lucky stars that he chose the one he did, because, later in the morning, the keyholder opened the second centre for normal business and found the boy dead on the stage, having fallen through the roof. I doubt if we would have used the stage and if we had taken over the Centre, he could have lay there within feet of the officers and not been found. Although this enquiry was over almost before it started, I had sent Family Liaison Officers to the family and again we were invited to the funeral.

Though I was not conscious of it, the stress of these incidents was building up on me as the regular call-outs for firearms incidents and prisoner issues continued on a regular basis. The screw was about to take another turn. An important trial was to be held at Northampton Crown Court and the defendants and some witnesses were all Category 'A' prisoners at Whitemoor Prison in Cambridgeshire, where many of the most dangerous prisoners are held. The trial was moved from Peterborough Crown Court to Northampton because security was felt to be better there. The nature of the charges is not significant to this story but they centred on the kidnapping and holding as hostage of a prisoner by other prisoners in the jail.

Andy Dickson was on holiday and the command was all to fall to me. Whenever Category 'A' prisoners are moved, they have to be accompanied by armed officers and this meant that we were effectively running a firearms incident each day of the trial, which began on a Monday morning. This meant that I had to be on duty at Force Headquarters at 6am to brief the firearms team and supporting officers, then go to my own Headquarters to run a Silver Control from 8am until 5pm when the court ended and the prisoners were returned to prison. I then had to do my own office work and check the status of the Andy's tray before going home at 8pm with a briefcase full of papers to work on at home. There I continued work until 12 midnight before grabbing a few hours sleep and returning to repeat the whole process on the Tuesday.

This was repeated again on the Wednesday and again I worked at home until midnight. On this day, I had taken the unusual step for me, of having a fried breakfast with the team before going to the Silver Control. I had then had a sandwich on the run at lunchtime and by unlucky co incidence, tea at home was again a fried meal.

When, at midnight, I began to feel pains in my chest, I thought it must be indigestion, though I was obviously well aware of the dangers of a heart attack. I decided to sit and watch TV for a while but the pain did not abate and at 3am I awoke Jackie. I took some indigestion relief and the pain did stop, so I had a couple of hours sleep before going back to work again.

The court adjourned early that day and I had arranged for another Superintendent to cover it the following day, as I was due to be Duty Superintendent for the weekend. However, the pain had returned and, at 4pm, I spoke to a Police Surgeon who happened to be in the Station. Although he was not my own doctor, he did agree to check my chest and he pronounced that he could find nothing wrong but he wanted me to go to Northampton General Hospital for an ECG test. I said I would drive there so I could go straight home after but he would not hear of that and I had to have an Inspector drive me there.

The test revealed nothing wrong but the doctors wanted me to stay in hospital overnight. This was one of the worst nights I have spent. In the Cardiac Unit there was one man with angina who snored all night, one who had just had a triple by pass and was in pain. A third, in the next bed to me was a regular town centre drunk.

I had been given a drug, administered under the tongue, which is designed to relieve heart symptoms and which expands the arteries of the brain and can cause severe headaches. In my case it did so.

I had barely slept by 6am when I was awakened by a nurse who told me that I was likely to be on the ward for five days, despite the fact that a second ECG was also normal. When Jackie visited me later that morning, I said I had to escape from all these sick people and go to the coffee shop. The pain was gone by now but the nurse would not consider letting me leave the ward and only allowed me to take 20 steps, accompanied by her before sitting down again. It was a massive relief when the Consultant visited me to say that there was nothing wrong with my heart and the pain was caused by indigestion and stress. I was therefore allowed to go home at once.

I resolved not to do the Duty weekend and I then received a very considerate telephone call from the Chief Constable who said that he had suffered a similar problem and I was now to do as he did and, if I had an early start to the day, I was to finish early or if I knew I had a late finish, I was to start late. I was grateful for this but could not, in all honesty, see how it could work.

Shortly afterwards, I received another call, this time from the ACC and when I told him what the Chief had said, he agreed and advised me that, instead of a fourteen hour day, I should cut down to twelve! And there was me thinking I had an eight-hour day.

It was this incident that forced me to conclude that I definitely would retire after thirty years. Just before Christmas 1998, I was visited in my office by the Chief Constable, who asked me if I would be prepared to stay on beyond thirty years to undertake a further full financial year that would end in April 2000. I said that I could not guarantee to stay that long and he said that he needed someone who would be there to see the budget right through so, if I was staying for less than the year, he would have to move me to a less vital post at the end of the current financial year. I told him that, in that case, I would definitely leave the Force at the end of the financial year.

In addition to the many serious incidents going on in that year, we were also wrestling with the problem of too many demands with insufficient resources. The Area was divided into six Sectors, each with its own Inspector and complement of Sergeants In theory, this should provide good local cover and offer the kind of contact with the Police management that the public demand. Unfortunately, it does not sit well with the need to provide 24-hour cover. The Sectors were too small to have a sufficient force of Constables and the number of Sergeants available meant that, frequently, there would be no Sergeant on duty on a Sector.

As a Management Team, we could not allow this to continue because the Constables were receiving neither the supervision nor the support they

The Author on his last day of Police Service at Campbell Square
Police Station, Northampton

needed. We therefore decided to reduce the number of Sectors to four, retaining the two Inspectors released by this move and providing ourselves with a planning capability and supervision for the busy Custody suite. Few people outside the Police Service have any idea how many prisoners are being held at any time in a busy Police Station. The unfair and untrue image generated largely by the press, that the Police rarely make arrests and actively seek to avoid work, could not be further from the truth.

At Northampton, there were rarely less than eight prisoners in the cells at any time of the day or night and I have seen the number rise as high as thirty, with some of them lodged at other stations around the county. Normally, we would have about fourteen officers available for duty and frequently they would all be committed to a job with one or two subsequent jobs waiting for them. The reduction from six to four Sectors had eased the supervision problem slightly and I had insisted that there would never be less than three Sergeants on outside duty at any time.

However, it had done little for the problem of the volume of work and we had begun to seek a solution by altering shift patterns to put more officers on duty at the busiest times. The issue of police shifts had never been properly resolved because of the need to provide cover 24 hours per day and 365 days per year. For years, officers had been forced to work two 'quick changeovers' per month. This entailed finishing work at 10pm and returning for the next shift at 6am – clearly most unsatisfactory and impossible if the late shift had to work any overtime.

I commissioned an Inspector to offer some new alternatives, including different lengths of shift. The Traffic Division already worked 12-hour shifts with 4 days on and 4 off but this required the full agreement of all staff because it was clearly outside regulations.

Many Senior Officers did not like the idea of 12-hour shifts and it was widely felt that the officers themselves would not like it. Consequently, it was not one of the options my Inspector came up with, although there was quite a swell of opinion that it should have been an option.

When the options were finalised, I invited all staff to attend a meeting. If they were on duty they could attend but if off duty they would have to come in their own time. I was, therefore, a little surprised when almost 300 of my staff turned out one evening.

Andy Dickson was suffering with severe back pain on the day but even he managed to get to the meeting. I set the agenda with an introduction from me, a presentation from the Inspector who had devised the options and an opportunity for comments from the floor before the Management Team would withdraw and leave the staff to have a Federation meeting, at the end of which we would come back together to decide the way forward.

The first part of the meeting was quite fraught and at one stage I had to warn some of the more outspoken members to curb the vitriol and remember to be polite when addressing senior officers, in particular the poor Inspector who had been tasked to offer options. We then withdrew to allow the Federation meeting to take place but we had only been out for about ten minutes when the Federation Representatives asked me to bring the Management Team back in to hear what they had to say. When we were seated, they asked their members to vote on the system they wanted. They unanimously voted against each of the options on offer but then the Reps asked who would prefer a 12-hour system and they voted unanimously in favour. They expected me to reject this out of hand but in fact, I felt that it had much to offer, in addition to the morale question. It also enabled us to have more staff on duty at any time and even more

Sergeants available on each shift.

The evening had a curious end because the meeting had been held in the gymnasium at Headquarters, which is about 10 steps below the ground level. The bar is upstairs and quite a large number adjourned there at the end. Unfortunately, as we left the gymnasium and climbed the steps, Andy's back totally gave way and he collapsed onto the stairs with his face against the wall. He was completely unable to move and I, together with several members of the Management Team, was trying to help him when a large group of officers descended from the bar. I was amazed and later thought it hilarious that they all called a cheery, "Goodnight Sir" as they left, completely ignoring the Chief Inspector who lay, as if drunk, on the steps with his face pressed to the wall. Of course, the situation was not at all funny at the time and Andy had to be given a pain relief injection before the ambulance crew could even get him to hospital. (I am pleased to report that he made a full recovery.)

I still had to sell the 12-hour shift idea to my successor, whose name was known by then, and also the ACC, who I knew was not a fan of the concept. I was surprised to find that both were willing to try the scheme, particularly as we found a way to release 23 Constables to act as Community Beat Officers aligned with the Ward boundaries of the Borough Council. This enabled the local Councillors to have a liaison point and someone to work with to resolve local problems.

A full referendum of the staff affected, confirmed their support for the scheme and it was to be my legacy to the Area, because it came into force the week after I finally retired. Its popularity was such that it has since been adopted throughout Northamptonshire and I believe many other Forces use it too.

I did retire on 14th May 1999, although I left my post at the end of the financial year on 30 March because I was owed that time from missed rest days and holidays.

So what was I to do after the Police Force? There is life in retirement, indeed, it is a very good life and some of us can even find the time to write a book about their experiences, though I am so busy that this tome has taken four years to write – but that is another story.